THE ETHICS OF
JOURNALISM

THE ETHICS OF JOURNALISM

INDIVIDUAL, INSTITUTIONAL AND CULTURAL INFLUENCES

Edited by WENDY N. WYATT

REUTERS
INSTITUTE for the
STUDY of
JOURNALISM

Published by I.B.Tauris & Co. Ltd in association with
the Reuters Institute for the Study of Journalism, University of Oxford

The Reuters Institute would like to acknowledge the assistance of Kevin Rafter and Ian Hargreaves as readers on behalf of the Institute.

Published in 2014 by I.B.Tauris & Co. Ltd
6 Salem Road, London W2 4BU
175 Fifth Avenue, New York NY 10010
www.ibtauris.com

Distributed in the United States and Canada Exclusively by Palgrave Macmillan
175 Fifth Avenue, New York NY 10010

ISBN: 978 1 78076 673 7 (HB)
         978 1 78076 674 4 (PB)

A full CIP record for this book is available from the British Library
A full CIP record is available from the Library of Congress

Library of Congress Catalog Card Number: available

Typeset in Great Britain by Data Standards Ltd, Frome, Somerset
Printed and bound in Great Britain by T.J. International, Padstow, Cornwall

Contents

Part IV Emerging Issues in a Global, Digital Age

Acknowledgements

Thanks, first, to Robert Picard, Director of Research at the Reuters Institute, for asking me to edit this volume. It has been an honour and a pleasure to help bring the work of my colleagues to an audience beyond the scholars and journalists who attended the Oxford conference. Thanks, also, to the faculty in the Department of Communication and Journalism at the University of St Thomas, who were patient with me when I put aside my administrative duties to work on this book. Third, thanks to Tom Clasen, my partner in writing and in life, who is a great supporter and critic (in all the right ways), not to mention a walking dictionary and the best copy editor I know. He has given me incredible help with this project. Finally, on behalf of the book's contributors, thanks to the journalists throughout the world who do ethically admirable work. Good journalism does matter.

Wendy N. Wyatt
January 2014

Figures

Contributors

David S. Allen is an associate professor in the Department of Journalism, Advertising, and Media Studies at the University of Wisconsin-Milwaukee where he currently serves as chair of the department. He is the author of *Democracy, Inc.* (2005) and co-editor (with Robert Jensen) of *Freeing the First Amendment* (1995).

Thomas H. Bivins is the John L. Hulteng Chair in Media Ethics in the School of Journalism and Communication at the University of Oregon where he is the head of the media studies major and graduate certificate programme in communication ethics. He is the author of numerous articles and books on subjects ranging from media ethics to public relations writing.

Elizabeth Blanks Hindman is an associate professor in the Edward R. Murrow College of Communication at Washington State University where she teaches undergraduate and graduate courses in media ethics. She is the author of *Rights vs. Responsibilities: The Supreme Court and the Media* (1997).

Jan Lauren Boyles is a PhD fellow and adjunct professor at American University's School of Communication in Washington, DC. In addition to her work as a professional journalist, Boyles has served as a Google Journalism Fellow and as a researcher with the Pew Internet and American Life Project.

Tom Clasen is a writer, editor, and media observer with particular interests in media economics and media literacy. His perceptions of the news industry are influenced by his 35-year career in the business world.

Robert E. Drechsel holds the James E. Burgess Chair in Journalism at the University of Wisconsin-Madison, where he is also an affiliated professor of law. His work has focused on the relationship between media law and media ethics, and it has appeared in communication and legal journals. He holds a PhD in mass communication from the University of Minnesota.

Tobias Eberwein is a visiting professor of journalism at the Technische Universität Dortmund where he teaches courses in international journalism, online journalism, and media ethics. He acts as scientific officer of the international research project 'Media Accountability and Transparency in Europe' (MediaAcT). His research interests include journalistic quality, media accountability, literary journalism, and comparative journalism research.

Susanne Fengler is a professor of international journalism at the Technische Universität Dortmund and the academic director of the Erich Brost Institute for International Journalism where she coordinates the international research project 'Media Accountability and Transparency in Europe' (MediaAcT). Besides media accountability, her research interests include comparative journalism studies, political journalism, development communication, and economic theory of journalism.

Yael de Haan is a senior researcher at the Utrecht University of Applied Science in the Netherlands. In 2011 she completed her PhD on media accountability and journalism ethics. In addition to her work as a researcher and senior lecturer at the school of journalism in Utrecht, she is a member of the Dutch press council.

Ejvind Hansen is a research director at the Danish School of Media and Journalism where he focuses on the cultural implications of digital communication. In 2005 he defended his PhD dissertation, *Embedded Critique in a Tensed World*, in which he investigates the conditions for critique in the late modern societies. His work is generally situated in the field of critical and post-structuralist theory.

Tony Harcup has worked in mainstream journalism, alternative media, and journalism education. Currently a senior lecturer at the University of Sheffield in the UK, he is the author of *The Ethical Journalist* (2007), *Journalism: Principles and Practice* (2009), *Newspaper Journalism* (2010, with Peter Cole), and *Alternative Journalism, Alternative Voices* (2013).

Dejan Jontes is an assistant professor in the Department of Media and Communication Studies, Faculty of Social Sciences, at the University of Ljubljana. His areas of interest include communication theory, media studies, and critical/cultural approaches to popular culture and journalism. His most recent book, published in Slovene, is *Journalism as Culture: Myths and Values* (2010).

Annemarie Landman is a professional journalist, currently working as a reporter for one of the leading broadcast news organisations in the Netherlands. In addition to her journalism study at the Utrecht University of Applied Science, she passed the master examination (cum laude) in Communication Science at the University of Amsterdam where she researched the influences of the digital era on newsroom collaboration in the Netherlands.

Julia Lönnendonker is a researcher at the Erich Brost Institute for International Journalism. She acts as coordination officer of the international research project 'Media Accountability and Transparency in Europe' (MediaAcT). Her research interests include international and European journalism, foreign correspondence, and European identity studies.

Carlos Maciá-Barber is an associate professor and vice-chair of the Journalism and Media Studies Department at the Carlos III University of Madrid. He is the author of the first doctoral thesis in Spain about news ombudsmen. He is also lead researcher for two journalism ethics projects funded by the Spanish National Research, Development, and Innovation Plan.

Mireya Márquez Ramírez is an assistant professor of journalism studies and media theory at Universidad Iberoamericana, Mexico City. She holds a PhD in Media and Communications from Goldsmiths, University of London, and an MA in Journalism Studies from Cardiff University, UK. Her research areas include the study of post-authoritarian journalism cultures; reporting practices, news routines, and press history in Mexico; and global media policy in Latin America. She is currently a team member of the Worlds of Journalism Study in Mexico.

David Pritchard is a professor at the University of Wisconsin-Milwaukee. He has been a Fulbright research scholar, a visiting professor at Laval

University in Canada, and a visiting professor at the French Press Institute in Paris. Before moving into the academic world, Pritchard was a journalist for seven years.

Laura Schneider-Mombaur is a researcher at the Erich Brost Institute for International Journalism. She acts as administrative officer of the international research project 'Media Accountability and Transparency in Europe' (MediaAcT). Her research focuses on accountability, transparency, and self-reflection in journalism, journalism cultures, and comparative journalism research. She also works as a freelance journalist.

Karen L. Slattery chairs the Department of Journalism and Media Studies at Marquette University, Milwaukee, Wisconsin. She received her doctorate from the University of Wisconsin. Her work has appeared in *Journalism and Mass Communication Quarterly*, *Journalism and Communication Monographs*, *Journal of Mass Media Ethics*, and *Journal of Broadcasting and Electronic Media*.

Bastiaan Vanacker is an associate professor at Loyola University Chicago where he teaches and researches media ethics and law and serves as Director of the Center for Digital Ethics and Policy.

Lee Wilkins, chair of the Department of Communication at Wayne State University, focuses her research on media ethics, media coverage of the environment, and hazards and risks. She is a co-author of one of the country's best-selling college ethics texts, *Media Ethics: Issues and Cases*, now in its eighth edition with McGraw Hill. Wilkins is the editor of the country's leading academic journal on media ethics, the *Journal of Mass Media Ethics*.

Wendy N. Wyatt is an associate professor of media ethics and chair of the Department of Communication and Journalism at the University of St. Thomas, Minnesota. Much of her research focuses on issues of media and democracy. She is the author of *Critical Conversations: A Theory of Press Criticism* (2007) and co-editor (with Kristie Bunton) of *The Ethics of Reality TV* (2012). She is also book review editor for the *Journal of Mass Media Ethics*.

Introduction

Wendy N. Wyatt

For anyone interested in making journalism better, it is essential to first sort out what makes journalism the way it is. What are the influences that contribute to journalists' attitudes and actions – to their ethics? Without an understanding of those influences, it is difficult to make recommendations for change meaningful. Through the contributions of nearly two dozen scholars and journalists, this volume aims at building understanding of three primary influences: the individual, the cultural, and the institutional. The book considers not only how the three work independently, but, importantly, how they interact to affect the moral compasses of journalists and the moral standing of the practice as a whole.

Much has been said about individual, institutional, and cultural influences. The autonomous moral agent – the rational individual – forms the basis of Western moral philosophy's three primary traditions: those of the good, the right, and the virtuous. For the Greeks, for Enlightenment thinkers, and for many modern-day ethicists, the focus is on the individual; if we can foster in individuals strong characters or if we can give them the tools to figure out how to do the good or the right thing, we will create moral communities. Therefore, when it comes to theorising about journalism ethics, a focus on individual influences is a solid way forward.

But individuals are not islands, and the extent to which they act independently of other factors can – as we are reminded by ethicists in the feminist and communitarian traditions – be overstated. We are who we are and we act as we do because of others. In other words, we are not as autonomous as we'd like to think we are. Institutional influences, particularly those in the news industry, can be incredibly strong, and robust socialisation can affect even the most independent of journalists. Put simply, an institution can change a person – for better or for worse.

What's more, an institution can take on an ethical life of its own. Scholars who have written about collective moral agency contend that organisations themselves can be assigned moral personhood. An organisation as a collective (not simply a group of individuals) acts as a moral agent with concomitant rights, duties, and accountabilities.

On top of individual and institutional influences, we add those that derive from culture. Journalists are part and parcel of the culture in which they live and work, and they reflect their own culture's worldview. We readily see this when, for example, we compare journalists from democracies with those from authoritarian states. But differences can be found even among journalists from two like cultures. Journalists in the United Kingdom certainly have ethical compasses that differ from their peers in other democracies. What is justified as ethically acceptable in one place may look quite different in another.

The discipline of journalism ethics developed with a focus on professional ethics – on the values, guiding principles, and codes of the journalism profession. During the last 35 years, questions have revolved around who journalists should be and what those journalists should do, and these questions have almost always considered journalism in a particular situated context. Today, however, foundations are being reimagined: first, by ethicists who contend that we need a global media ethics, which transcends the limitations of place, and, second, by ethicists who advocate for a return to a common morality that focuses on our general moral commitments and our obligations as human beings, rather than our particular role-related responsibilities as journalists. All of this leaves journalism ethics in an interesting theoretical place. What is the proper way – or ways – forward to best understand the influences on journalism ethics? And once that is established, what is the proper way – or ways – forward to make normative claims about fostering the most ethically justifiable practice of journalism?

As media ethicists grapple with these questions, they are constantly reminded that the questions are not only abstract and theoretical. Real life intervenes – sometimes with examples of ethically praiseworthy behaviour, the kind that makes us proud to be associated with journalism. We don't focus on those exemplars here (most ethics texts don't) but we can't ignore that journalists and journalism organisations do good work every day. On the other hand, the reason that media ethicists have steady jobs is that the examples we would call ethically praiseworthy are often overshadowed by examples of another kind – behaviour that makes those ethicists and their journalist colleagues cringe. What's more, these behaviours are what tend to attract the public's attention. Even if news people and news organisations act daily to serve the public's best interest, that public notices when something goes wrong. It is one of these examples – the phone hacking scandal in the UK and the subsequent Leveson Inquiry into the culture, practice, and ethics of the press – that serves as the origin for this book.

As Lord Justice Leveson, together with his panel of six independent assessors, considered how to best 'guard the guardians', ethicists around the world grappled with what went wrong and how a repeat of history could be prevented. Should the focus be placed on changing the ethical standards of individual journalists? Was this a problem with a single institution, one that tended towards ethical recklessness? Was there something in the culture of UK journalism – one marked by intense competition and more than a little bombast – that led to the scandal? Or, more plausibly, was it some combination of influences? And, of course, what happens next? How can journalism ethicists earn their keep by offering a path forward?

For many, the phone hacking scandal provided yet another concrete example of journalism ethics gone wrong. Interestingly, Lord Leveson noted that the report resulting from his inquiry was the seventh of its kind in fewer than 70 years. The questions it raised were more than interesting academic exercises. Regardless of what transpired during the scandal and what the Leveson Inquiry would later propose, if journalism was to successfully justify itself in the face of harsh and understandable critique, it would need answers or, at the very least, a plan.

So, in September 2012, just as Lord Leveson wrapped up more than a year's worth of evidence collected for his inquiry, a group of nearly 50 scholars and journalists convened at the invitation of the University of Oxford's Reuters Institute for the Study of Journalism to discuss and debate a particularly timely theme: 'Journalism Ethics: Individual, Institutional or Cultural?' When participants met in Oxford with Reuters Director of Research Robert Picard, the tale of the phone hacking scandal – and all of its gruesome details – had unfolded in front of the Leveson Inquiry, but the judgement was still out. Conference participants weren't sure what the end result would be, but we were all interested in exploring what got journalism to that regrettable place and how we could help it make a new turn.

Over the course of two full days at St Anne's College – plus some evening indulgences at the Reuters Institute and at Balliol College – we grappled with issues of where journalists get their ethical compasses, what leads to ethically problematic behaviour in newsrooms around the world, and how we might foster more ethically praiseworthy journalism. This volume illustrates just some of the good thinking that went on in Oxford.

The chapters in the book certainly stand on their own; any one could be read in isolation. But there's something to be said about reading the collection as a whole: individual chapters give glimpses; the entire collection gives a more complete story. As you work through, you'll find that journalism ethics is driven by a multitude of complex forces that rank in importance by time, by place, and by other contextual factors. The story, of course, is never a simple one, which, in my mind, is what makes ethics so endlessly intriguing.

Recurring themes

A number of themes serve as threads that connect the individual chapters and help make sense of the multiple ideas presented:

- *Both the descriptive and normative realms matter.* Typically, scholarship in journalism ethics falls into two categories: (1) work that describes the ethical landscape and helps make sense of it; (2) work that enters the normative realm by prescribing ethical values, principles, standards, and behaviours. Both approaches are useful; clearly, we must understand before we can recommend. Contributors to this volume help us with both. Some chapters reside in the realm of the descriptive, establishing the landscape of journalism ethics and building the all-important foundations. Others make the move to the normative, offering prescriptions aimed at making journalism better.
- *Theory and practice can and should intersect.* Moral philosophy serves as the theoretical underpinning of much scholarly work in journalism ethics. Unless that theory can connect to practice, however, the work is merely an academic exercise. Several chapters in the book address how theory can – and, normatively speaking, should – inform practice and how practice can and should exemplify theory. In addition, the volume stretches beyond moral theory and considers the contributions that other kinds of theory – democratic, legal, organisational – can make to the practice of ethical journalism.
- *The global, digital age affects journalism ethics.* Perhaps the top item on the agenda of media ethicists today is the nature of the global,

digital age; a sophisticated discussion of journalism ethics requires consideration of the context in which journalists now work. Chapters throughout this book both predict and prescribe how the bases of journalism ethics will and should evolve in today's global, digital age.

- *International perspectives are crucial.* Until recently, much scholarship on journalism ethics has come out of the United States and United Kingdom. The topic, however, is a global one that should be examined through multiple cultural lenses. Contributors to this volume come from nine countries in Europe and North America. Although a number of shared foundational values emerge in their work, authors offer a range of perspectives on the practice of journalism and journalism ethics.

- *Newsrooms are important sites for investigation.* A good deal of scholarly work has been done on the sociology of the newsroom, and it demonstrates the importance of the newsroom to journalists' work. Most of this scholarship, however, has not focused on ethical implications. Several chapters in this book both illuminate the strong influences of the newsroom on journalism ethics and make suggestions for how newsrooms of the future (either real or virtual) can become ethically healthier workplaces.

- *Journalism ethics is individually, institutionally, and culturally based.* The chapters in this volume demonstrate that an exploration of journalism ethics does not lead to a single influence but rather to multiple influences that work together in complex ways. David Pritchard's first essay, which presents the concept of normative ecologies, makes this argument explicitly, but it is implicit throughout the book. As all of the chapters demonstrate, journalism ethics is the result of multiple competing and complementary forces.

A book in four parts

If the book's themes serve to connect the chapters, the structure divides them. The book is organised into four parts, although the division is admittedly somewhat arbitrary; several of the chapters could easily fit into more than one part. As noted, David Pritchard's short first essay sets the stage for the four parts and 14 chapters that follow. In his essay, Pritchard discusses the domains that determine journalistic behaviour and the complex journalism ecologies that result from the interplay of those domains. Keep his ideas in mind as you move through the rest of the book.

Part I. Spheres of influence: Fostering (or not) ethical journalism

Part I focuses squarely on the topic of the Reuters conference and the title of the book: individual, institutional, and cultural influences – or domains – and the effects those can have on journalism ethics. The first two chapters, by Tony Harcup and Lee Wilkins, aim inward, exploring ethics in the newsroom and the forces that both contribute to and detract from ethical behaviour. Both authors use the News Corp phone hacking scandal as an example of the strong socialisation effects of the newsroom. In work that sparked passionate discussion at the Reuters conference, Tony Harcup uses testimony from the Leveson Inquiry to explore the tensions between individual and collective approaches to journalism ethics, and he argues that the two can coexist within an institutional setting. Drawing on feminist theory, Harcup contends that, if a culture of dialogue, openness and mutual respect can be fostered in newsrooms, both individual and collective responsibility can be called upon to create a framework for more ethical journalism. Lee Wilkins usefully takes ethicists outside of their normal comfort zone, examining the literature on business ethics and organisational change for insights into how organisational culture affects individual ethical choice. She finds that, although organisational culture does not replace individual thinking, it can either enhance or degrade individual ethical choice. Wilkins closes her chapter with a set of questions that can help scholars understand the influence that a newsroom's organisational climate can have on ethical decision-making.

Next, Part I turns to three short chapters by Mireya Márquez Ramírez, Bastiaan Vanacker, and Dejan Jontes that demonstrate the multiple influences journalists experience in their daily work. Each one features a case study that brings the cultural domain into the spotlight, while also recognising the role of individual and institutional forces. Mireya Márquez Ramírez gives us an intriguing glimpse into the changing nature of journalism in Mexico, particularly as it relates to attitudes about journalists accepting cash, gifts, and perks in exchange for news. Although the new generation of journalists working in post-authoritarian Mexico sees itself as a group of professionals committed to principles of autonomy and independence, Márquez Ramírez illustrates how these journalists work within nuanced and constantly changing standards. Her chapter reminds us that values, principles, and behaviours do not change overnight; history can be a powerful legacy. Bastiaan Vanacker reports on interviews he conducted with journalists in the United Kingdom, the Netherlands, and the Flanders region of Belgium that illuminate both shared and separate perspectives on journalism ethics, particularly as it relates to privacy issues. Vanacker's thought-provoking conclusion is that institutional factors contribute to a shared conception among journalists of their professional role and the principles that guide it. However, cultural differences lead to divergent ways of putting these shared principles into practice. Journalists in each country disagree about the limits of telling a particular story. Wrapping up Part I, Dejan Jontes engages in an insightful unpacking of journalism values in post-socialist Slovenia using two unusual but important sources: texts of award presentations and journalism textbooks. Through these two kinds of texts, Jontes finds an embrace of democratic journalistic values such as objectivity that have been imported from elsewhere and also, importantly, an understanding of non-partisanship that means resisting socialism and any remnants of it; this resistance, in fact, is represented as Slovene journalism's most important ethical value.

Part II. Accountability mechanisms

Part II includes three chapters that explore mechanisms of media accountability. Susanne Fengler, Tobias Eberwein, Julia Lönnendonker, and Laura Schneider-Mombaur begin with a broad look at journalists' perceptions of both traditional and emerging media accountability instruments. The results of their study, which impressively includes journalists from 14 countries, are somewhat discouraging. As they report, the impact of media accountability instruments is moderate at best. However, the authors offer some interesting ideas for approaches that could lead to more effective media accountability, including partnerships with the state – what they call government regulation of self-regulatory efforts. In his chapter, Carlos Maciá-Barber examines the role of a particular accountability instrument – the news ombudsman – and argues that this role can help reinforce the professional ethics of journalists while simultaneously promoting audience participation, media literacy, and the public's right to information. Maciá-Barber, who has studied the ombudsman function in news organisations around the world, outlines the most important conditions for effective ombudsmen and ends with a plea that, even in the face of ongoing challenges, ombudsmen should make all efforts to persevere. To finish Part II, Robert Drechsel, an accomplished media law scholar, looks at accountability from a legal perspective and poses an important question: has the professionalisation of journalism in America, which is centred on the idea of serving the public interest and is accompanied by ethical codes and standards, led journalism to a legally dangerous – and less free – place? In a systematic examination, Drechsel investigates two specific legal contexts – negligence and confidentiality – and the ways in which these ethical standards may be transforming into legal standards. He ends with an exploration of the American context vis-à-vis Canada and the United Kingdom.

Part III. Intersections: Theory and practice

Part III includes three chapters that focus directly on the intersections between theory and practice. In their two chapters, Karen Slattery and Thomas Bivins apply the moral philosophies of deontology and virtue ethics – two philosophies firmly grounded in the autonomy of the individual as a moral agent – to journalism. David Allen and Elizabeth Blanks Hindman examine democratic theories and the different kinds of journalism each requires.

Karen Slattery's chapter focuses on the codes of ethics from three American journalism associations and the relationship between the principles expressed in those codes and the moral principles identified by deontologists such as Immanuel Kant and W. D. Ross. Slattery makes a persuasive and logical argument that, when journalism codes fail to offer clear resolutions to ethical dilemmas, deontological theory and the prima facie duties it presents can help clarify the most ethically justifiable choice. Thomas Bivins also examines American codes of ethics, but he chooses to look at the language of the earliest codes from the first part of the twentieth century. Language, Bivins argues, is central, and he takes the claim to heart in his compellingly written chapter. In the early codes, Bivins sees an appeal to virtue and good character that is missing from many of today's codes, which tend to be rules-based. This virtue-based approach, which is experiencing a resurgence thanks to the work of neo-Aristotelians such as Alasdair MacIntyre, may serve journalists and the public better. Bivins, therefore, recommends a return to a philosophical framework based on virtue that would allow individual journalists the leeway to make their own decisions based on overarching human virtues such as sincerity, competency, thoroughness, mercy, and moderation. Rounding out Part III is David Allen and Elizabeth Blanks Hindman's chapter on the centrality of democratic theory to journalism ethics. Their chapter succinctly and clearly describes three broad perspectives on democratic theory – elitist, discursive, and communitarian – and applies them to questions of journalism ethics. The authors then take a normative turn by suggesting that there is room for multiple conceptions of democracy along with multiple roles and responsibilities for journalism. The chapter ends with a nice pay-off: specific ideas about what roles different types of media may play based on the normative assumptions of the three different perspectives on democratic theory.

Part IV. Emerging issues in a global, digital age

The book's final chapters take a glimpse into journalism's future by investigating emerging issues in the global, digital age. Yael de Haan, Annemarie Landman, and Jan Lauren Boyles study real journalists' experiences in a rapidly changing work environment. Two other chapters – the first by Ejvind Hansen and the second by me and my co-author Tom Clasen – might be better categorised as thought experiments: Theoretically speaking, how can and should journalists adjust to this new landscape?

Yael de Haan, Annemarie Landman, and Jan Lauren Boyles focus on journalists in one Dutch newsroom, examining how the online era has introduced entirely new categories of news and information creators. From internet journalists who work in a traditional newsroom to citizen journalists who have no newsroom at all, the three authors demonstrate how these new creators of news are forcing legacy journalists to examine the standards upon which they have historically relied. The authors, who worked together after the Reuters conference to combine their two research projects, make a useful move from the descriptive – the focus of de Haan and Landman's work – to the normative – the focus of Boyle's work. To deal with the challenges arising from both within and outside the newsroom and to help ensure ethical journalistic practices, the authors propose a knowledge-centred newsroom model, which is focused on the ethics of collaboration. Ejvind Hansen's chapter also explores how journalism standards will be negotiated into the future. In one of the most philosophically sophisticated chapters of the book, Hansen asks whether the idea of journalism as the 'Fourth Estate', which is linked with clearly defined political nation states, can be transferred to an informational, economic, and political setting that has little affiliation with specific political units. In other words, if the Fourth Estate loses relevance in a transnational setting, what will ethical journalism mean, and who will – and should – get to decide? Adopting a proceduralist approach, Hansen argues that journalists from across the world need to articulate a set of rules that don't prescribe specific standards but rather provide for the possibility of deliberating disagreements about those standards. The book closes with the chapter I co-wrote with Tom Clasen. Both of us have followed with interest and disappointment the steady reports of newsroom cutbacks. What, we wondered, would happen if the newsroom – the site that has been so central to journalists' identities – goes away? And what will it mean for journalism ethics if journalists find themselves working in more solitary settings? In the chapter, we investigate how the newsroom has affected journalism ethics in both beneficial and harmful ways. We end our chapter with a position we didn't expect going in: if journalism in the solitary age can hold onto the best parts of newsroom culture while leaving behind those that inhibit ethical practice, the solitary age could, in fact, enhance journalism ethics.

Join the conversation

During the Reuters conference, participants joined in a number of lively conversations through which we found much common ground. We certainly, however, didn't always agree. Questions about the strongest theoretical approaches, the most influential ethical forces, and the possibility of global standards took us in different directions. You'll find the same thing in this book: many points of agreement across the chapters but some disagreements as well. The point is not to solve all of the issues but rather to contribute to the conversation about journalism ethics – to get us a step closer to more fully understanding the multiple forces that influence journalists, news organisations, and media systems. Everyone in the room at Oxford and in this volume appreciates the essential role that journalism plays in people's lives. We are critics but also fans. It's my hope that others who care deeply about journalism will find our observations and ideas meaningful and that, together, we can offer ideas for making journalism better.

1

The Norms that Govern Journalism: An Ecological Approach

David Pritchard

The principal determinants of journalistic behaviour in any society come from four domains: legal rules, professional standards, market forces, and technology. Although the domains are conceptually distinct, in practice they constantly evolve and interact to create a dynamic ecology of norms. It is impossible to fully understand a given society's journalism without first understanding the society's normative ecology for news.

This brief essay has five parts. The first introduces the normative ecology concept in the context of journalism. The second focuses on the domain of law. The third examines the broad area of professional standards. The fourth discusses the market as a regulator of journalism. The fifth notes the influence of digital technology.

Normative ecologies

Some influences on the practice of journalism have the form of rules. Laws that enable journalists to be sued for libel or invasion of privacy are examples of such rules, as are journalistic norms such as accuracy and objectivity. Although it may be difficult to define the precise contours of such rules, the rules are explicit and widely understood (if not always followed). Other influences on journalistic behaviour are less explicit, though no less important. The behaviour of the market for news and other media products is not decided by any court or decreed by any self-regulatory body, but it is as powerful an influence on journalistic behaviour as any law or ethics code. The design of communication technology by the companies that manufacture hardware and software also plays a role in influencing twenty-first-century journalistic behaviour. The normative ecology that results from the interaction of these forces governs journalism by shaping, channelling, constraining, and enabling various practices.

Scholarship about journalism standards (including, but not limited to, journalism ethics) is generally theoretical and prescriptive, rarely testing ideas in the bubbling cauldron of day-to-day newswork. Inevitably, such scholarship reveals more about a scholar's preconceived ideas than about the reasons for actual journalistic practices. As Lippmann noted, 'For the most part we do not first see, and then define, we define first and then see' (Lippmann, 1922: 54–5). Careful empirical research on journalistic behaviour not only would help bridge the gap between abstract theory and concrete reality, but would reveal the normative ecology of news in operation.

In recent years an increasing number of scholars have adopted 'ecology' as an appropriate metaphor for the multifaceted system of intertwined rules and processes of varied origin and varying levels of formality that governs journalism at any given time and place. Among the first to explicitly use the ecology metaphor in discussing media governance was a Canadian scholar who described a 'range of seemingly disconnected institutions, issues and practices' that constitutes 'a complex ecology of interdependent structures' (Raboy, 2002: 6). A few years later, two journalism researchers in the Baltic region proposed an 'ecological approach' to media accountability (Harro-Loit and Balčytienė, 2005), though they did not incorporate market forces or technology into their framework. A Spanish scholar included media literacy schemes to empower media audiences in her conception of a 'regulatory ecology' (Ariño, 2007: 132).

Researchers who focus on the internet have been especially attuned to the ecological metaphor. A study of internet regulation by a group associated with Oxford University's Programme in Comparative Media Law and Policy noted the 'emergence of a fertile ecology of rule-making, regulatory competition, alternative dispute resolution and a complex interaction between state, co- and self-regulatory practices in the media sectors' (Tambini et al., 2008: 3). A report to UNESCO's Division for Freedom of Expression, Democracy and Peace by a different team of British researchers carried the subtitle, 'The Changing Legal and Regulatory Ecology Shaping the Internet' (Dutton et al., 2011). A 2013 chapter in a media law handbook noted 'evolutionary trends' in the media 'governance ecology' (Burri, 2013: 335). The author noted that the ecology 'not only draws together horizontally different domains but is also unevenly vertically spread along a multi-layered structure that mobilises various actors at the local, national, regional and international levels' (Burri, 2013: 327).

The legal domain

Although, in theory, formal law applies evenly to everyone in a given political unit, in practice, the force of law in any given situation varies with the relative power and status of parties to disputes (Black, 1976). The behaviour of law also varies with more macro-level factors such as cultural, social, and political contexts (Engel, 1984; Pritchard, 1989).

In other words, journalism law is variable and dynamic, open to influences that may have nothing to do with either journalism or law. This fact helps explain why journalists who work for community media in small towns have, for all practical purposes, less law at their disposal than do journalists who work for large news organisations. The small-town journalists are less likely to assert their legal right to publish material that authorities want suppressed or to frame a request for public documents in terms of an access-to-information law (see e.g. Hansen and Moore, 1990; Sanders, 2000).

The contextual variability of journalism law makes it difficult to isolate law's influence on journalists. That said, law's effect may be weaker than many scholars believe. A survey of journalists in 17 countries found that media law was not amongst the strongest influences on their behaviour (Hanitzsch et al., 2010). Nor does law seem to be particularly important to those who actually sue the media. The authors of a landmark study of libel litigation in the United States, for example, noted that 'legal theories and rules appear only to have the most tenuous relationship to the actions of the plaintiffs' (Bezanson et al., 1987: 212).

Professional standards

The most important source of journalists' knowledge about professional standards is learning on the job (Weaver et al., 2007: 159), but what journalists at different news organisations learn is not necessarily uniform. What is more, newsroom socialisation processes are not open to public scrutiny. The lack of uniformity and transparency means that core principles such as objectivity may be poorly understood both by journalists and the public. Nonetheless, such principles are important determinants of journalistic behaviour (Hanitzsch et al., 2010).

In the twentieth century the news industries in North America and Western Europe developed a variety of self-regulatory mechanisms intended to explain journalism and its standards to the public (Nemeth, 2003), to resolve disputes between news organisations and members of the public (Pritchard, 1992), and to provide accountability via press criticism (Bunton, 2000). Much of this self-regulation arose during times of state scrutiny of the press; virtually all press councils in the United States and Canada, for example, were created to block the threat of direct government regulation of the news industry (Pritchard, 1992). The Australian Press Council was created in similar circumstances (O'Malley, 1987a).

Although press self-regulation may be conceptually appealing as a presumed middle ground between the worrisome extremes of state control on the one hand and unconstrained press irresponsibility on the other, in practice self-regulation has not been notably successful in curbing journalistic excesses. No country has more experience with the limits of self-regulation than Britain, where the Press Council's inability to rein in the press led to its replacement in 1991 by a Press Complaints Commission that would monitor compliance with a formal code of conduct. The *News of the World* phone hacking scandal highlighted the impotence of the Press Complaints Commission, and in July 2011 the prime minister announced a public inquiry into the culture, practices, and ethics of the British press. The inquiry, headed by Lord Justice Brian Henry Leveson, issued its report of nearly 2,000 pages in November 2012. The report recommended the creation of an independent self-regulatory body that would adopt a code of standards for the press and have the power to impose sanctions, including fines of up to £1 million. As of June 2013, however, none of the inquiry's recommendations had been adopted.

Despite the fact that the threat of state control has been at the root of many mechanisms of news self-regulation, it appears that self-regulation is not simply state control by other means. Instead, self-regulation attempts to balance the interests of the news industry with those of other sectors of society (O'Malley, 1987b; Ugland, 2008). That is not to say, however, that there are no interactions between journalism law and self-regulatory mechanisms. Courts sometimes cite the decisions of self-regulatory bodies (Trudel and Abran, 2006), and self-regulatory bodies sometimes change their practices in reaction to court decisions (Bernier, 2005). Some scholars who are sensitive to any hint of censorship express the concern that self-regulation may give courts a rationale for limiting freedom of the press (Drechsel, 1992; Gajda, 2009).

Market forces

Market forces have always been part of the normative ecology for news in the sense that news content is always influenced by journalism's 'funders' – subscribers, advertisers, organisations, and sometimes governments – along with the competition for the revenue they provide (Shoemaker, 1987). Web 2.0 has added a new and different kind of market to the normative ecology: competition for primacy in defining the meaning of the news. This new market manifests itself via reader comments about stories posted on online news sites and social media platforms, as well as via blogs. The comments, generally anonymous and often rude, have two kinds of effects. First, they 'can significantly distort what other readers think was reported in the first place', which is 'a surprisingly potent effect' (Brossard and Scheufele, 2013; see also Anderson et al., in press). Second, they act as virtually instantaneous media criticism that can influence how a journalist frames a story (Santana, 2011).

Blogs increasingly compete with traditional news organisations to be the first to report an important story (Gant, 2007). Bloggers often distinguish their standards from those of traditional journalism. They contrast what some call 'horizontal editing' – posting an initial version of a story and then relying on peer review and rapid self-correction – with the 'vertical editing' common at legacy news organisations (Wischnowski, 2011). Traditional journalism standards inevitably adapt to competition from the blogosphere, resulting in changes to the normative ecology for news.

Technology

The widespread belief that the internet not only is unregulated but cannot be regulated is patently false. In the United States, for example, laws that permit filtering internet content, enabling restrictive digital rights management schemes, allowing internet service providers to discriminate against certain categories of content, and undermining copyright's fair-use provisions via the guilty-until-proven-innocent mandatory take-down provisions of the Digital Millennium Copyright Act are the part of the regulatory scheme that Lessig calls the 'East Coast Code' (2006: 72). The East Coast Code is traditional law and policy as adopted by legislators and administrative agencies. Though it is the product of inefficient deliberative processes, it is transparent and subject to a system of checks and balances, including the First Amendment.

West Coast Code, by contrast, is not a governmental product. Product developers simply build it into software or hardware. There is no public deliberation and no transparency. West Coast Code reflects corporate interests, not the public interest (though the two can sometimes overlap). Few scholars question the ascendance of West Coast Code. An American law professor wrote that 'decisions about technological design, legislative and administrative regulations, the formation of new business models, and the collective activities of end-users' have become more important than the First Amendment in influencing the future of freedom of expression (Balkin: 2009, 427). Does this mean that digital technologies determine journalism standards? Not in any direct way, but digital technologies raise the stakes and change the ethical discussion in the sense that they represent powerful new tools that journalists can use for good or ill (e.g. the British phone hacking scandal). More research on the relationship between digital technologies and journalism standards is urgently needed.

Conclusion

Anyone who wishes to understand the standards that govern journalism – and, therefore, journalism ethics – in the twenty-first century must consider not only the importance of technological design and the emergence of new kinds of markets, but also how those factors interact with the other components of the normative ecology for news. Research on this topic is necessarily contextual because ecologies are dynamic rather than static. Knowledge that is both broad and deep is far more likely to emerge from an accumulation of careful case studies than from any single research project.

The chapters that follow explore the domains that determine journalistic behaviour and the journalism ecologies that result from the complex interplay of these domains. Some chapters focus on a single domain; others explore multiple domains. Some focus on one particular context; others are more broad. Finally, some authors speak specifically to the domains identified here; others introduce new domains (e.g. culture or individual morality). The point is that, to fully understand journalism ethics, we must look at how all of these domains work together. The contributors to this volume help us more fully conceptualise the dynamic ecology of norms – the powerful web of influences that forms the basis for journalism ethics.

Note

All web addresses in this chapter were last accessed in March 2013.

References

Anderson, Ashley A., Brossard, Dominique, Scheufele, Dietram A., Xenos, Michael A., and Ladwig, Peter (in press) 'Crude Comments and Concern: Online Incivility's Effect on Risk Perceptions of Emerging Technologies', *Journal of Computer-Mediated Communication*.

Ariño, Monica (2007) 'Content Regulation and New Media: A Case Study of Online Video Portals', *Communications and Strategies*, 66(2): 115–35.

Balkin, Jack M. (2009) 'The Future of Free Expression in a Digital Age', *Pepperdine Law Review*, 36: 427–44.

Bernier, Marc-François (2005) *L'ombudsman de Radio-Canada: Protecteur du public ou des journalistes?* (Quebec City: Presses de l'Université Laval).

Bezanson, Randall P., Cranberg, Gilbert, and Soloski, John (1987) *Libel Law and the Press: Myth and Reality* (New York: Free Press).

Black, Donald (1976) *The Behavior of Law* (Orlando, FL: Academic Press).

Brossard, Dominique, and Scheufele, Dietram A. (2013) 'This Story Stinks', *New York Times*, 3 Mar.: SR5.

Bunton, Kristie (2000) 'Media Criticism as Professional Self-Regulation', in David Pritchard (ed.), *Holding the Media Accountable: Citizens, Ethics, and the Law* (Bloomington, IN: Indiana University Press), 68–89.

Burri, Mira (2013) 'Controlling New Media (without the Law)', in Monroe E. Price, Stefaan G. Verhulst, and Libby Morgan (eds), *Routledge Handbook of Media Law* (Abingdon, Oxon: Routledge), 327–42.

Drechsel, Robert E. (1992) 'Media Ethics and Media Law: The Transformation of Moral Obligation into Legal Principle', *Notre Dame Journal of Law, Ethics and Public Policy*, 6: 5–32.

Dutton, William H., Dopatka, Anna, Hills, Michael, Law, Ginette, and Nash, Victoria (2011) *Freedom of Connection – Freedom of Expression: The Changing Legal and Regulatory Ecology Shaping the Internet* (Paris: UNESCO).

Engel, David M. (1984) 'The Oven Bird's Song: Insiders, Outsiders, and Personal Injuries in an American Community', *Law and Society Review*, 18: 551–82.

Gajda, Amy (2009) 'Judging Journalism: The Turn toward Privacy and Judicial Regulation of the Press', *California Law Review*, 97: 1039–1105.

Gant, Scott. (2007) *We're All Journalists Now: The Transformation of the Press and the Reshaping of the Law in the Internet Age* (New York: Free Press).

Hanitzsch, Thomas, Anikina, Maria, Berganza, Rosa, Cangoz, Incilay, Coman, Mihai, Hamada, Basyouni, Hanusch, Folker, Karadjov, Christopher D., Mellado, Claudia, Virginia Moreira, Sonia, Mwesige, Peter G., Plaisance, Patrick Lee, Reich, Zvi, Seethaler, Josef, Skewes, Elizabeth A., Noor, Dani Vardiansyah, and Yuen, Kee Wang (2010) 'Modeling Perceived Influences on Journalism: Evidence from a Cross-National Survey of Journalists', *Journalism and Mass Communication Quarterly*, 87: 5–22.

Hansen, Elizabeth K., and Moore, Roy L. (1990) 'Chilling the Messenger: Impact of Libel on Community Newspapers', *Newspaper Research Journal*, 11(Spring): 86–99.

Harro-Loit, Halliki, and Balčytienė, Auksė (2005) 'Media Accountability Systems: An Ecological Viewpoint', in Richard Baerug (ed.), *The Baltic Media World* (Riga: Flera Printing House), 25–39.

Lessig, Lawrence (2006). *Code: Version 2.0* (New York: Basic Books).

Lippmann, Walter (1922) *Public Opinion* (New York: Macmillan).

Nemeth, Neil (2003) *News Ombudsmen in North America: Assessing an Experiment in Social Responsibility* (Westport, CT: Praeger).

O'Malley, Pat (1987a) 'Regulation, Pseudo-Regulation and Counter-Regulation: The Operation of the Australian Press Council', *Media, Culture and Society*, 9: 77–95.

O'Malley, Pat (1987b) 'Regulating Contradictions: The Australian Press Council and the "Dispersal of Social Control"', *Law and Society Review*, 21: 83–108.

Pritchard, David (1989) 'Beyond the Meese Commission Report: Understanding the Variable Nature of Pornography Regulation', in Susan Gubar and Joan

Hoff (eds), *For Adult Users Only: The Dilemma of Violent Pornography* (Bloomington, IN: Indiana University Press), 163–77.

Pritchard, David (1992) 'Press Councils as Mechanisms of Media Self-Regulation', in Jacques Zylberberg and François Demers (eds), *L'Amérique et les Amériques/America and the Americas* (Quebec City: Presses de l'Université Laval), 99–116.

Raboy, Marc (2002) 'Media Policy in the New Communications Environment', in Marc Raboy (ed.), *Global Media Policy in the New Millennium* (Luton: University of Luton Press), 3–18.

Sanders, Craig (2000) 'Newspapers' Use of Lawyers in the Editorial Process', in David Pritchard (ed.), *Holding the Media Accountable: Citizens, Ethics, and the Law* (Bloomington, IN: Indiana University Press), 138–53.

Santana, Arthur D. (2011) 'Online Readers' Comments Represent New Opinion Pipeline', *Newspaper Research Journal*, 32(3): 66–81.

Shoemaker, Pamela J. (1987) 'Building a Theory of News Content: A Synthesis of Current Approaches', *Journalism Monographs*, 103: 1–38.

Tambini, Damian, Leonardi, Danilo, and Marsden, Chris (2008) *Codifying Cyberspace: Communications Self-Regulation in the Age of Internet Convergence* (Abingdon: Routledge/UCL Press).

Trudel, Pierre, and Abran, France (2006) *Le statut et les processus décisionnels du Conseil de presse du Québec.* Report commissioned by the Quebec Press Council: www.chairelrwilson.ca/cours/drt3805/conseildepresse(juillet).pdf.

Ugland, Erik (2008) 'The Legitimacy and Moral Authority of the National News Council (USA)', *Journalism: Theory, Practice and Criticism*, 9: 285–308.

Weaver, David H., Beam, Randal A., Brownlee, Bonnie J., Voakes, Paul S., and Wilhoit, G. Cleveland (2007) *The American Journalist in the 21st Century: U.S. News People at the Dawn of a New Millennium* (Mahwah, NJ: Lawrence Erlbaum).

Wischnowski, Benjamin J. (2011) 'Bloggers with Shields: Reconciling the Blogosphere's Intrinsic Editorial Process with Traditional Concepts of Media Accountability', *Iowa Law Review*, 97: 327–46.

Part I

Spheres of Influence: Fostering (or Not)
Ethical Journalism

2

The Ethical Newsroom: Where the Individual and the Collective Work Together

Tony Harcup

Ethical horror stories within journalism are often blamed on the moral shortcomings of individual journalists who can find themselves represented rather in the manner of manipulative reporter Chuck Tatum in the classic 1951 film *Ace in the Hole*: flawed individuals who are 'irredeemably wicked, amoral, worthless' (McNair, 2010: 27). Perhaps the most notorious recent example of how this blame game plays out in real life came when the Murdoch empire and its supporters spent years pinning responsibility for phone hacking at the *News of the World* newspaper on a single 'rogue reporter'. That defence was ultimately breached, not by the forces of law or regulation, but by dogged, questioning, investigative reporting most notably by the *Guardian* (not forgetting the *New York Times*).

More subtle variations on the lone wolf theme may perhaps be detected in some academic literature that emphasises the 'highly individualistic' nature of journalism and journalists (Hargreaves, 2003: 167). Yet during 2011–12, the Leveson Inquiry into the culture, practice, and ethics of the UK press heard compelling evidence that individual journalists do not *on their own* determine the ethics of their job; the power to establish ethical standards within any newsroom is more likely to reside 'not at the bottom, where the majority work to get the job done', but rather 'at the top' (Stanistreet, 2011).

This chapter will explore these tensions between the individual, the institutional, and the collective approach to the relationship between ethics and journalism. It will examine evidence that collective and individual responsibility for ethics are not contradictory, that they can coexist within an institutional setting and that, together, in a culture of dialogue, openness, and mutual respect, the individual and the collective can create a framework and an atmosphere within a newsroom whereby more ethical journalism might be encouraged, facilitated, and expected. The primary evidence examined below will be accounts by journalists themselves given to the Leveson Inquiry, although some earlier ethical interventions by journalists are also drawn upon to help contextualise more recent material (Harcup, 2002, 2005, 2007, 2012).

In an effort to make sense of such accounts, the evidence from journalists will be analysed not only within the context of recurring arguments about the *individual* responsibility of journalists (Frunza and Frunza, 2011) but also by drawing on feminist thinking concerning the roles of the individual and the collective in democratic participation and in active citizenship (Dietz, 1992; Harcup, 2011, 2013; Lister, 1997, 2003). The argument will be advanced that a newsroom culture with a degree of openness, one that ensures space for some collective discussion of ethical issues, can have the effect of encouraging individuals to express their own ethical concerns, even if – perhaps, especially if – those individuals appear out of step with the thinking of the majority. In this sense, the individual and the collective can work together; indeed, such a collective *requires* the input of individuals. If an active citizen within a democracy is 'somebody who *acts* as a citizen, who conceives of herself as a participant in a collective undertaking' (Mouffe, 1992: 4; emphasis in original) then so too is a journalist within an ethical newsroom.

A dialectic relationship

The responsibility of the individual journalist has been a recurrent theme in debates about ethics, with the argument being advanced that ethical responsibility for journalistic output rests 'as much with the individual journalist as with any institutional framework' (Hargreaves, 2003: 167). Although 'almost all modern journalism takes place within a corporate setting, which limits and influences what journalists do', it has been argued that individuals are still responsible for preserving the 'moral compass' they learned before entering journalism (Hargreaves, 2003: 140, 227). At the very least, individual journalists have the power to decide for whom they can stomach working (Randall, 2000: 133) and, even once employed, they retain the ability to exercise what John O'Neill calls 'principled resignation' (1992: 28) by resigning from any organisation of which they disapprove. Sandra Borden (2000: 161) describes this as the 'take this job and shove it' form of resistance, but she adds: 'To stand up for professional ideals, journalists should not be *required* to be moral heroes, however *desirable* heroism may be' (p. 151; emphasis in original). A focus on individual responsibility can be problematic because, by leaving their jobs, individuals might well be able to end their own contribution towards what they see as an unethical undertaking, but they are unlikely to prevent others from continuing. As for the alternative option of remaining in post whilst trying to effect change from within, Deirdre O'Neill argues: 'To expect individuals to make a stand at the expense of their careers is unrealistic – what is needed is a collective response' (2004: 48).

Of relevance here is the issue of agency – that is, the ability to act, to intervene, to make a difference. Although journalists as individuals do have some degree of agency and 'are free to act in one way or another', as Karen Sanders (2003: 15) notes, they are not 'autonomous moral agents. They must work within business enterprises whose owners and managers are concerned, as much as anything, with profits, increased circulation, audience figures and, in some cases, disseminating propaganda' (Sanders, 2003: 27). It is in this sense that human agency may be understood not in splendid isolation but as existing 'in a dialectic relationship with social structures' and 'embedded in social and cultural relations', as Ruth Lister (2003: 38) puts it. That is, citizens may have individual agency, but they are also *social* beings who may engage in 'collective activities directed towards collective as well as individual ends' (Lister, 2003: 38). This theoretical conceptualisation of the fluidity, interplay, and tension between the roles of the individual, the institution, and the collective within a social structure may be seen in practice by reading the sometimes painful testimony of those flesh-and-blood journalists from real, concrete (and glass) work-places who gave evidence during the course of the Leveson Inquiry.

'It's not an open dialogue'

In light of the above, let us now consider a little of the voluminous evidence that was presented to Leveson, all of which remains available as a valuable resource on the inquiry's website (www.levesoninquiry.org.uk). We are not concerned here with the testimony that attracted most media coverage, that of celebrities, other victims of phone hacking, proprietors, high-profile editors and ex-editors, senior police officers, or politicians. Instead, we will examine some of the sorry tales told by 'ordinary' journalists who have worked in the pressurised and highly competitive world of the UK's tabloid press. Consider this example from one such journalist:

> *I worked for the* News of the World *for over three years ... It was a very intimidating culture ... People lived in fear. There's a real military chain of command. You do what you're told when you're told ... It takes a pretty brave person to take a stand ... If you want a career in the future you shut up and you keep quiet ... The culture is macho, it pervades the industry ... The culture is such that you don't question it ... I can't tell you how high the levels of paranoia and pressure were. It's an insidious environment to work in. During the time I worked there I kept my mouth shut like everyone else there. No-one wants to hear it.*
> *(Quoted in Stanistreet, 2012a)*

Those are the words of a journalist with 30 years of experience across the industry in the UK, who would only give evidence by means of being interviewed by the General Secretary of the National Union of Journalists (NUJ) and guaranteed anonymity (Stanistreet, 2012b). It is worth noting that such anonymous evidence was heard only after lawyers for the NUJ fought off employers' attempts to block it.

Another of the journalists interviewed – this one with six years' experience – described the culture at the *News of the World* in the following terms: 'The atmosphere was poisonous, it was unchecked bullying. When your boss said jump, it was a case of how high and where do you want me to jump from.' Other experienced journalists referred to 'constant ritual humiliation' and 'a deliberate climate of fear and tension', within which the unwritten rules were 'never complain publicly and never refuse an order' (quoted in Stanistreet, 2012a).

A journalist with experience working on two unidentified national newspapers gave a sense of the internal conflicts felt by some within such an environment:

> *The bullying that goes on has to be seen to be believed. A lot of the time it's shouting and swearing, being humiliated and made to feel really*

stupid. I've been so tempted to just walk out so many times, but I just bite my tongue and put up with it. I can barely make ends meet as it is. I can't afford to lose my job ... But I've seen other people being treated much worse than me – literally reduced to tears – and in a way that makes me feel worse because I've not intervened to stop it. (Quoted in Stanistreet, 2012a)

Some journalists *have* intervened on occasion, the inquiry was told. A journalist on one title 'made my dissatisfaction with the continued anti-Islam agenda within the pages very clear', explaining:

On numerous occasions, knowing all too well that whatever balance or neutrality I incorporated into my stories would be changed or removed, I asked the news editors to remove my byline from the final piece. This earned me the reputation and nickname of the 'token leftie' in the newsroom – and in what was often portrayed as a 'joke', solely for the amusement of the news editors and reporters, I was targeted to produce the highest number of anti-Muslim stories ... This didn't stop, even when I was in tears because I hated what I was being forced to do so passionately. (Quoted in Stanistreet, 2012a)

That journalist resigned. Another experienced journalist, referring to stress and a 'genuine sense of fear' amongst staff at the *News of the World*, offered the opinion that 'having independent trade union representation at News International might well have affected the culture at the *News of the World* ... Having the NUJ represented would have given staff more confidence in dealings with management and, almost certainly, fostered a greater sense of openness' (journalist quoted in Stanistreet, 2012a). It might be countered that such journalists would say that (wouldn't they?), as they were giving evidence anonymously, via the offices of the NUJ itself. Yet these individuals were not alone in painting a picture of a culture within national tabloid newsrooms in general, and the *News of the World* in particular, that might be thought of as inimical to human rights at work and an employer's duty of care towards employees, let alone to the concept of ethical journalism.

The Leveson Inquiry heard evidence from Richard Peppiatt (2011a) who said he felt he would have been 'laughed out the door' of the *Daily Star* newsroom had he ever attempted to use the Press Complaints Commission Editors' Code of Practice to raise an ethical issue during his time on the newspaper. He added: 'The spectre of being "let go" at any moment is a powerful deterrent against sticking your head above the trench if you disagree with something that is occurring' (Peppiatt, 2011a). So he kept his head down and contributed towards what he now considers to be unethical journalism before eventually walking out and going public with his concerns

Asked whether he had expressed disquiet over the 'Muslim-bashing stories' that he admitted writing for the newspaper, Peppiatt told the inquiry:

> I certainly did towards the end when I was very much sort of really disheartened with what was going on, but about a year beforehand, there had been a casual reporter like myself who had expressed disquiet over the tone of the coverage and because she did that, she was given every anti-Muslim, every anti-immigrant story to write from then on for about two weeks until it became so much that she quit, and that was the – you know, it certainly deterred me, and I am – you know, certainly to this day, I am deeply ashamed of myself that I didn't walk out the door with her but instead I stuck my head down and thought: 'I don't want to end up like that, I can't afford to be'. That's the atmosphere. You toe the line or you get punished. It's not an open dialogue. (2011b)

It was not an open dialogue. Precisely. If Peppiatt might be dismissed by some as having courted publicity in the way he eventually walked out on his job – with an open letter to his proprietor published on the website of a rival newspaper (Peppiatt, 2011c) – the same cannot be said about Matt Driscoll. He was very much the ordinary journalist, an experienced sports reporter who quietly got on with his job. In his witness statement to Leveson, he described being shocked at some of the 'darker arts' of the *News of the World*, such as the paper obtaining an individual's private medical records and engaging an actor to pretend to be somebody else for the purpose of obtaining confidential personal information (a practice known in the trade as 'blagging'). Of the latter, he recalled: 'The general attitude to this in the newsroom was one of mirth' (Driscoll, 2011a). His statement continued:

> At the time I felt very uneasy about such methods. However, I knew I could not bring up my concerns on the editorial floor for fear of being seen as a trouble maker. Any writer who questioned the morality of these methods used by executives would have been a marked man ... There was an ever-growing trend to get the big story or headline by any means

*possible ... I feel that for many years some newspapers have been on
course for destruction. Editors were handed far too much power and
their egos were allowed to run wild. Some that I worked for often became
pampered peacocks who only ever wanted to hear the word 'yes' and
would shout and scream if they heard anything else ... And the closure
of one of the world's oldest newspapers was, in my view, is [sic] born of
the collective responsibility of a culture of neglect at executive level to look
at themselves from the public's perspective. (2011a)*

Driscoll told the inquiry how he suddenly found that his face did not fit at
the paper, and he was dismissed after being subjected to what his
subsequent (successful) employment tribunal found to have been a culture
of bullying at the paper. In his oral evidence to Leveson, he expanded on
the above theme that – in some newsrooms, at least – the climate is one in
which compliant 'yes' people are encouraged (and promoted) whilst
ethical qualms are actively discouraged:

*I've thought about it long and hard, it would be a very brave journalist,
certainly in the early years of his career on the paper, to suddenly say,
'I'm not happy with these techniques that are being used'. You'd be
basically making a decision over your career there. Anyone on that floor
who complained too much would find themselves pushed out, certainly.
(Driscoll, 2011b)*

Such attitudes were not confined to the *News of the World* or other
Murdoch titles and could be found throughout much of the national press,
according to Driscoll, who explained:

*It's a kind of bizarre world that the editors and big executives on
newspapers work in. They rarely get questioned by anyone, certainly
[not] their staff. Most of the people they're surrounded by are people who
are going to say 'yes' and are going to agree with them most of the time. I
can think of a few examples where most of the staff would be thinking:
'Why have we got that on the front page? Why is that story being used?
It's not going to sell papers. It's the wrong story to have this week or this
day'. But no one was brave enough to actually say that to the editor, and
editors would lead a very cossetted life. (Driscoll, 2011b)*

Driscoll worked in sport, an environment in which some might think a
testosterone-fuelled bullying culture goes with the territory. But the
atmosphere was not all that different in news, if the *News of the World's*

former news editor Ian Edmondson is to be believed. He told the Leveson Inquiry that he had to carry out tasks about which he felt uneasy or uncomfortable because 'I was told to', even though he had the title of news editor. He explained where he saw power residing within the newspaper:

> Every part of the paper is dictated and controlled by the editor ... You don't do anything unless you are told to do something ... it's a case of you will do as you are told and you live in that environment ... It's not a democracy at a newspaper. Autocratic. (Edmondson, 2012)

All the evidence cited above may be rare and extreme examples of newsroom culture. The evidence may come from a succession of disgruntled journalists who, their erstwhile employers may feel, just couldn't hack it (pun intended) in the cut and thrust of a tabloid newsroom. But it is worth noting that an employment tribunal found that Matt Driscoll had indeed been the victim of a bullying regime at the *News of the World*, and also that the company lost its appeal against the tribunal's ruling of unfair dismissal, with compensation plus legal costs totalling in the region of £800,000 (Driscoll, 2011b). In other words, Driscoll's version of events was found to be credible by an independent body that examined the evidence.

That is just one case, and it could be suggested that anonymous journalists whose testimony was recorded by their trade union ought to enjoy less credibility than that. But if even a tiny fraction of their evidence is accepted at face value, then that is surely sufficient to suggest, to put it no higher, that something has on occasion gone seriously wrong in some of the newsrooms of the UK national press. The above examples may be extreme, but perhaps they represent one end of a continuum within journalism rather than a total aberration from what has become the norm.

A citizen among other citizens?

Reading the testimony above, two questions spring immediately to mind: What on earth is going on in such newsrooms, and how can people let it happen? A clue may be provided by the fact that, although Matt Driscoll, for example, now has plenty to say about what went wrong at his former newspaper, he did not exactly choose to put his head above the parapet whilst he was still there. He is speaking out only after he found that his face no longer fitted, after he himself became a victim of the paper's culture, and after ceasing to be employed there. If his conscience did trouble him before that moment then, by his own account, he kept any such concerns to himself. As he says, it would take a 'brave' journalist to question, openly, practices that seem to be accepted by peers and superiors alike. It appears that he did not do so whilst he was in the midst of it all.

When considering the position of the individual within the social and economic structure of such a media company, the role of – and constraints upon – human agency can be seen as assuming a crucial importance, as can the question of what rights and responsibilities (or obligations) the individual and the collective may have towards each other. Therefore, the experiences of the journalists quoted above might usefully be considered not merely as a sorry series of individual tales but as evidence of how a social structure (in this case, the newsroom) can bear down on individuals, constrain their sense of agency, and militate against ethical qualms being expressed in an open manner. To this end, we are less concerned with examining the behaviour of these individual journalists than we are with exploring ideas of how a newsroom full of intelligent and inquiring people can become a place in which only a particularly 'brave' – or foolhardy? – employee is likely to ask awkward questions about what is going on in his or her place of employment. A fruitful line of such inquiry might be to consider the witnesses' accounts within the context of discussions about our roles as individual citizens participating in a wider collective undertaking (aka society) and, in particular, to draw on theorising that has emerged amongst feminist thinkers in recent decades about the interplay between the individual and the collective in the form of 'active citizenship'.

Why look to feminist theories to help make sense of the journalists' testimony? Partly because such theorising has much to say that is relevant to issues of democracy, informing discussion of how alternative and participatory forms of journalism can be seen as citizenship in action (Harcup, 2011, 2013; Rodriguez, 2002). And partly because, given mainstream journalism's own claims about the key role it plays in enabling the democratic participation of a well-informed citizenry (Kovach and Rosenstiel, 2003; Lloyd, 2011), the inclusive nature of such feminist thinking on citizenship might help broaden our perspective or, at the very least, provide a small side window through which we might view issues from a different angle. Thirdly, given the 'macho' culture that seems to have pervaded some of the newspapers in which unethical journalism has apparently flourished, a feminist perspective on events might also provide a useful counter-balance (or counter-narrative) to some of the mainstream explanations of the events under consideration. After all, evidence suggests that, even though many of today's newsrooms have more of a gender balance than in decades gone by, that is not enough on its own to preclude the existence of a 'macho' culture.

For Mary Dietz, 'the power of democracy rests in its capacity to transform the individual as teacher, trader, corporate executive, child, sibling, worker, artist, friend or mother' – and, we might add, as journalist, source, or reader – 'into a special sort of political being, a citizen among other citizens ... Its relation is that of civic peers; its guiding virtue is mutual respect; its primary principle is the "positive liberty" of democracy and self-government' (1992: 75). Furthermore, for Dietz, such a participatory and democratic notion of active citizenship based upon mutual respect 'must be conceived of as a continuous activity and a good in itself' (p. 76). The absence of even a semblance of such mutual respect on the editorial floors of the newspapers described above perhaps points to why so few internal voices seemed to be raised against what other citizens might regard as alarmingly unethical practices. The evidence suggests that, in certain newsrooms at certain times, journalists who were supposed to be society's fearless watchdogs on behalf of fellow citizens were not themselves trusted or allowed to be citizens, or to have a voice of their own.

The *News of the World* was manifestly not operating as a democracy, just as the *Daily Star* newsroom was clearly not the place for open dialogue, as Ian Edmonson (2012) and Richard Peppiatt (2011b), respectively, testified. And who would ever have expected anything different, given that they were/are commercial publications operating in a marketplace not of ideas but of commodities, namely a newsprint product bought by readers who are in turn 'sold' to advertisers? Such newspapers do not claim to be internal democracies or to operate as if they are workers' co-operatives, so what is the big deal about them being run in what Edmondson (above) described as an 'autocratic' fashion?

The big deal is that journalism *does* lay claim to a democratic role for itself, operating as 'a check on the powerful', in the words of the editor of *The Times* newspaper, who adds: 'In a democracy, journalists should ask politicians questions, not answer to them' (Harding, 2012). Journalism owes its first loyalty to a society's citizens, according to the Committee of Concerned Journalists (cited in Harcup, 2007: 181). Given such claims, journalists' own accounts of being denied a voice at work are surely worth listening to at a time when society is still wondering how things could have gone quite so badly wrong in the press. Is it not at least possible, even plausible, that discouraging journalists themselves from speaking out has been damaging to the role of journalists as enablers and champions of democracy? And is it not likewise the case that journalists' role of acting as a check on the powerful might be compromised if power relations within the newsroom itself are left unexamined and unquestioned? As Maurizio Passerin d'Entreves argues, 'the ability of citizens to enlarge their opinions and to test their judgments can only flourish in a public culture of democratic participation that guarantees to everyone the right to action and opinion' and in which 'individuals can act collectively and engage in common deliberation' (1992: 165). If we substitute the word journalists for citizens in d'Entreves's argument, we can see what a contrast such an ideal offers to the 'bizarre' workplaces described by Driscoll (2011b) and others.

If having the freedom and space within which people can exercise their voice is 'crucial to their possibilities of acting as citizens' (Couldry, 2006: 326), we need to ask: are journalists not citizens too and, if so, how might they assert such citizenship (Harcup, 2005)? Lister argues that a more active form of citizenship must be conceptualised as a process rather than a status, seeing citizens not as 'atomised individuals but in the context of the wider society' (2003: 36). For her, citizenship can become 'an expression of human agency' (p. 37) through 'struggle' (p. 6), although she recognises that not all citizens will be engaged in struggle all of the time (p. 42). Indeed, some may seek a quiet life or keep their heads down some of the time. But the *possibility* of action – of agency – remains, and 'to *act* as a citizen involves fulfilling the full potential of the status' (Lister, 2003: 42; my emphasis).

Informed by such thinking, it perhaps becomes a little easier to understand how a collection of individuals in a particular workplace may end up allowing unethical practices to continue unchecked: people who are in effect denied the right to speak (as citizens or journalists) may feel little responsibility or obligation (as citizens or journalists) towards activities of which they are aware or even in which they are engaged. In many UK newspapers, it seems that ethical issues were too often considered above the pay grade of the individual journalists who were required simply to carry out instructions. This attitude is perhaps symbolised by the insistence of the UK's Press Complaints Commission throughout its two decades of existence that no journalist below the rank of editor should have a say either in its deliberations on complaints or in the formulation of its Code of Practice, which it always referred to, pointedly, as the *editors'* code. Clearly editors play a key role in the production of most journalism, but if their system of 'self-regulation' effectively denies their subordinates the right to speak, is there not something missing?

The dangers of leaving ethics in the hands of senior editors and company executives were clearly demonstrated at the *News of the World*, according to Matt Driscoll, who referred to a 'collective responsibility' at the senior level (Driscoll, 2011a). Others might consider the phrase 'collective irresponsibility' to be more accurate in that particular case. Either way, based on the evidence, the *News of the World* does not appear to have been a workplace in which ordinary journalists felt they had much of a voice either individually or collectively. Yet the Leveson Inquiry heard evidence of some such interventions at other newspapers. At the *Daily Express*, journalists twice joined forces via the NUJ to complain about their newspaper's coverage of asylum-seekers (in 2001) and gypsies (in 2004). In addition, an anti-Muslim spoof page was pulled from the *Daily Star* at the last minute (in 2006) after a group of the paper's journalists met to express their collective disquiet (Stanistreet, 2011). It is also worth noting that the biggest strike in UK television occurred when workers took action not over pay, pensions, or job losses, but over an issue of journalistic ethics: the 1985 *Real Lives* strike over censorship of a BBC documentary about events in Northern Ireland (Harcup, 2007: 133). A small number of other examples of ethical intervention could be cited (Frost, 2012; Harcup, 2002; White, 2008), but at least as significant as such showdowns might be the smaller actions that we rarely hear about, the quietly expressed concern, even the raising of a collective eyebrow at a superior's dubious suggestion.

Bravery in the newsroom

When extracts of witness testimony were read aloud at the Reuters Institute conference on journalism ethics in September 2012, the journalists, scholars, and journalism educators assembled in Oxford were 'inevitably left with goosebumps', according to one of the participants (Russ-Mohl, 2012). Certain words and phrases leap out from the journalists' evidence to Leveson: fear, military chain of command, do what you're told, shut up, keep quiet, macho, insidious, poisonous, bullying, ritual humiliation, climate of fear and tension, never complain, never refuse an order, tears, targeted, uneasy, ashamed, compliant, marked man, autocratic, and finally – as mentioned by several witnesses – brave. That last (but not least) word was used, it is worth recalling, by way of explaining that it would have taken a very brave journalist to have stood up and objected to what was going on. But these are journalists speaking – people who have survived for years, in some cases decades, at the sharp end of a trade that is not renowned for being populated with shrinking violets or people who are easily intimidated. So what on earth *was* going on?

If journalism is about speaking truth to power, as that heavily eroded yet durable cliché tells us it is, then journalists should be expected to be brave, even those of us who work in liberal democratic societies where the risk of being arrested, tortured, or assassinated for our efforts is, thankfully, relatively slight. Journalists *should* be brave in all sorts of ways, within our workplaces as well as with those on whom we are reporting. As individuals we should not let ourselves off the hook by saying we are only following orders, only doing our job, only doing what someone else surely will if we don't. Employees at the bottom of the hierarchical ladder do retain *some* agency, even if it may sometimes seem as if the only choice is between the boss's way or the highway. As Lister notes, 'people can be, at the same time, both the subordinate objects of hierarchical power relations *and* subjects who are agents in their own lives, capable of exercising power' (1997: 35; emphasis in original).

After hearing the journalists' stories as recounted in this chapter, the resulting discussion among those in Oxford was empathetic, critical, and insightful, as if to demonstrate there and then the way that individuals and a collective can work together productively. Karen Slattery from Marquette University in the United States (and a contributor to this volume) spoke of parallels between the dysfunctional newsrooms described above and research into so-called horizontal or 'lateral violence' among nurses who, feeling powerless within the workplace, sometimes take out their frustrations on each other. Herman Wasserman from Rhodes University in South Africa pointed out that the sort of internal bullying described within newsrooms could be seen as mirroring the bullying approach that some journalists display externally towards the wider public; he also highlighted the connection between having a voice and feminist thinking on 'active listening'. Others contributing to the discussion underlined the difficulty of any individual speaking out against unethical practice at work when, for economic reasons, the person does not wish to risk losing his or her job. Yet others at the Oxford conference spoke of feeling personally 'inspired' to go back to their own workplaces more prepared to voice concerns and to show bravery.

Creating a healthier culture

We ought to be brave, of course, in academe as much as in journalism. The Leveson Inquiry heard evidence that some individual journalists *have* raised their voices on occasions. However, an occupation and an industry that *relies* for its sense of ethical responsibility on a few brave souls speaking out and putting their jobs on the line is an occupation and an industry that is almost bound to fail to live up to its high ideals or to meet the ethical standards that journalists routinely demand of others.

Individuals have a role to play in creating a healthier newsroom culture, whether that means being prepared to speak out occasionally, actively offering support for others who do so, or merely assuming a more passive role and not ganging up on someone or taking part in the bullying or victimisation of a colleague. But individuals do not act in a vacuum, and frequently there *is* a form of a collective at work in a newsroom, even if it does not see itself as such. It is the collective of the 'yes man' and (perhaps less prevalent) the 'yes woman'. The question arises whether newsrooms would be healthier places for journalists and citizens alike if they had a more collective spirit of 'yes, but …' and even occasionally 'no, because …'. What's needed is further recognition that journalists ought to be given voice within the workplace just as citizens are given voice within wider society. Anna Yeatman refers to this as 'dialogical rights', namely 'a right to give voice and be listened to within the dialogical process of decision-making' (quoted in Lister, 1997: 40). Speaking, in this sense, is only part of the necessary process because, as Carol Gilligan points out, 'speaking depends on listening and being heard; it is an intensely relational act' (1993: xvi). And, as Fiona Robinson writes, such dialogue 'does not have a clear beginning or end, but is instead a long process of moral learning' (2011: 855).

Research that has explored horizontal violence or 'silencing' in the nursing profession shows that such a process has the potential to alter established working relationships and transform the culture within a workplace (Dong and Temple, 2011; Fletcher, 2006; Roberts et al., 2009). The concept of horizontal violence draws on the work of anti-colonial writers Frantz Fanon and Paulo Freire, who both described how oppressed people sometimes hit out at those nearest to them rather than support each other against those responsible for their oppression (Fanon, [1961] 1967: 40 and 248; Freire, [1970] 1972: 38). Thus, the oppressed could in effect become 'sub-oppressors' (Freire, [1970] 1972: 22), a phenomenon that might be recognisable to some employees who have seen former colleagues promoted to middle-management positions.

Studies of nursing suggest that workplace cultures can change and that dialogue helps promote such change. It may not be inevitable, but it is possible, argues Karen Fletcher:

> [I]t is easy, and understandable ... to feel victimised and have a cynical outlook, and believe that no amount of effort will make our world more liveable. Yet, we have seen that there is some possibility for change. We have seen that social structural factors in the workplace are important conditions for empowering nurses to accomplish their work ... The development of self-awareness through reflection, in itself, can begin to break the cycle of oppression and lead to changes in the structures that oppress nurses. However, it is only through dialogue and engaging in a healing relationship that empowerment can occur. (2006: 57–8)

If we also conceive of newsrooms as places in which such dialogue can take place, and if we conceive of journalists as citizens with rights as well as obligations, we might conclude that change can happen in newsrooms too. If so, the idea of the individual and the collective working together to create a more ethical newsroom culture need not be pie in the sky.

Nor would it require the journalistic production process to be constantly halted to allow for endless ethical discussions. Journalism already involves a complex intellectual effort, the production of which necessitates more-or-less constant communication and cooperation within editorial teams, so journalists ought to be able to reflect upon and 'scrutinise their own actions, exposing the processes and underlying values in their work *while* they are doing it', as Lynette Sheridan Burns puts it (2002: 44; emphasis in original). And if the atmosphere is such that ethical (and other) qualms can be expressed internally prior to publication, a considerable amount of time, trouble, angst, money, and reputation may be saved in the long run.

Outspokenness or collective discussion will not automatically produce collective wisdom, and allowing people to speak up and be listened to can be challenging, involving as it does the possibility of 'conflict, dissonance, and persuasion' (Dreher, 2009: 449). Individuals may still feel the need to stand out against the crowd, and a strong newsroom will have to be able to accommodate the maverick, the loner, the one-person awkward squad. But the evidence suggests that a workplace climate in which ethical concerns can be discussed openly by journalists – informally and/or formally, individually and/or collectively – will *ultimately* be good for journalistic standards. Let's not forget that we have seen what happens in the absence of such a climate.

There are power relations at work here, and they must be acknowledged if we hope to make sense, not just of what went wrong at the *News of the World*, but of how we can move forward to create more ethical forms of journalism. As Mary Dietz contends:

> [F]eminists have long recognised as imperative the task of seeking out, defining and criticising the complex reality that governs the ways we think, the values we hold, and the relationships we share ... If context is all, then feminism in its various guises is committed to uncovering what is all around us and to revealing the power relations that constitute the creatures we become ... We are indeed conditioned by the contexts in which we live, but we are also the creators of our political and social constructions and we can change them if we are so determined ... First, however, the urgency must be felt, and the spirit necessary for revitalizing citizenship must be enlivened in the public realm. (1992: 63 and 79)

That seems to be a useful way of looking at journalists and ethics too, although Dietz was writing more than 20 years ago not about journalism but about wider social relations. That same year, Carl Bernstein put it more bluntly, more journalistically:

> Good journalism requires a degree of courage in today's climate, a quality now in scarce supply in our mass media ... We need to start asking the same fundamental questions about the press that we do of the other powerful institutions in this society – about who is served, about standards, about self-interest and its eclipse of the public interest and the interest of truth. (1992: 28)

Having examined evidence that has emerged from some of the newsrooms of the UK national press in recent years, it might be concluded that, when it comes to asking those hard questions, to critiquing power relations, and revitalising citizenship based on mutual respect, there is no better place to start than in those very newsrooms and no better time than now. As Ruth Lister argues, 'To act as a citizen requires first a sense of agency, the belief that one can act; acting as a citizen, especially collectively, in turn fosters that sense of agency' (2003: 39). To which we might add, to act as an ethical journalist requires not merely a willingness to reflect but also the belief that one can act – whether individually or collectively – and such action can in turn foster a more reflective practice and a sense of human agency, leading ultimately to more ethical forms of journalism.

Note

All web addresses in this chapter were last accessed in June 2013.

References

Bernstein, Carl (1992) 'The Idiot Culture', *New Republic*, 8 June: 22–8.

Borden, Sandra (2000) 'A Model for Evaluating Journalist Resistance to Business Constraints', *Journal of Mass Media Ethics*, 15(3): 149–66.

Couldry, Nick (2006) 'Culture and Citizenship: The Missing Link?', *European Journal of Cultural Studies*, 9(3): 321–39.

Dietz, Mary (1992) 'Context is All: Feminism and Theories of Citizenship', in Chantal Mouffe (ed.), *Dimensions of Radical Democracy: Pluralism, Citizenship, Community* (London: Verso), 63–85.

Dong, Doris, and Temple, Beverley (2011) 'Oppression: A Concept Analysis and Implications for Nurses and Nursing', *Nursing Forum*, 46(3): 169–76.

Dreher, Tanja (2009) 'Listening across Difference: Media and Multiculturalism beyond the Politics of Voice', *Continuum*, 23(4): 445–58.

Driscoll, Matthew (2011a) 'Witness Statement of Matthew Driscoll', *Leveson Inquiry: Culture, Practice and Ethics of the Press*: www.levesoninquiry.org.uk/evidence/?witness=matthew-driscoll.

Driscoll, Matthew (2011b) 'Transcript of Afternoon Hearing 19 December 2011', *Leveson Inquiry: Culture, Practice and Ethics of the Press*: www.levesoninquiry.org.uk/evidence/?witness=matthew-driscoll.

Edmondson, Ian (2012) 'Transcript of Morning Hearing 9 February 2012', *Leveson Inquiry: Culture, Practice and Ethics of the Press*: www.levesoninquiry.org.uk/evidence/?witness=ian-edmonson.

d'Entreves, Maurizio Passerin (1992) 'Hannah Arendt and the Idea of Citizenship', in Chantal Mouffe (ed.), *Dimensions of Radical Democracy: Pluralism, Citizenship, Community* (London: Verso), 145–68.

Fanon, Frantz ([1961] 1967) *The Wretched of the Earth* (London: Penguin).

Fletcher, Karen (2006) 'Beyond Dualism: Leading out of Oppression', *Nursing Forum*, 41(2): 50–9.

Freire, Paulo ([1970] 1972) *Pedagogy of the Oppressed* (London: Penguin).

Frost, Chris (2012) 'Ethics and the Newsroom Culture', in Richard Keeble and John Mair (eds), *The Phone Hacking Scandal* (Bury St Edmunds: Abramis), 250–61.

Frunza, Sandu, and Frunza, Mihaela (2011) 'The Ethical Fundamentals of the Responsibility of the Journalist', *Journal of Media Research*, 4(1): 31–41.

Gilligan, Carol (1993) *In a Different Voice* (Cambridge, MA, and London: Harvard University Press).

Harcup, Tony (2002) 'Journalists and Ethics: The Quest for a Collective Voice', *Journalism Studies*, 3(1): 101–14.

Harcup, Tony (2005) 'Citizens in the Newsroom: Democracy, Ethics and Journalism', *Ethical Space*, 2(3): 25–31.

Harcup, Tony (2007) *The Ethical Journalist* (London: Sage).

Harcup, Tony (2011) 'Alternative Journalism as Active Citizenship', *Journalism*, 12(1): 15–31.

Harcup, Tony (2012) 'Standing up for Standards', in Richard Keeble and John Mair (eds), *The Phone Hacking Scandal* (Bury St Edmunds: Abramis), 240–9.

Harcup, Tony (2013) *Alternative Journalism, Alternative Voices* (London: Routledge).

Harding, James (2012) 'Don't Force the Press into Politicians' Arms', *The Times*, 27 Nov.: 18.

Hargreaves, Ian (2003) *Journalism: Truth or Dare?* (Oxford: Oxford University Press).

Kovach, Bill, and Rosenstiel, Tom (2003) *The Elements of Journalism: What Newspeople Should Know and the Public Should Expect* (London: Atlantic).

Lister, Ruth (1997) 'Citizenship: Towards a Feminist Synthesis', *Feminist Review*, 57: 28–48.

Lister, Ruth (2003) *Citizenship: Feminist Perspectives* (2nd edn, Basingstoke: Palgrave).

Lloyd, John (2011) *Scandal! News International and the Rights of Journalism* (Oxford: Reuters Institute for the Study of Journalism).

McNair, Brian (2010) *Journalists in Film: Heroes and Villains* (Edinburgh: Edinburgh University Press).

Mouffe, Chantal (ed.) (1992) *Dimensions of Radical Democracy: Pluralism, Citizenship, Community* (London: Verso).

O'Neill, Deirdre (2004) 'The Challenge for Journalism Educators', in *Journalism and Public Trust* (London: NUJ Ethics Council and Mediawise), 47–9.

O'Neill, John (1992) 'Journalism in the Market Place', in Andrew Belsey and Ruth Chadwick (eds), *Ethical Issues in Journalism and the Media* (London: Routledge), 15–32.

Peppiatt, Richard (2011a) 'Witness Statement of Richard Peppiatt', *Leveson Inquiry: Culture, Practice and Ethics of the Press*: www.levesoninquiry.org.uk/evidence/?witness=richard-peppiatt.

Peppiatt, Richard (2011b) 'Transcript of Morning Hearing 29 November 2011', *Leveson Inquiry: Culture, Practice and Ethics of the Press*: www.levesoninquiry.org.uk/evidence/?witness=richard-peppiatt.

Peppiatt, Richard (2011c) 'Richard Peppiatt's Letter to *Daily Star* Proprietor Richard Desmond', *Guardian*, 4 Mar.: www.guardian.co.uk/media/2011/mar/04/daily-star-reporter-letter-full?INTCMP=SRCH.

Randall, David (2000) *The Universal Journalist* (2nd edn, London: Pluto).

Roberts, Susan Jo, Demarco, Rosanna and Griffin, Martha (2009) 'The Effect of Oppressed Group Behaviours on the Culture of the Nursing Workplace: A Review of the Evidence and Interventions for Change', *Journal of Nursing Management*, 17: 288–93.

Robinson, Fiona (2011) 'Stop Talking and Listen: Discourse Ethics and Feminist Care Ethics in International Political Theory', *Millennium: Journal of International Studies*, 39(3): 845–60.

Rodriguez, Clemencia (2002) 'Citizens' Media and the Voice of the Angel/Poet', *Media International Australia*, 103: 78–87.

Russ-Mohl, Stephen (2012) 'Media Mafia', *European Journalism Observatory*, 6 Nov.: http://en.ejo.ch/5850/ethics/media-mafia.

Sanders, Karen (2003) *Ethics and Journalism* (London: Sage).

Sheridan Burns, Lynette (2002) *Understanding Journalism* (London: Sage).

Stanistreet, Michelle (2011) 'NUJ Submission to Leveson Inquiry', *National Union of Journalists: Campaigns*, 16 Nov.: www.nuj.org.uk/innerPagenuj.html?docid=2310.

Stanistreet, Michelle (2012a) 'MS Exhibit 1', *Leveson Inquiry: Culture, Practice and Ethics of the Press*: www.levesoninquiry.org.uk/evidence/?witness=michelle-stanistreet.

Stanistreet, Michelle (2012b) 'Second Witness Statement of Michelle Stanistreet', *Leveson Inquiry: Culture, Practice and Ethics of the Press*: www.levesoninquiry.org.uk/evidence/?witness=michelle-stanistreet.

White, Aidan (2008) *To Tell You the Truth: The Ethical Journalism Initiative* (Brussels: International Federation of Journalists).

3

My Newsroom Made Me Do It: The Impact of Organisational Climate on Ethical Decision-Making

Lee Wilkins

> *Perhaps the single greatest key to the medical function of the Auschwitz self was the technicising of everything. That self could divest from immediate ethical concerns by concentrating on the purely technical or purely professional. (Lifton, The Nazi Doctors)*

Ethics has always focused on the individual. Classical ethical theory – from the virtue ethics of Aristotle through the deontology of Kant and the utilitarianism of Mill – has also focused on individual decision-making. Yet within that classical realm, there is a contradiction. Aristotle believed that humans were social animals. Mill linked the common good with community, and it is impossible to conceptualise duty without considering duty to whom … or to what. People live in groups; they do not exist in isolation. Ethical theory has always conceptualised the essential human being as part of a group, even if that group connection was overshadowed by the individual.

This chapter argues that groups – for the purposes of this project, news organisations – may influence ethical decision-making in three distinct ways. First, news organisations form a culture, or what contemporary literature refers to as a climate. That climate, in turn, provides a kind of solidarity; it allows organisations to relate to the 'outside' world – other institutions, other news organisations, and audiences – all of which are subsumed under the concept of institutional role. Climate also provides a tangible internal support network. Second, organisational climate sets up formal and informal behaviour standards, including standards for individual ethical behaviour. Those boundaries do not dictate or predetermine precisely what it is that individuals will do; rather, climate establishes the boundaries of acceptable acts. Third, organisations, through their leaders, emphasise certain values that subtly permeate the organisation and its employees. The values of individuals acting within organisations are negotiated. Organisations may summon some values yet modify or dismiss others. These negotiated values are often instrumental in nature; they serve a larger organisational end, which may or may not be in alignment with individual understanding of values, standards, and goals. Organisational climate does not replace individual thinking or the emotional components of ethical decision-making. But organisational ethical culture can enhance or degrade individual ethical choice in both inconsequential and fundamental ways. In fact, case studies (Adams and Balfour, 2004) suggest that this impact can supersede individual, logical decision-making.

This chapter applies insights from the business ethics and organisational change literature to what is known about News Corp and the phone hacking scandal. After reviewing the News Corp case and the relevant literature on organisational ethical decision-making, the chapter explores a template for evaluating organisational culture and its impact on ethical decision-making. The chapter ends with an important caveat that ethical values alone do not lead to an ethical organisation.

Murdoch's mess: Individual and/or organisational culpability?

Rupert Murdoch, who was born in Australia but became a US citizen, had been building his media empire – News Corp – since the 1950s. By 2007, News Corp's holdings included major newspaper publishing groups in Australia, the United Kingdom, and the United States. It also had a sizeable financial stake in BSkyB, the most lucrative broadcast holding in the UK, and it owned the news and entertainment divisions of the US Fox network. Murdoch and News Corp had built the Fox network in a highly competitive economic environment, accomplishing something most believed was impossible: an economically viable fourth US television network.

The phone hacking story, which revolved around Mudoch's *News of the World* newspaper, began in late 2005 when Buckingham Palace suspected interference with the voicemail of Prince William and the royal staff. *News of the World* royal editor Clive Goodman and private investigator Glenn Mulcaire were arrested and later jailed after pleading guilty in January 2007 to intercepting phone messages. That same month, *News of the World* editor Andy Coulson resigned, although he claimed to know nothing about the hacking. (He was appointed David Cameron's media adviser in July 2007 and his communication director in May 2010.) Official word from News International, the British subsidiary of News Corp and owner of *News of the World*, was that Goodman acted alone and that no one else at the newspaper knew what was going on. This claim was backed up by a Press Complaints Commission report in May 2007 that 'effectively cleared the *News of the World* of any illegal conspiracy' (Brook, 2007).

For more than two years, the public heard nothing more. But the story wasn't dead. Since early 2008, *Guardian* reporter Nick Davies had been doggedly investigating whether there was more going on. And in July 2009, the *Guardian* published the results of Davies's investigation in a story headlined: 'Murdoch Papers Paid £1m to Gag Phone-Hacking Victims'. In addition to reporting that other journalists – not only Clive Goodman – engaged in phone hacking, Davies also uncovered evidence 'suggesting thousands more had been victims, ranging from celebrities to politicians to ordinary people' (Guardian News and Media, 2011: 16). News Corp called the allegations irresponsible and unsubstantiated, and a second Press Complaints Commission report concluded that the *Guardian*'s stories 'did not quite live up to the dramatic billing (p. 17).

Through much of 2010 and 2011, the *Guardian* continued to cover the story with new evidence of widespread phone hacking at the *News of the World*, but it wasn't until July 2011 when the *Guardian* reported that the *News of the World* had hacked into the voicemails of murdered British schoolgirl Milly Dowler that the UK – and the world – truly took notice. The response was immediate; major advertisers withdrew from *News of the World*, and many others threatened to follow. On 10 July 2011, the 168-year-old paper published its last edition. About 200 journalists lost their jobs, and James Murdoch, Rupert Murdoch's son and heir apparent, conceded that the paper had been irrevocably 'sullied by behaviour that was wrong' (Robinson, 2011).

On 13 July, Murdoch announced he was withdrawing his bid to take over BSkyB. The announcement was made just a few hours before the British Parliament was scheduled to debate a resolution, supported by all political parties, calling on Murdoch to withdraw from the process. Despite the announcement, the House of Commons unanimously passed the resolution. On 16 and 17 July, Murdoch published full-page apologies to the British public. The next month, Wireless Generation, a News Corp subsidiary, lost a no-bid contract with the state of New York to build an information system to track student performance. New York State comptroller Thomas DiNapoli said the revelations of corporate and individual malfeasance had made awarding the bid to Wireless Generation 'untenable'.

The elder Murdoch was politically influential on both sides of the Atlantic, but his power reached to the highest levels in the UK. News reports detailed Murdoch's connections to the upper echelons of the British government regardless of party affiliation and the relationships of Rebekah Brooks, Murdoch's third-in-command, with government officials. Most of these reports emphasised the apparent 'cronyism' and 'class' bases of the relationships. Many news stories also noted that Brooks had no journalistic training and that she had moved up the Murdoch organisational ladder through her personal relationships. Brooks, however, was still considered a fine journalist by many of her competitors.

Rupert and James Murdoch and several other long-time employees were called before Parliament. Both Murdochs admitted to the hacking, but each denied the existence of a corrosive organisational culture that could have led to widespread ethical and legal breaches. In fact, Rupert Murdoch testified that he was a victim of a cover-up. Concurrently, high-level resignations occurred throughout the Murdoch empire, including that of Les Hinton, who had been serving as the chief executive of Dow Jones, owner of the *Wall Street Journal* and a long-time Murdoch employee. Hinton had testified to Parliament that there was never any evidence of phone hacking beyond the actions of a single employee. However, as the scandal continued to unfold, it became apparent that other Murdoch employees had engaged in similar newsgathering tactics.

In May 2012, a committee of British parliamentarians ruled that Murdoch was not a 'fit person to exercise the stewardship of a major international company' (BBC, 2012). This ruling led to the question of whether media regulator Ofcom would allow BSkyB, still 39% owned by News Corp, to hold a broadcasting licence. (In September 2012, Ofcom determined that, despite the phone hacking scandal, BSkyB remained a 'fit and proper' owner of a broadcast licence (Davies, 2012).) In the meantime, approximately 2,000 lawsuits were filed over the scandal, and the Murdoch empire paid more than £1 million to settle some of them. As of this writing, more than 90 public employees and current or former Murdoch employees have been arrested.

On 29 November 2012, the Leveson Inquiry released a 1,900-page report which stated that Murdoch's leadership suffered from 'a failure of systems of management and compliance' and that the news organisations were governed by 'a general lack of respect for individual privacy and dignity' (Leveson Report, 2012). Shortly thereafter, Murdoch began the necessary legal and corporate moves to split his media empire into two parts: the first, a newspaper-centred entity (with holdings in Australian television) and the second, the more profitable entertainment corporation. That corporation would include Murdoch's son, James, as a corporate officer, although not the CEO. On 10 January 2013, the first criminal conviction in the hacking scandal concluded when a high-ranking officer in Scotland Yard was found guilty of accepting a bribe in exchange for information (Burns, 2013). The court did not accept her defence – that she was whistleblowing for the public good – a decision that may have a significant impact on other criminal defendants making the same claim.

Among the most significant consequences of the scandal was a call by the Leveson Inquiry to establish an independent press regulatory body that would have the power to levy fines (up to £1 million) and provide a 'first-stop' for newspaper libel proceedings. In March 2013, under an all-party agreement, the British Parliament established a royal charter to implement the Leveson recommendations relating to regulation. This would be the first time a free press had been regulated in this way by government in hundreds of years – a true change in the institutional relationships between government and the media. The following month, however, the newspaper industry launched a bid to set up its own royal-charter-backed body. At the time of writing, the fate of the royal charter – either parliament's or the news industry's – was yet to be determined.

Rupert Murdoch has been called the last of the media barons, and the criticisms of him and his business practices parallel those levelled against Joseph Pulitzer and William Randolph Hearst at the height of the 'yellow journalism' era in the USA. All were accused of building media empires that lacked an ethical foundation. In a column, Watergate reporter Carl Bernstein noted:

> This scandal and all its implications could not have happened anywhere else. Only in Murdoch's orbit. The hacking at News of the World was

> *done on an industrial scale. More than anyone, Murdoch invented and established this culture in the newsroom, where you do whatever it takes to get the story, take no prisoners, destroy the competition, and the end will justify the means. ... In the end, what you sow is what you reap. Now Murdoch is a victim of the culture that he created. It is a logical conclusion, and it is his people at the top who encouraged lawbreaking and hacking phones and condoned it. (Bernstein, 2012)*

While many were willing to blame Murdoch personally, other critics noted that the 24/7 nature of competitive news on the internet had created the sort of atmosphere in which hacking was not merely tolerated but encouraged. These critics noted that using hidden cameras, lurking on websites, publishing stories before checking facts – all in the drive to increase web hits – were merely less illegal, but not less ethically questionable.

The morality of groups

Philosopher Larry May (1987) takes what he calls a middle position on the existence and ethical implications of social groups. May founds this position ontologically, noting that 'the capacities of individuals change when they are mixed together with other individuals' (p. 17). Societies and cultures are generated out of collective beliefs and traditions that, while passed on by individuals, are seldom changeable by individuals acting singly. 'Other groups, such as corporations and professional associations, come to have a life of their own as the collective beliefs and traditions of the group become deeply embedded in the psychologies of the individual members' (p. 19). May adds that the social relationships that comprise groups, through structure and purpose, allow individuals to act in different ways and have different interests than they could on their own. This emphasis is important because May bases his middle position on real-world acts, not theoretical postulates. 'A social group does not have to have a formal decision procedure in order to be assigned the status of moral agency' (p. 29). Group solidarity can promote a purposiveness distinct from individuals acting independently.

May distinguishes two types of solidarity: mechanical – where the individual is subsumed into the group – and organic, where 'the group is more effective the more individuals develop and retain their own individualities' (1987: 62). Some evidence (Bem et al., 1965) suggests that certain goals set by groups tend to be more risky than those set by individuals acting alone. Group success can also be a motivator that stands apart from the motivation of individual success. This organic group solidarity can promote ethical thinking and decision-making, plus provide a foundation for it.

This notion of an individual gaining additional power from affiliation is well accepted in journalism. A reporter from the *New York Times* will almost assuredly be treated differently by a variety of sources than will a reporter from a small-town radio station. Further, the *New York Times* reporter will have an organisational history that captures not just organisational standards and practices (Wilkins and Brennen, 2004) but the sort of organic solidarity May describes. In part because of the prestige of the organisation for which they work, *New York Times* reporters have taken well-documented risks in covering the news. The motivation of the group with which one is professionally affiliated – be it the *New York Times* or the *News of the World* – sustains individual choice.

Assigning moral agency – and hence responsibility – to a group does not, in May's thinking, let the individual assume free-rider status. Rather, it provides a richer and philosophically based context in which to understand ethical choice, including a profession-based way to describe a circumscribed range of decision options distinct from the autonomy asserted by classical ethical theory. The literature refers to this conceptualisation as bounded rationality. This bounded organisational rationality, together with professional responsibility, describes the ethical world of journalists.

Promoting an ethical organisational climate

The ways in which groups influence ethical decision-making was initially explored as part of a larger effort to understand organisational climate. In their seminal work, Victor and Cullen (1988) theorised that organisational ethical work climates would have bases that are separate from individual perceptions and evaluations, linking this postulate to Kohlberg's moral development theories (1976, 1981, 1984), which cited 'moral atmosphere' and 'just community' as factors in ethical decision-making. Victor and Cullen defined ethical climate as a 'normative system' institutionalised within the organisation. Rather than being based exclusively in workers' individual values, the system reflects the values of leaders. It specifies behaviours modelled in the workplace and is made tangible through the organisation's reward system. Ethical climate includes several dimensions: self-interest, company profit, efficiency, friendship, team-interest, social responsibility, personal morality, rules and standard operating procedures, and laws and professional codes (Treviño et al., 2001).

Organisational change theory suggests that individuals operate within a bounded rationality established by the organisation itself (Diamond, 2008). Intra-organisational communication patterns (i.e. flat as opposed to more hierarchical lines of authority), toleration of differences in thinking and behaviour (dissent), and the level of formalisation regarding attention to moral concerns are consistently noted as marks of ethical organisational climate (Ethics and Compliance Officer Association, 2012; Vogel et al., 2008).

Victor and Cullen (1988) developed – and initially tested – a typology of organisational ethical climates which allowed them to consider both the general ethical approach to decision-making and whether the decision was viewed as important to the individual, the intermediate group or corporation, or the social system in which the organisation operated. The general ethical approaches outlined were labelled egoism, benevolence, and principled, while the locus of responsibility was labelled individual, local, and cosmopolitan. Nine types of ethical climates emerged. When tested on more than 800 employees working for four different firms, Victor and Cullen found: (1) managers were statistically more likely to have a distinct perception of organisational ethical climate than were lower-level employees; (2) employee organisational satisfaction was statistically higher if employees perceived the ethical climate to be a caring one; (3) employee organisational satisfaction was statistically lower if the ethical climate was perceived to be an instrumental one, particularly if that instrumentalism was connected with profit. Caring and instrumentalism had more impact on employee satisfaction than the benevolent ethical climate. Employee satisfaction with ethical climate also had an effect on worker retention: 'Those who fail to fit in an organisation's climate probably turn over while others operate in their "zone of indifference"' (Victor and Cullen, 1988: 119).

Victor and Cullen's work became a launching pad for subsequent work. Treviño (1986) theorised a link between a manager's stage of moral development (Rest and Narváez, 1994) and the effect of external pressures on leadership and ethical decision-making. These pressures include: the influence of the behaviour of 'referent others' (particularly authority figures); the potentially salutary impact of codes; the potentially negative impact of time, competition, and scarce resources; and the lack of enforcement of ethics codes and guidelines. Managers who operated in Kohlberg's stages 3 and 4 – what Kohlberg labelled conventional moral reasoning characterised by conformity to external rules – were those most likely to be influenced by external, and negative, organisational factors. In 1994, Wimbush and Shepard theorised that behaviour within the organisation is influenced by others in that organisation, specifically supervisors, and suggested that 'Overall workgroup performance will be lower when an instrumental ethical climate dimension predominates and higher when caring, independence, law and code, and rules dimensions are most characteristic' (p. 642). Supervisors establish through verbal and non-verbal acts with subordinates what is acceptable and what is not (p. 643).

In 2000, these postulates were tested on members of the American Marketing Association (Barnett and Vaicys, 2000). The three types of ethical climate – egoism, benevolence, and principled – were linked explicitly with moral philosophy: egoism equated with self-interest and was linked to profit and efficiency; benevolence equated with utilitarianism and was linked to friendship, team interest, and social responsibility; and principled equated with deontology and was linked with personal morality, internal rules, external laws, and professional codes. These approaches were embedded in scenarios, and participants' responses were analysed. The researchers found a single egoistic ethical climate, two climates that were characterised as benevolent, and a single principled ethical climate. They noted:

> There were relatively strong negative correlations between the egoistic climate of self-interest and the other three ethical climates. This is as expected, since the self-interest climate has both an individual focus and an egoistic ethical dimension, as opposed to the other ethical climates. In contrast, the correlations among the team/friendship, social responsibility and rules/codes climates were all positive. This suggests that companies that have egoistic climates are not likely to have high levels of the other ethical climate characteristics, but that characteristics of the utilitarian and deontological climates can co-exist in organisations. (Barnett and Vaicys, 2000: 358)

Barnett and Vaicys then tested whether these climates had an influence on individual ethical decision-making. Their findings suggested that ethical climate had an indirect – moderating – effect in two kinds of organisations. In those organisations marked by a beneficent or principled climate, individuals who believed that specific acts were ethical were less likely to agree to them when they worked for organisations where those same acts would be ethically condemned. In other words, the organisation influenced individual ethical choice. However, Barnett and Vaicys found no moderating effect in organisations with an egoistic climate. Therefore, the authors contend:

> *One possible implication of this for managers and organisations is that rather than attempting to change individual-level ethical judgments about ethically ambiguous actions, they should attempt to develop ethical climates that encourage the individual to look outside themselves (to organisational policies, societal considerations) for guidance ... organisations can positively influence ethical behaviour by establishing climates characterised by a utilitarian ethical criterion directed toward external constituencies. (p. 360)*

Although Barnett and Vaicys do not make this claim, their data suggest the inverse also might be true. Organisations characterised by internal and external competition, by a largely egoistic focus on profit and efficiency, and by an atmosphere in which unethical acts are tolerated by supervisors might develop an organisational climate where the moderating effect is one that condones unethical workplace behaviour, even if the individuals involved would not consider making the same choices in their personal lives.

In a number of studies, Vardi examined whether ethical climate has any impact on unethical behaviour – from deliberate substandard performance to internal sabotage. In weak organisations, standards and values may be informed by the standards and values of subgroups. Climate had both positive and negative impacts on employee attitudes and behaviour, and a climate that emphasised rules and procedures deflected employee unethical behaviour (Vardi, 2001, 2004). Citing a separate study (Vardi and Weiner, 1996), Vardi noted that in strong organisations where the cultural values are directed toward deviation, organisational employee misbehaviour will 'become normative and may put the organisations' existence in danger for the long run' (Vardi, 2001: 326).

In concert, these research findings foreshadow much of what has been published about Murdoch-owned and -managed news organisations. First, stressors are common among news organisations, particularly where there is a focus on efficiency, profit, and the commonplace – but largely untested – notion that individual journalists should develop a 'brand'. Murdoch properties are fierce competitors, and continuing corporate acquisitions reveal a strong focus on profit; clearly, Murdoch journalism on both sides of the Atlantic has an unmistakable 'brand'.

At the helm of News Corp, Murdoch established an organisation that responded to his individual ego. In fact, based on published reports, it is reasonable to assume that this egoistic approach permeated all Murdoch properties. Throughout his career, Murdoch has made it clear that he is in control, particularly in terms of internal promotions, long-term planning for organisational succession, and membership on corporate governance boards. This fits the pattern of a strong, hierarchically organised workplace where communication is more top-down than horizontal and where dissent appears to have been poorly tolerated. Couple this with the fact that the organisation's leaders are among the more than 30 journalists currently under criminal investigation, and it is difficult not to conclude that the sorts of organisational characteristics that blunt ethical thinking found a home in Murdoch's media empire. The Leveson Inquiry concluded as much when it cited Murdoch for a failure of management and compliance. This failure was amplified, and deeply rooted, in the organisation itself.

Research on the effect of leadership on organisational culture further illuminates the connections between organisational climate and ethical thinking and behaviour. Historian James MacGregor Burns (1978) grounds his theory of leadership in morality and ethics, noting:

> Leadership is a process of morality to the degree that leaders engage with followers on the basis of shared motives, values and goals – on the basis, that is, of the followers' 'true' needs as well as those of leaders . . . Ultimately the moral legitimacy of transformational leadership, and to a lesser degree transactional leadership, is grounded in conscious choice among real alternatives. (p. 36)

Transactional leadership emerges when all parties to the process are aware of the resources and attitudes of others involved; the leadership bargain is conscious, and it recognises the others involved as persons of worth in their own right. Transformational leadership, on the other hand, happens when leaders and followers raise one another to higher levels of moral actions.

Other scholars, too, have placed values at the centre of understanding the impact of leaders within organisations. The enhancement and encouragement of an organisational 'embodiment' of ethical values is the role of leaders who demonstrate how the leaders' values integrate 'personal values and the needs of the social system in the development' of an organisation's ethical culture (Grojean et al., 2004: 226). These studies have not ignored the values of non-leaders; the assumption is that leaders have an effect on the values of employees and that, sometimes, the reverse is also the case. Holding positions of leadership and authority does not, in most of these studies, suggest that the values of leadership will always or even often overwhelm the values of individuals.

The following have been found to be the most central mechanisms by which leaders communicate values within an organisation: modelling behaviours (based on social learning theory); establishing expectations of conduct (including both formal and informal socialisation); providing feedback regarding ethical behaviour; recognising and rewarding specific behaviours, being aware of individual differences among subordinates; and establishing leadership training and mentoring. Grojean et al. (2004: 233) suggest that:

> strategic leaders transmit values and ethics via four primary transmitting mechanisms. First leaders used the idealised influence and inspirational motivation aspect of transformational leadership to convey the importance of ethical values, and inspire members to link their own personal values and self-concepts to the organisation. Second, members are likely to have less direct contact with strategic leaders. However, these leaders' actions serve as a model … Third, strategic leaders establish structure and policies that provide clear expectations regarding ethics. … And, fourth, strategic leaders develop and mentor direct leaders.

Employees also contribute to values transmission by trusting in their leadership, forming strong in-group bonds and examining who is being mentored for leadership roles and the ethical choices those future leaders are making.

The scholarship cited above is essentially concerned with the positive qualities of leadership and of an ethical climate in which leaders and organisations/governments are entwined. As Burns notes:

> *To watch one person absolutely dominate another is horrifying; to watch*
> *one person disappear, his motives and values submerged into those of*
> *another to the point of loss of individuality, is saddening . . . Submersion*
> *of one personality in another is not genuine merger based on mutual*
> *response. Such submersion is an example of brute power subtly applied,*
> *perhaps with the acquiescence of the victim. (Burns, 1978: 21)*

How much this description fits Rupert Murdoch the human being, or those he chose to hire and promote, is beyond the scope of this chapter. However, published accounts do suggest that Murdoch himself is ambitious and something of a control freak – the phrase 'brute power subtly applied' may be quite applicable in Murdoch news organisations. These ingredients, in the right context, put an organisation at risk.

The power of organisational corruption

Burns's comments about the impact of leadership focus on the individual, but organisations themselves can amplify that impact in important ways. Almost all studies of corruption focus on the relationship between the individual and the larger organisational and cultural structure. As Adams and Balfour (2004) note, 'It is an easy to make – but important – error to personalise evil in the form of the exceptional psychopath … This proclivity draws a cloak over social and organisational evil' (p. 17). They emphasise that organisations, because they help make or give meaning to events, are socially constructed (Berger and Luckmann, 1967) and hence subject to the influences of culture and history that are only imperfectly accounted for by a reliance on rationality. According to Miller et al. (2005), corruption begins with the individual, but it is amplified and promoted within organisations (or societies) in which there is a high level of conflict, an unequal distribution of wealth and status, and an imbalance of power. 'In times of rapid social and economic transition, stable moral practices are upset, and a degree of moral confusion can set in' (Miller et al., 2005: 31).

Adams and Balfour uncovered some common patterns in organisations they characterise as the locus of administrative evil: an emphasis on technological and professional competence at the expense of a more expansive ethical framework; an organisational mission that is dominated – often for decades – by the vision of a single individual who focuses on organisational or personal success, essentially unmodified by the thinking of others; and an organisational structure that tends to be administratively hierarchical as opposed to flatter and somewhat more participatory. These dysfunctional (at least in ethical terms) organisational characteristics are also emphasised by scholars who explore moral violence in organisations. Diamond and Allcorn (2004: 23) note that:

> 21st-century organisations (public, private and non-profit) are stressful climates … organisational change in the form of downsizing and reengineering actually serves to diminish creativity and resources that otherwise might be available to respond to problems.

Wilkins (2010) suggests that corruption occurs on three levels: individual, institutional (organisational), and systemic. Second-level corruption is defined as a corrupt individual who either helps to create or sustain a corrupt system. It emerges where the enforcement or encouragement of moral norms is either weak or lax. Second-level corruption, particularly, promotes taking advantage of the weaker party; in an organisational sense, a stronger organisation may take advantage of individuals or of organisations that are more fragile. Third-level corruption is corruption that is so systemic that it taints even those individuals with good hearts and moral purposes. It alters the moral purposes of those who work within it. The *News of the World* newsroom, based on published accounts, appears to have been at the second level of corruption and moving up the scale.

The foregoing authors accept Noddings's (1989) contention that most organisational systems include some corrupting elements. Her caution echoes that of Adams and Balfour (2004), who emphasise that understanding organisational corruption should not be reduced to locating blame and castigating a single individual. Combating corruption cannot be left exclusively to individuals or whistleblowers but also must include elements of organisational transparency, decision-making processes that are open to multiple points of view, and leadership that acknowledges the ethical value of social relations both within and outside the organisation itself. A strong external regulatory structure, including codes and laws, is also essential. As Diamond and Adams (1999: 246) note, fostering consistency between ethical claims and actual behaviour, at the organisational level, can provide a 'good enough' container for ethics.

Potential problems loom when ends are focused on power and profit; means are highly centred on efficiency and technique; and an organisational structure, including the structure of promotion and reward, is internally hierarchical and subject to significant cultural stress. These insights are clearly applicable to multinational organisations such as media conglomerates that are under serious pressure to perform financially. This is happening at the same time that media organisations' legacy financial model has disintegrated due to technological innovations that are also exerting enormous pressures on another legacy: content production. Scholars have noted that, when it comes to ethics, organisations may espouse one pattern of behaviour: a laudatory version of providing the news as an essential part of democratic functioning. Simultaneously, they are actually promoting and rewarding another pattern: seeking power through wealth and influence, which is essentially anti-democratic. It is this lack of alignment that promotes unethical conduct (Diamond and Adams, 1999). Interestingly, scholars have also noted that contemporary journalistic organisations are out of alignment with deeply held normative standards (Gardner et al., 2001). This contradiction of aspirational and actual goals seems to have characterised the Murdoch-owned and run British newspapers, at least as personified by Murdoch himself.

To some degree, all organisations possess one or more of these characteristics. Thus, the issue becomes, first, understanding the complex and nuanced mechanisms that contribute to organisational ethical climate – including its opposite, the corrupt organisation – and, second, developing systemic approaches to forestall universal tendencies that lead to unethical behaviour. One way to begin this effort is to understand 'moral exemplars' of what went wrong and factors that contributed to the ethical morass. This is the approach of Adams and Balfour (2004), and it is to that effort that this project now turns.

Applying theory to practice

Although the literature includes case studies of ethical decision-making within single journalistic organisations (see e.g. Borden, 1997), broader insights regarding organisational climate have yet to be applied to news organisations and specifically to ethical decision-making within those organisations. This lack of theoretical depth is noteworthy because there is a significant body of literature that documents the impact of newsroom socialisation (Berkowitz, 1997) on non-moral professional routines (e.g. gatekeeping) and a less robust body of literature that implicates socialisation for professional standards (Filak, 2004; Hardt and Brennen, 1995; Killebrew, 2003).

Scholars attempting to understand the impact of news organisational climate on ethical decision-making can begin their work by asking the following set of questions based on both the literature and case studies:

- How is organisational solidarity developed (May, 1987)? How do leaders and employees articulate the organisation's sense of purposiveness through work product and corporate governance? How do employees and managers define 'good work'?

- Based on employee response, how would organisational climate be characterised – as one that is predominantly instrumental in nature or one that is more benevolent or principled? How do internal patterns of professional reward – promotion, retention, prestigious assignment – align with publicly stated values?

- In what ways is the organisational structure hierarchical, and in what ways is it 'flat'? How are creativity and dissent promoted and/or tolerated? Do managers and employees believe they have space for dialogue? If so, with whom?

- What leadership values do acts of promotion and hiring reflect? Why do those who leave the organisation leave it? How did those who became leaders achieve their positions?

- How do employees and managers evaluate the traditional components of climate, tolerance of diversity of staff and of ideas, cultivation of emerging leaders, team building, and the ability to be involved in and have influence on decision-making?

- Understanding that all organisations, to greater or lesser extents, have the capacity for corruption, how is professional misbehaviour handled? Are there different standards for different categories of employees? Are there structural mechanisms – e.g. a union or informal subgroups – that either counter or promote corrosive tendencies?

As the facts of the phone hacking scandal have become progressively more public, what seems clear is that, on many of these dimensions, the newsroom that produced the *News of the World* would have responded in a way that allowed corruption to flourish and, in many cases, be rewarded. However, what is needed is not just this single case study but a range of cases that can begin to detail the relative impact of certain organisational qualities on newsroom ethical climate.

A caveat: The necessary but insufficient nature of values

An extensive body of research – some of it case-study-based and some of it more traditionally generalisable – links formal and informal organisational structure with employee responses to ethical questions. While this literature never suggests that values are unimportant, it also notes that strong values – by themselves – are insufficient to ensure long-term ethical behaviour. The fundamental reason for this is a philosophical one. As Noddings (1989) and others have noted, all organisations have some capacity for corruption and all organisations have some capacity for building solidarity. In addition, in the current era, news organisations particularly are subject to meaningful internal and external stressors. The result is that many news organisations have intensified a focus on speed, personal branding, and technological sophistication. These are hallmarks of an egoistic organisational culture, as exemplified by *News of the World*.

But not all news organisations have a similar newsroom culture. As Borden (1997) notes in her study of a single newsroom and as scholars of organisational change have found more generally, an ethical climate can be developed and sustained by promoting flatter lines of authority, a reward system that considers and acknowledges ethical choice, and a daily operation that opens up a space for dialogue, even under the pressure of content production. What the field itself lacks is a systematic investigation of how organisational characteristics influence ethical decision-making – across news organisations. Right now, the answer to this broader question resides in anecdote alone. As Lowry and Hanges (2008: 2) contend:

> A healthy organisation has policies, practices and procedures that empower employees and emphasise the importance of continual learning and innovation to meet the demands of an ever-changing environment. It is one in which customer service, employee diversity, and organisational justice are all recognised as critical imperatives that will determine the effectiveness of the organisation in the long run.

If the research in business ethics is correct, such an organisational culture can actually promote ethical reflection and response, even when individual values inform different decisions.

Values, then, are a necessary building block of journalistic ethical choice. But all ethical choice takes place in a context, and some contexts are far more conducive to ethical thinking and doing than others. Being an ethical journalist requires the sort of organic solidarity of which May (1987) speaks. Values plus organisational heft are necessary and sufficient for sustained ethical professional performance. One without the other is incomplete.

Note

All web addresses in this chapter were last accessed in July 2013.

References

Adams, Guy B., and Balfour, Danny L. (2004) *Unmasking Administrative Evil* (Thousand Oaks, CA: Sage).

Barnett, Tim, and Vaicys, Cheryl (2000) 'The Moderating Effect of Individuals' Perceptions of Ethical Work Climate on Ethical Judgments and Behavioral Intentions', *Journal of Business Ethics*, 27: 351–62.

BBC (2012) 'Rupert Murdoch "Not a Fit Person" to Lead News Corp – MPs', BBC News, 1 May: www.bbc.co.uk/news/uk-politics-17898029.

Bem, Wallach, N., and Kogan, M. (1965) *Risky and Cautious Shifts in Group Decisions: The Influence of Widely Held Values* (Cambridge, MA: MIT Press).

Berger, Peter L., and Luckmann, Thomas (1967) *A Social Construction of Reality: A Treatise in the Sociology of Knowledge* (New York: Open Road).

Berkowitz, Daniel A. (1997) *The Social Meaning of News* (Beverly Hills, CA: Sage).

Bernstein, Carl (2012) 'Why the U.S. Media Ignored Murdoch's Brazen Bid to Hijack the Presidency', *Guardian*, 20 Dec.: www.theguardian.com/comment isfree/2012/dec/20/bernstein-murdoch-ailes-petreaus-presidency.

Borden, Sandra L. (1997) 'Choice Processes in a Newspaper Ethics Case', *Communication Monographs*, 64(1): 65–81.

Brook, Stephen (2007) '*News of the World* in the Clear over Goodman Case', *Guardian*, 18 May: www.theguardian.com/media/2007/may/18/newsofthe world.pressandpublishing.

Burns, James M. (1978) *Leadership* (New York: Harper & Row).

Burns, John F. (2013) 'Officer at Scotland Yard is Guilty in Hacking Trial', *New York Times*, 10 Jan.: www.nytimes.com/2013/01/11/world/europe/scotland-yard-officer-guilty-in-phone-hacking-trial.html?_r=0.

Davies, Lizzy (2012) 'Sky is a Fit and Proper Broadcaster, Rules Ofcom', *Guardian*, 20 Sept.: www.theguardian.com/media/2012/sep/20/sky-fit-and-proper-rules-ofcom.

Diamond, Michael A. (2008) 'Telling them What they Know: Organizational Change, Defensive Resistance, and the Unthought Known', *Journal of Applied Behavioral Science*, 44(3): 348–64.

Diamond, Michael A., and Adams, Guy B. (1999) 'The Psychodynamics of Ethical Behavior in Organizations', *American Behavioral Scientist*, 43: 245–63.

Diamond, Michael A., and Allcorn, S. (2004) 'Moral Violence in Organizations: Hierarchic Dominance and the Absence of Potential Space', *Organizational and Social Dynamics*, 4(1): 22–45.

Ethics and Compliance Officer Association (2012) *Ethical Culture Building: A Modern Business Imperative*: www.ethics.org/files/u5/ECOA-Report-FINAL. pdf.

Filak, Vincent F. (2004) 'Cultural Convergence: Intergroup Bias among Journalists and its Impact on Convergence', *Atlantic Journal of Communication*, 12(4): 216–32.

Gardner, Howard, Csikszentmihalyi, Mihaly, and Damon, William (2001) *Good Work: When Ethics and Excellence Meet* (New York: Basic Books).

Grojean, M. W., Resick, C. J., Dickson, M. W., and Smith, D. B. (2004) 'Leaders, Values and Organizational Climates: Examining Leadership Strategies for Establishing an Organizational Climate Regarding Ethics', *Journal of Business Ethics*, 55: 223–41.

Guardian News and Media (2011) *Phone Hacking: How the Guardian Broke the Story* (London: Guardian shorts, ibook).

Hardt, Hanno, and Brennen, Bonnie (1995) *Newsworkers: Toward a History of the Rank and File* (Minneapolis, MN: University of Minnesota Press).

Killebrew, K. C. (2003) 'Culture, Creativity and Convergence: Managing Journalists in a Changing Information Workplace', *International Journal on Media Management*, 5(1): 39–46.

Kimmel, David M. (2004) *The Fourth Network: How FOX Broke the Rules and Reinvented Television* (Chicago: Ivan R. Dee).

Kohlberg, Lawrence (1976) 'Moral Stages and Moralization: The Cognitive Developmental Approach', in Thomas Lickona (ed.), *Moral Development and Behavior* (New York: Holt, Rinehart & Winston), 31–53.

Kohlberg, Lawrence (1981) *The Philosophy of Moral Development: Moral Stages and the Idea of Justice* (Cambridge, MA: Harper & Row).

Kohlberg, Lawrence (1984) *The Psychology of Moral Development: The Nature and Validity of Moral Stages* (San Francisco: Harper & Row).

Leveson Report (2012) *An Inquiry into the Culture, Practices, and Ethics of the Press*, 29 Nov.: www.official-documents.gov.uk.

Lifton, Robert Jay (2000) *The Nazi Doctors: Medical Killing and the Psychology of Genocide* (New York: Basic Books).

Lowry, Charles B., and Hanges, Paul J. (2008) 'What is a Healthy Organization? Organizational Climate and Diversity Assessment', *Libraries and the Academy*, 8(1): 1–5.

May, Larry (1987) *The Morality of Groups: Collective Responsibility, Group-Based Harm, and Corporate Rights* (Notre Dame, IN: University of Notre Dame Press).

Miller, Seumas, Roberts, Peter, and Spence, Edward (2005) *Corruption and Anti-Corruption: An Applied Philosophical Approach* (Upper Saddle River, NJ: Pearson/Prentice Hall).

Noddings, Nell (1989) *Women and Evil* (Berkeley, CA: University of California Press).

Rest, James R., and Narváez, Darcia (eds) (1994) *Moral Development in the Professions: Psychology and Applied Ethics* (Hillsdale, NJ: Lawrence Erlbaum Associates).

Robinson, James (2011) 'News of the World to Close as Rupert Murdoch Acts To Limit Fallout', *Guardian*, 7 July: www.theguardian.com/media/2011/jul/07/news-of-the-world-rupert-murdoch.

Treviño, Linda K. (1986) 'Ethical Decision Making in Organizations: A Person-Situation Interactionist Model', *Academy of Management Review*, 11(3): 601–17.

Treviño, Linda K., Butterfield, Kenneth D., and McCabe, Donald L. (2001) 'The Ethical Context in Organizations: Influences on Employee Attitudes and Behaviors', *The Next Phase of Business Ethics*, 3: 301–37.

Vardi, Yoav (2001) 'The Effects of Organization and Ethical Climates on Misconduct at Work', *Journal of Business Ethics*, 29: 325–37.

Vardi, Yoav (2004) *Misbehavior in Organizations* (Mahwah, NJ: Lawrence Erlbaum).

Vardi, Yoav, and Weiner, Yoash (1996) 'Misbehavior in Organizations: A Motivational Framework', *Organization Science*, 7(2): 151–65.

Victor, Bart, and Cullen, John B. (1988) 'The Organizational Bases of Ethical Work Climates', *Administrative Science Quarterly*, 33: 101–25.

Vogel, S., Holt, J. K., Silgar, S., and Leake, E. (2008) 'Assessment of Campus Climate to Enhance Student Success', *Journal of Postsecondary Education and Disability*, 21(1): 15–31.

Wilkins, Lee (2010) 'The Ethics of Professional Corruption', in Robert Fortner and Mark Fackler (eds), *Ethics and Evil in the Public Sphere: Media, Universal Values and Global Development* (Cresskill, NJ: Hampton Press), 117–30.

Wilkins, Lee, and Brennen, Bonnie (2004) 'Conflicted Interests, Contested Terrain: Journalism Ethics Codes Then and Now', *Journalism Studies*, 5(3): 297–309.

Wimbush, J. C., and Shepard, J. M. (1994) 'Toward an Understanding of Ethical Climate: Its Relationship to Ethical Behavior and Supervisory Influence', *Journal of Business Ethics*, 13: 637–47.

4

Professionalism and Journalism Ethics in Post-Authoritarian Mexico: Perceptions of News for Cash, Gifts, and Perks

Mireya Márquez Ramírez

After a long-standing history of corruption and complicity between the press and the state in Mexico, a changing environment of political democratisation and commercialism in the 1990s allegedly instilled new standards of professionalism in journalism. Scholars in certain disciplines claimed that greater autonomy, a universalisation of ethical codes, and the rapid decline of news for cash practices – known locally as *embute* and *chayote* – were slowly eroding the corrupt journalistic culture of the previous authoritarian era (Hughes, 2006; Lawson, 2002; Rockwell, 2004, Wallis, 2004). This view, however, disregards the micro human relations that take place in the source–journalist interaction and in everyday reporting practices. Rather than a wholesale adoption of professionalism and its accompanying ethical values, we instead find a gradually changing discipline in which practices are negotiated within a context marked by new ideals but also by strongly established traditions.

Two of these practices – both of which involve journalist–source relations – are often problematised in the literature as ethical dilemmas that would fall into the category of bribery in many contexts: first, news for cash and, second, gifts and other perks. Both are ordinary forms of journalist–source exchanges and both are influenced by the personal, organisational, and structural forces that help define post-authoritarian journalistic culture in Mexico.

The authoritarian legacy

Mexican press development contrasts with that of the USA and other Western countries in that it never experienced a rapid process of industrialisation and mass readership, a clear shift towards commercialism, or the 'professionalisation' of the journalistic occupation via technological advances that rendered objectivity and political neutrality the norm (Allan, 1997; Chalaby, 1996; Hallin, 2000a; Schudson, 2001, 2005). Instead, throughout most of its history, the Mexican press has consistently remained an instrument of either contesting political factions or, later, the single-party authoritarian system. These state–press relations impacted the culture of reporting and significantly undermined professional autonomy and ethical principles. As political scientist Chappell Lawson notes, 'a web of subsidies, concessions, bribes, and prerequisites created a captive media establishment that faithfully reflected ruling party priorities' (2002: 173). Through subtle and effective instruments of control, a culture of collusion – one that didn't require formal or official state intervention in the media – developed (Fuentes-Beráin, 2002; Orme, 1997; Trejo Delarbre, 1998). Indeed, editors and publishers frequently claimed to enjoy freedom and independence (Martínez S., 2005; Monsiváis 2003) while simultaneously receiving enormous governmental benefits. In return, the government expected congratulatory reporting of official events as well as the minimisation or silencing of critical and oppositional voices (Monsiváis, 2003; Rodríguez Castañeda, 1993; Rodríguez Munguía, 2007).

In this context, dispensing *chayote* – one-off payments – or *embute* – regular pay-offs given in return for planting stories, twisting story lines, or spiking embarrassing pieces (Fromson, 1996: 117) – were two typical means of controlling information. Editors and reporters received payment for interviews or as a supplement for their low wages. News organisations would respond by either turning a blind eye or agreeing *de facto* that their reporters and journalists should seek alternative sources of income (Baldivia et al., 1981; Cleary, 2003; Fromson, 1996; Rodríguez Munguía, 2007). Through this, news organisations saved considerable amounts of money. Therefore, as Daniel Hallin claims, 'the officialist character of the Mexican press result[ed] not simply from government pressure, but from collusion between political and economic elites' (Hallin, 2000b: 101).

During the authoritarian era, many of the most notable bylines in Mexican journalism were from authors who rose to privilege, rubbing shoulders with the literati and intelligentsia and enjoying comfortable lifestyles – often at the expense of taxpayers. However, when lecturing others about good journalism, many of these veterans frequently appealed to ethical and professional values – integrity, ethics, independence, or impartiality – to describe their jobs and career trajectories, even if their own political columns generously praised the government. Indeed, these journalists' close ties with those in political power and their claims of ethical behaviour were seen as unproblematic (Martínez S., 2005; Scherer García and Monsiváis, 2003), and so far remain as such. Journalist Raymundo Riva Palacio observes that 'for the bulk of Mexican journalists, the concept of "conflict of interest" does not exist in theory or practice ... The absence of this concept is a fundamental ingredient in the collusion between the media and the authorities' (Riva Palacio, 1998: 113). Understanding these historical issues helps us trace the cultural development of journalism ethics in Mexico.

The clash of generations: Bribery and news for cash

For journalists in transitional or post-authoritarian democracies, a clash of values and beliefs is often evident among different generations. Scholars have concluded that, in many countries, younger generations of journalists, many of whom have university degrees, are imbued with a more 'professional' mindset and ethical values – or with principles and values that best adapt to the new commercial business models (Canel and Piqué, 1998; Pasti, 2005; Shamir 1988). In Mexico, the older generation of journalists is widely perceived as uneducated and corrupt; this sharply contrasts with the view that most contemporary journalists hold of themselves: highly skilled, committed, and educated professionals.

The scholarly emphasis on journalists' generational differences is normally connected to the quest for a professional identity – one that is distanced from the media's notorious and well-documented bad reputation and low credibility. The low esteem in which journalists are held by Mexican society is historically symbolised by the *chayote*. These infamous pay-offs were distributed through most governmental branches, and, as noted earlier, journalists viewed them as an entitlement that not only supplemented their low salaries, but compensated them for poor working conditions and job insecurity (Baldivia et al., 1981; Fromson, 1996; Hernández López, 1999). The institutionalised distribution of the *chayote* and *embute* meant that 'reporters did not have to chase after a story: it was handed to them by the (official party government) PRI on a silver plate, along with an envelope containing *el chayote*' (Cleary, 2003: 65). Even today, the *chayote* remains the icon of an easily manipulable generation that had to bow to both its sponsor politicians and its newsroom bosses.

Contemporary journalists recall how editors and publishers were not only aware of the situation, but encouraged their staff to seek pay-offs because they conveniently relieved those editors and publishers from having to increase staff salaries. Likewise, bosses would let reporters negotiate advertisement contracts with their assigned newsbeats in return for a fee. Although the *chayote* is currently a subject of journalists' mockery and newsroom banter, journalists also tacitly complain that they have been unfairly stigmatised; in reality, editors, managers, publishers, and owners' names have also featured on the government's payroll, but they have carried none of the public shame (see Hernández López, 1999).

Testimonies from political journalists tell of the days when journalists travelled to provincial cities to cover 'Affairs of State' ceremonies or election days, with the full knowledge that, with the help of thankful politicians, envelopes would soon follow (Márquez Ramírez, 2005, 2012a, 2012b). Therefore, reporters competed with each other to get sent to the top-rank political beats, which distributed the biggest cheques. At their peak in the 1970s and 1980s, pay-offs to reporters became institutionalised, with editors' and executives' names often appearing alongside those of reporters in the fortnightly payroll lists. At the upper level of the newsroom hierarchy, loyalty was rewarded with luxury gifts or personal favours – taxi licences, bar memberships, housing privileges, junkets to resorts – and by means of more government advertisements to ensure the organisation's survival (Fromson, 1996: 117).

Fifteen years after *chayote* began to earn widespread disfavour, the public continues to apply the word to any journalist whom they perceive as biased. Still, some elite journalists – newspaper columnists, radio presenters, TV executives, and anchors – are named and shamed for belonging to 'the black list' of those accepting pay-offs. These elites have no problem accepting *chayote* and will happily shift their party loyalties to the highest bidder. Public criticism and political scandals, therefore, become commodities to be traded.

Predictably, most journalists today quickly deflect the blame and portray themselves as part of a new 'professional' generation that has defied the vices of the so-called 'old guard'. Nonetheless, some younger journalists with university credentials still implicitly admit to having accepted pay-offs; *chayote* and *embute* were, they claimed, not only supplementary sources of income, but also the safest tools of survival in the journalism profession. Agreeing to accept pay-offs was sometimes the only way to be actively welcomed onto official tours and reporters' pools, to be able to socialise with sources and colleagues, and to be given access to exclusive and privileged information.

Journalists, gifts, and perks

Another ethical dilemma that routinely affects journalists' perceptions of ethical standards is the acceptance of gifts, tokens, vouchers, all-inclusive tours, and other forms of 'media attention' provided by press officers and public relations managers. Accepting gifts from sources is a long-standing concern in journalism ethics; the received wisdom is that these gifts corrupt journalists and undermine the integrity of journalism (Day, 2003). However, there is no consensus on their practical significance. In contemporary Mexican journalism, it is commonplace for journalists from all news organisations and levels to be presented with small tokens and gifts on their birthdays or during the Christmas season.

For most journalists, such exchanges belong to the realm of public relations; it is a nice gesture, but rarely is it seen as obligating journalists to write or speak about their sources favourably. However, as sources strive to maximise coverage and visibility, other kinds of perks are being institutionalised, including payment for conventions, trips, and tours. Although Mexican journalists are aware of the ethical risks of attending all-expenses-paid trips, they often see it as the only way to cover important news events. Only the most affluent news organisations fully fund their staff's accommodation and travel expenses; many low-budget or more 'resource-savvy' organisations still rely on their news sources to pay reporters' expenses. In these cases, editors continue to adopt the attitude that it is the source's obligation to fund the reporter's expenses if the reporter is going to devote time to covering a story.

The most visible newsbeat for which reporters' travel is funded is the presidency; however, several other less prominent government ministries also take their reporter pools on tour. In this regard, the newspaper *Reforma* famously broke with the paradigm of accepting perks by setting new rules for its reporters and prohibiting or limiting practices that rival organisations tolerate and encourage. Not only does *Reforma* dismiss staffers if they accept pay-offs, it also refuses any invitations, meals, freebies, tokens, gifts, or anything that could be seen as compromising the newspaper's independence or integrity. *Reforma*'s 'not even a glass of water' policy has created a good deal of controversy. Staffers defend the policy with pride; for rivals, the policy has set a standard against which to measure one's own behaviour.

The mundane interactions between beat reporters and press officers, and the mutual dependence that leads to exchanges of favours, are two of the lesser-known aspects of Mexican journalism. However, journalists have come to question the ethical validity of the dependency that state-funded press offices, gifts, and all-expenses-paid trips create. It is in this micro-level of human interaction that ethical dilemmas often emerge. As the literature suggests, the most resourceful sources generate the most media attention; success depends upon the capacity of organisations 'to mobilise material and symbolic resources, and to exert control over the flows of information which may emerge from within their internal environments' (Manning, 2001: 138). Hence, it could be argued that reporters' attendance at well-catered events, in press offices, and on all-inclusive trips may positively affect the attention and coverage devoted to such events, regardless of their newsworthiness. In many cases, journalists would not have covered these events if their expenses had not already been paid.

Conclusion: Mexican journalism in the age of democracy

This chapter has introduced two instances in which ethical principles, journalistic practices, and newsroom dynamics come together to help shape professional journalistic identity at both the individual and collective level. Today, Mexican journalists see themselves as generational change agents. These journalists – many of whom are university graduates – stand in stark contrast to their corrupt, ill-equipped, trained-on-the-job predecessors who were fond of bribery and manipulation. Today's journalists define themselves as professionals who strive to counter established power, seek to impart the truth without bias, and endeavour to overcome ordinary pressures and provide politically relevant and reliable information to their audiences. However, political structures, occupational culture, and individual values clearly influence the extent to which this cherished autonomy and commitment to ethics can be practised. Therefore, it is not possible to speak about two separate generations – one unethical and the other ethical – but, instead, of one transitional generation where old and new elements blend. In Mexico, ethical and professional principles are contradictory and ambiguous (Márquez Ramírez, 2012b). They may not reflect an overarching normative philosophy but rather a set of nuanced and constantly changing standards that are set and legitimated by colleagues both past and present.

Note

All web addresses in this chapter were last accessed in March 2013.

References

Allan, Stuart (1997) 'News and the Public Sphere: Towards a History of Objectivity and Impartiality', in M. Bromley and T. O'Malley (eds), *A Journalism Reader* (London: Routledge), 296–329.

Baldivia, Urdininea, Planet, J. M., Riva, J. Solís, and Guerra, T. (1981) *La formación de los periodistas en América Latina: México, Costa Rica y Chile* (Mexico City: Nueva Imagen).

Canel, J. M., and Piqué, A. M. (1998) 'La evolución profesional de los periodistas españoles', *Comunicación y Sociedad*, 32: 107–34.

Chalaby, Jean K. (1996) 'Journalism as an Anglo-American Invention: A Comparison of the Development of French and Anglo-American Journalism, 1830–1920s', *European Journal of Communication*, 11(3): 303–26.

Cleary, Johanna (2003) 'Shaping Mexican Journalists: The Role of University and On-the-Job Training', *Journalism and Mass Communication Educator*, 58(2): 163–74.

Day, Louis A. (2003) *Ethics in Media Communication: Cases and Controversies* (Belmont, CA: Wadsworth).

Fromson, Murray (1996) 'Mexico's Struggle for a Free Press', in Richard Cole (ed.), *Communication in Latin America: Journalism, Mass Media and Society* (Wilmington, DE: Scholarly Resources), 115–37.

Fuentes-Beráin, Rossana (2002) 'Prensa y poder político en México', *Revista Iberoamericana de Comunicación*, 2: 61–79.

Hallin, Daniel C. (2000a) 'Commercialism and Professionalism in the American News Media', in James Curran and Michael Gurevitch (eds), *Mass Media and Society* (London: Arnold), 218–37.

Hallin, Daniel C. (2000b) 'Media, Political Power and Democratization in Mexico', in James Curran and Myung-Jin Park (eds), *De-Westernizing Media Studies* (London: Routledge), 97–110.

Hernández López, Rogelio (1999) *Sólo para periodistas: Manual de supervivencia en los medios mexicanos* (Mexico City: Grijalbo).

Hughes, Sallie (2006) *Newsrooms in Conflict: Journalism and the Democratization of Mexico* (Pittsburgh, PA: University of Pittsburgh Press).

Lawson, Chappell (2002) *Building the Fourth Estate: Democratization and the Rise of a Free Press in Mexico* (Berkeley, CA: University of California Press).

Manning, Paul (2001) *News and News Sources: A Critical Introduction* (London: Sage).

Márquez Ramírez, Mireya (2005) 'The Radio Journalist in Mexico: Practices, Notions and Attitudes to Professionalism', Master's thesis, Cardiff University.

Márquez Ramírez, Mireya (2012a) 'Change or Continuity? The Culture and Practices of Journalism in México (2000–2007)', PhD dissertation, Goldsmiths, University of London.

Márquez Ramírez, Mireya (2012b) 'Valores normativos y prácticas de reporteo en tensión: Percepciones profesionales de periodistas en México', *Cuadernos de Información*, 30: 97–110.

Martínez S., José Luis (2005) *La vieja guardia: Protagonistas del periodismo mexicano* (Mexico City: Plaza y Janés).

Monsiváis, Carlos (2003) 'Señor Presidente, a usted no le da vergüenza su grandeza?', in J. Scherer García and C. Monsiváis (eds), *Tiempo de saber: Prensa y poder en México* (Mexico City: Aguilar), 99–339.

Orme, William A. (ed.) (1997) *A Culture of Collusion: An Inside Look at the Mexican Press* (Boulder, CO: Lynne Rienner).

Pasti, Svetlana (2005) 'Two Generations of Contemporary Russian Journalists', *European Journal of Communication*, 20(1): 89–115.

Riva Palacio, Raymundo (1998) *Más allá de los límites: Ensayos para un nuevo periodismo* (México: Universidad Iberoamericana/Fundación Manuel Buendía).

Rockwell, Rick (2002) 'Mexico: The Fox Factor', in E. Fox and S. Waisbord (eds), *Latin Politics, Global Media* (Austin, TX: University of Texas Press), 107–22.

Rodríguez Castañeda, Rafael (1993) *Prensa vendida: Los periodistas y los presidentes. 40 años de relaciones* (Mexico City: Grijalbo).

Rodríguez Munguía, Jacinto (2007) *La otra guerra secreta: Los archivos prohibidos de la prensa y el poder* (Mexico City: Random House Mondadori).

Scherer García, J., and Monsiváis, C. (eds) (2003) *Tiempo de Saber: Prensa y Poder en México* (Mexico City: Aguilar).

Schudson, Michael (2001) 'The Objectivity Norm in American Journalism', *Journalism: Theory, Practice and Criticism*, 2(2): 149–70.

Schudson, Michael (2005) 'The U.S. Model of Journalism: Exception or Exemplar?', in H. De Burgh (ed.), *Making Journalists: Diverse Models, Global Issues* (London: Routledge), 94–106.

Shamir, J. (1988) 'Israeli Elite Journalists: Views on Freedom and Responsibility', *Journalism Quarterly*, 65: 589–96.

Trejo Delarbre, R. (1998) 'Veinte años de prensa', *Nexos*, 1 Jan.: http://bit.ly/PI8ETV.

Wallis, D. (2004) 'The Media and Democratic Change in Mexico', *Parliamentary Affairs*, 57(1): 118–30.

5

Covering the Private Lives of Public Officials: Comparing the United Kingdom, Flanders, and the Netherlands

Bastiaan Vanacker

In recent years, media ethics scholarship has shown an increased interest in global media ethics. Among other things, this interest stems from a conviction that a global media system requires a global media ethic. The chapter that follows does not take a position on this issue, but it is undeniably the case that globalisation highlights the differences in ethical standards between countries. For example, high-profile stories such as Dominique Strauss-Kahn's arrest and the Amanda Knox trial generated news columns in France, the United States, Italy, and the United Kingdom about which journalists cried foul at the ethical practices of their foreign colleagues. This begs the question: to what extent is journalism ethics determined by culture, and to what extent is it based on principles that stretch across borders?

In August 2011, I conducted face-to-face interviews with 18 journalism experts from the United Kingdom, the Netherlands, and the Flemish region of Belgium (henceforth Flanders) about journalistic standards in their countries. The interviews were open-ended and dealt with a number of topics, including the one this chapter explores: covering the private lives of public officials. Insights gathered from these interviews can help answer the question driving this book: is journalism ethics individual, institutional, or cultural?

Subjects were selected because they represent an important voice in their respective professional communities; they understand the unwritten laws and maxims of the discipline and can help give access to knowledge that is not readily available (Bogner and Menz, 2009). During the interviews, I explored how my subjects viewed journalism ethics practised in their country, not their own ethical decision-making per se. As a result, the data gathered for this project do not shine light on the *individual* nature of journalism ethics.

That leaves us with two levels – institutional and cultural – both of which need some clarification. For the purposes of this chapter, I equate *cultural* with national or regional culture and *institutional* with the professional norms, practices, and customs that define the journalism profession. I argue, then, that institutional and cultural forces are not mutually exclusive; rather, they interact with one another to shape journalistic ethical decision-making. The issue to examine, therefore, becomes the extent to which approaches to journalism ethics in these three closely related countries are shared. To explore this, I look to experts in the three countries and consider their views on the ethicality of writing about the private lives of public officials.

The private lives of public officials

Experts in each of the three countries were in agreement about general principles that should be applied when determining if and how to cover the private lives of public officials. They said that when a public official's private life interferes with his or her public duties, it is the journalist's obligation to report on that official's private life, even if it means violating privacy. My experts also agreed that when a public official's private behaviour is in direct conflict with his or her publicly professed beliefs, reporting on this is justifiable. (The textbook example of this is a politician who opposes gay rights but has a same-sex partner.) These general principles can also be found in the codes and guidelines of the respective press councils and, as such, seem to indicate a certain level of cross-border institutional agreement.

Below the veneer of ethical concordance, however, different applications of these principles emerge. By and large, British journalists are accustomed to a more aggressive press system in which public officials' privacy is not valued as highly as it is in Flanders and in the Netherlands. This doesn't mean there is no consideration for the value of privacy in the UK, but according to Jon Slattery, media blogger and former deputy editor of the *Press Gazette*, there is 'a presumption of openness' and a belief that the public can be trusted to make up its mind when presented with information that might be damaging to a politician's reputation and privacy. William Gore, who was at the time of his interview the public affairs director at the UK Press Complaints Commission, believes that journalists should trust the public rather than assume that information automatically harms and kills reputations and careers. According to Gore, as long as the press presents the information in a manner that refrains from judgement – allowing the public to make up its own mind – people should be entrusted with a wide range of information.

This attitude is not shared in Flanders or in the Netherlands; in both places, privacy invasion is considered a more fundamental harm that can only be overcome in extreme cases. For example, Wim Criel, publisher and president of the Flemish journalism council Raad voor de Journalistiek, dismisses the judgement-of-the-public argument as nothing more than a convenient excuse invoked by pulp media to justify invasions of privacy: 'We cannot move the limits of privacy because you are of the opinion that your reader can make a distinction'. For Criel, 'the UK is an example of a country where giving in to sensationalism creates a culture of sensationalism'. Dutch media expert and former assistant editor-in-chief Yvonne Zonderop calls this 'the laboratory position' and adds: 'It does not work that way. Journalists have to make a calculation between privacy and public interest.'

This difference in approach can also be seen in the justification for privacy invasion on the grounds that it reveals something about a public official's character. This more controversial justification was somewhat accepted by British experts, who were willing to entertain the justification and saw some validity to it, although they by no means totally agreed with it. Dutch and Flemish experts, on the other hand, flatly dismissed this justification and seemed much more tolerant of a certain level of hypocrisy and imperfection in their elected officials. As Guido Roelants, editor and journalist with *De Gazet van Antwerpen*, said 'I think there are very few ministers in this country or other countries who have NOT had affairs.'

Notably, my interviews took place shortly after Dominique Strauss-Kahn had been arrested in New York on rape allegations. Some British experts contended that a figure like Strauss-Kahn – who French journalists allegedly knew had been having numerous affairs – could not have climbed to as high a position in British politics without being exposed by the press. British experts argued that French journalists failed their readers by not exposing this dark side of Strauss-Kahn's character. According to Andrew Sparrow, senior political correspondent for the *Guardian*, there is an ongoing debate in English journalism about how far one can go in these matters, an issue he feels ambivalent about. Sparrow acknowledged that in British media one frequently sees aggressive invasions of public figures' privacy that cannot be justified on public interest grounds. While Sparrow feels conflicted about some of these privacy invasions, he does think there is a level of corruption in French politics that isn't found in the UK, precisely because of the UK's anti-establishment press.

Experts in Flanders indicated that their media system is not as overtly modelled on the watchdog role as in the Anglo-Saxon world. (Like the Netherlands, Belgium had a party press system until well into the 1970s.) These experts stated that, as a matter of principle, they agree that a public official's infidelity becomes newsworthy once it affects his or her public duties, but they also acknowledged that this principle is not always applied in the everyday practice of journalism. To know when exactly an official's private life affects his or her public duties, a journalist may have to do some digging into that official's private life, and Flemish journalists are reluctant to do this. Flemish interviewees agreed that, in this respect, the Flemish press is not very aggressive. Criel even acknowledged that, at one point in the past, there was a code of silence in Flemish media; he said that journalists simply did not write about the private lives of politicians. Period. Journalism council ombudsman Filip Voets also recognised that in the past the media had kept quiet for too long about the private lives of public officials, even when those private lives clearly affected their public lives.

Similarly, Dutch experts consider their press to be docile; their journalists are reluctant to investigate aspects of a public official's private life that may have an impact on his or her public performance. Award-winning political reporter Hans Wansink thinks Dutch journalists generally respect authority and, in that regard, share some similarities with French journalists; both, for example, are reticent to report on politicians with alcohol or fidelity problems. Political reporter Frits Bloemendaal gave examples of how, in the past, the media failed to report on ministers who clearly had an alcohol problem and even appeared drunk at official functions.

While institutional and cultural norms may be changing, it is clear that the values regarding privacy and respect for those in power cause Dutch and Flemish journalists to approach the issue in a different manner than their colleagues across the English Channel, despite their apparent allegiance to the same professional standards.

Cultural bias

The experts with whom I spoke had no qualms about recognising differences in cultural bias and did, in fact, explicitly refer to cultural values when explaining diverging journalistic standards. When asked about the French media ignoring Strauss-Kahn's alleged chequered past, experts explained it by referencing different French mores regarding privacy, sexuality, and the role of the press. Most of the interviewees considered their own media system a golden mean between the extremes provided by media systems in other countries.

Experts in Flanders and the Netherlands, for example, repeatedly mentioned the UK as a model *not* to emulate because of its sensationalism; they tended to position themselves as the reasonable mean between the extreme French position – where strict adherence to the value of privacy overrides public interest – and the sensationalism that permeates British media. In the UK, on the other hand, experts saw their media system as the mean between the French/continental media system – where journalists often are too cosy with politicians – and the sensationalism of the American media.

Of course, the whole purpose of these interviews was to discuss media ethics in a comparative framework; in many ways, the framework I provided, which referenced media practices in other countries, called for the experts to position their media system in reference to those of neighbouring countries. Nonetheless, the experts were comfortable explaining 'their' media system by referring to culturally determined values. For example, the relative lack of support by journalists for the Dutch Press Council was linked to – among other things – the anarchist bent of Dutch journalists, which the experts considered to be quintessentially Dutch. Numerous experts said that Dutch journalists are somewhat obstinate, stubborn, and unwilling to submit themselves to the judgement of a press council.

British experts – while repeatedly pointing out that, in terms of ethical decision-making, there are huge differences between the tabloids and the broadsheets – did not totally reject the notion of a 'British media'. Despite the obvious differences in methods and standards, the two types of

British media share a view of themselves as aggressive watchdogs, something the British experts see as non-existent (or at least far less prominently present) in continental Europe.

Shifting tides?

Whether approaches to journalism ethics are universal across cultures depends on how closely one cares to look. When deciding whether to report on the private life of a public official, the general principles are similar in the three countries I examined: reporting is justified if the public official's private life is affecting his or her public duties and if the person's private life stands in direct contrast to the official's publicly held beliefs. Below the surface of this broad agreement, however, cultural differences emerge.

But indicators point to a lessening of these cultural differences. Particularly in the Netherlands, experts see a shift towards an Anglo-Saxon model. Some high-profile cases about the marital infidelity of public officials made the front pages in Holland in the months before I conducted my interviews, and some interview subjects saw these stories as indicative of a change taking place in Dutch media. They pointed to increased competition and online media (lacking in ethical standards) as contributing factors to this perceived shift. Interestingly, the stories did not come about because of hard-nosed investigative journalism but rather because a scorned lover approached the press. In fact, upon receiving information about one case, the press did nothing with it for years until a rogue publication picked up the story and published it. As award-winning journalist and *Trouw* columnist Hans Goslinga pointed out, other media were then forced to follow suit. Dutch experts observed that, once the cat was out of the bag, the rest of the media descended on the stories with guns blazing. Experts in the Netherlands also pointed to popular scandal news sites like *Geen Stijl*, which they said is the Dutch equivalent of the British tabloids and a force that is driving their media system towards the Anglo-Saxon model and the wanton sensationalism they associate with it.

In Flanders, on the other hand, a similar story about alleged infidelities of the prime minister reported by a weekly gossip magazine was treated with great restraint by the mainstream media. They reported on the fact that the article had appeared, but the story was not picked up and further investigated. In Flanders, where the relatively new press council enjoys strong support within the journalistic community and where journalists – unlike their Dutch colleagues – are well organised in professional associations, the experts did not see a similar shift towards the Anglo-Saxon model.

Conclusion

To return to our initial question – is journalism ethics institutional or cultural? – this study found that, to the extent that journalism ethics converges, it does so because of institutional factors. By and large, journalists interviewed had similar views on the role of their profession, and they all tended to agree that serving as a check on those in power is an important function of journalism. This commonality of purpose explains why Wim Criel, who was instrumental in drafting a code of ethics for Flemish journalists, admitted that the code of the British Press Complaints Commission served as a model, despite the fact that Criel did not spare his criticism for the way journalism was practised in the UK. In other words, the commonalities he sees between journalism in Flanders and in the UK are based on the fact that journalism fulfils essentially the same role in Flanders as it does in the UK. Within this functionalist perspective, similar ethical principles rose to the top.

The differences in these three culturally similar countries emerged in the way that these principles were put into practice. That a politician's private life can be relevant to report when it affects his or her public duties is generally accepted, but at what point this in fact becomes the case seems to depend on cultural sensibilities. The question then becomes: at what level of abstraction do these generally applicable principles start to follow their own culturally determined directions?

A larger question, not answered here, is whether it is desirable to have journalists agree not just on the principles that guide their profession, but also on how these principles are applied. In an ever more globalised media environment, an argument could be made that this is a worthwhile endeavour. However, journalists interviewed for this project did not seem to see much value in this; instead, they tended to regard their media's response to privacy issues as superior to the responses of their colleagues across the borders. It's clear that media ethicists who promote a global approach have their work cut out for them.

Reference

Bogner, Alexander, and Menz, Wolfgang (2009) 'The Theory-Generating Expert Interview: Epistemological Interest, Forms of Knowledge, Interaction', in Alexander Bogner, Beate Littig, and Wolfgang Menz (eds), *Interviewing Experts* (Basingstoke: Palgrave Macmillan), 43–80.

6

Ethics (of Objectivity) and Cultural Authority: Metajournalistic Discourse in a Post-Socialist Context

Dejan Jontes

Even though criticism of the press by the press is, according to Lule (1992), extremely rare, it is nevertheless gaining in importance (Hass, 2006). Despite this trend, very little attention has been directed to how journalists talk about their work in public ways (Carlson, 2011). This chapter explores how journalistic professional ideology in Slovenia is produced and reproduced through the discourse of journalism awards and through journalism textbooks.

Both awards and textbooks can be considered an important part of 'metajournalistic discourse'. As Carlson argues:

> [A]s an object of inquiry, metajournalistic discourse reveals attempts by journalists to articulate, negotiate, defend, and even obscure their cultural, social, and political significance. This is not idle banter, but one means by which journalists actively seek to define the boundaries of journalistic practice, locate their profession within society, and shape how their work should be received. (2011: 268–9)

Conducting a discourse analysis of these 'texts' (awards presented between 1990 and 2010 and books published since 1988) helps illustrate how the core values of occupational ideology are reinforced. Interpreted historically, such analyses can provide important insights into the meaning of journalistic culture and, therefore, journalism ethics. These metajournalistic discourses can, therefore, speak to the question posed in this book: from where does journalism ethics emerge?

Journalistic discourses and cultural authority

As Deuze emphasises, the twentieth-century history of (the professiona-lisation of) journalism can be typified by the consolidation of a consensual occupational ideology among journalists in different parts of the world (2005: 444). Conceptualising journalism as an ideology means under-standing journalism in terms of how journalists give meaning to their newswork. The ways in which journalists do this are important because of journalism's cultural authority. Anderson defines journalistic authority as a cultural form of power 'possessed by journalists and journalistic organisations that allows them to present their interpretations of reality as accurate, truthful, and of political importance' (2008: 250). Therefore, the discourse of journalism awards and textbooks can be seen as one of the mechanisms through which journalists shape their own self-image and legitimise their authority. According to Zelizer (1993) this discourse provides a locus where journalists have been able to come together as a community but not necessarily in accordance with formalised professional cues. The metajournalistic discourse is not 'univocal, uniform or uncontested, but on-going, persistent and contradictory' (Carlson, 2011: 268).

Journalism awards can be seen as an important part of the mainstream debates and power struggles about journalistic quality, and because there are two competing awards for outstanding journalistic achievements in Slovenia, an analysis of the awards is a good starting point for observing the tensions within the journalistic community – tensions about what constitutes 'quality' and 'professional' journalism. Journalism textbooks can be viewed as a primary guide for future practitioners – one way in which those future practitioners are introduced to the values and norms of the practice.

Journalists about journalism

In Slovenia, two competing awards for outstanding journalistic achieve-ment are presented. The first is the award of the Association of Slovenian Journalists, which has been presented since 1952. Initially, it was named after Tone Tomšič, a pre-war communist leader who was captured and killed by Italians in 1942; it was renamed in 1990 as Consortium Veritatis (Brotherhood of Truth). Honours are presented in different categories, including outstanding debutant, lifetime achievement, outstanding journalistic achievement, outstanding photojournalism, etc. Among the laureates are the most prominent Slovene journalists. The second award, named after Slovene writer Josip Jurčič, was established in 1993 by *Nova revija* (the main journal of the right-wing intelligentsia) and the Association of Slovene Writers. The Jurčič awards have been presented primarily to journalists who, because of dissatisfaction with the Association of Slovenian Journalists, established the Association of Journalists and Commentators in 2007. Anti-socialism is one of the main themes in these awards. At risk of oversimplifying, it could be said that the Consortium Veritatis awards are primarily presented to more liberal journalists and the Jurčič awards to right-wing journalists. The fact that only two journalists have received both awards supports that claim.

When an award is presented, a lengthy explication is typically published. For this chapter, more than 50 examples of such texts were analysed.

Key characteristics of a professional self-definition of journalism can be summarised as a set of discursively constructed ideal-typical values: public service, objectivity, autonomy, immediacy, and ethics (cf. Deuze, 2005: 458). Journalists feel these values give legitimacy and credibility to what they do. In the case of Slovenia, the public service ideal is a very powerful component of journalism's ideology, and both awards share a sense of 'doing it for the public'. Here, it is useful to bear in mind Hallin's (2000: 220) comment that the ideology of public service is connected with the notion of objectivity – 'the faith that it [is] possible to report events from a non-political and non-sectarian point of view, relying on neutral criteria of news-worthiness to make the inevitable choices gatekeepers must make'.

The journalism described in awards texts clearly presents itself within what Fiske (1989) calls the 'transparency fallacy' – the idea that journalism is a window on the world. Even in the thoughtful discussions of journalism described in the texts of the awards, the idea that journalism can paint an unmediated picture of reality still figures prominently. Ettema and Glasser argue that, even if the term objectivity is out of vogue, its legacy endures:

> What specifically endures is an allegiance to the ideal of language as strictly denotative and purely referential – language as the medium for a clear picture, an undistorted image or a full depiction of all the mind and

> *language independent objects that presumably constitute social reality.*
> *(1998: 184)*

The often-used metaphor of the window is important because, as Fiske reminds us, it invokes a sheet of glass as an impersonal, non-cultural medium of reproduction; the human or cultural agency in the process is masked. This means that the finished representation is naturalised. It is made to appear as the result of a natural rather than a cultural process. It is taken away from the realm of history and culture and moved towards that of the universal truth (Fiske, 1989).

According to Ettema and Glasser (1998), even when acknowledging the inevitability of some distortion in any narrative, journalists turn to metaphors of glass to defend the authenticity of news. In such metaphors, an entire conception of what journalism ought to be is conveyed in a simple figure of speech that can encompass no moral imperative other than the accurate reflection of facts.

The repeated references to journalism as a window on the world reinforce Slovene journalists' commitment to an ethics of objectivity. Elsewhere, Jontes (2010) has shown how the notion of objectivity as a cornerstone of professional knowledge has been understood by Slovene journalists. Put simply, in a post-socialist journalistic culture, to be ethical means to be objective, no matter how that concept is understood. In this respect, the commitment to the imported norm of objectivity also opens up the question of the pressure of globalising forces, which 'may be acting to homogenise journalistic practices internationally' (Thomson et al., 2008: 227).

Despite its problematic status, objectivity is still the key element of Slovene journalists' professional self-perception. Through its elements of detachment, balance, non-partisanship, and facticity, objectivity represents the main component of journalism's self-definition. Numerous examples of detachment and balance can be found in the discourses of journalism awards. What is interesting, however, is the way non-partisanship is defined in each award. For the Association of Slovenian Journalists, non-partisanship is noted only occasionally in the award texts; in the Jurčič award, on the other hand, non-partisanship is the most important value, and it can be found in almost every analysed example. In this award, non-partisanship is defined not only as excluding political party preferences but also as resistance to socialism and any remnants of it. Socialism, therefore, is redefined, and resistance to it is seen as the most important journalistic ethical value.

News sense is another notable concept in award discourses. One can find metaphors of the 'sixth sense' and a 'nose for news', both of which imply that journalistic skills are innate and cannot be learned. This reinforces an observation made by Zelizer (2004) that news sense figures prominently in journalists' discussions of what they do and how they do it. This is important; as Glasser and Ettema (1998) have noted, the question of how journalists decide what is news is the main question of the epistemology of journalism.

Finally, both prizes see the main threat to the dominant paradigm as sensationalism; the 'yellow threat' is used as a rhetorical ritual for maintaining and repairing the dominant, objective journalism paradigm. 'Serious' journalism, therefore, tries to differentiate itself from the tabloids through the use of strategies such as emphasising epistemological and methodological differences between serious and tabloid journalism, and ritually isolating individuals who breach ethical standards.

Journalism textbooks: Individualising responsibility

Journalism textbooks can also provide important insights into the norms and practices guiding the Slovene journalism community. Vos (2011) argues that journalism educators have a unique authority to construct and maintain morally potent occupational norms; therefore, textbooks serve as important metajournalistic discourses. Analysis of the nine Slovene textbooks published since 1988 reveals a number of themes. First, the textbooks align closely with the codes of ethics of both Slovene professional journalism organisations. Second, they are extremely 'American' in that they overwhelmingly import key concepts of the dominant American journalism paradigm without considering local specificities. Third, analysed textbooks deal primarily with ethics on an individual level.

To cite two illustrative examples, Manca Košir, one of the main figures of journalism education in Slovenia, argues that to ensure freedom of the press, we need journalists

as personalities with specific biographies, psychological structure, world views, interests and motivations ... A good journalist needed for the

> *freedom of the press is a* good person *who is familiar with the rules of journalistic communication. (1991: 383; emphasis added)*

Three years earlier, in the first journalism textbook that did not address journalism from a socialist perspective, Košir emphasised:

> *It is no coincidence that objectivity is part of codes of ethics as it is also a moral question. Will the journalist be honest and report everything he knows about the subject? Journalists faces a constant choice: will he be honest or opportunistic? (1988: 12)*

In these examples, objectivity is defined as a moral question and a matter of individual journalistic intent.

Dealing with ethics on the individual level – as the analysed textbooks tend to do – has been criticised by Trapp (1978). She argued that the point is not that individual action is wrong or impossible – or that an individual sense of responsibility is wrong or impossible – but that institutional constraints set definite limits on individual action and also help shape an individual's sense of responsibility:

> *Such a basic change in ethical perspective, from individualist to contextualist, could provide the necessary foundation for development of a theory of journalistic responsibility which would reflect both the limits and possibilities of the process of journalism. (Trapp, 1978: 23)*

Trapp concludes that writing on press ethics tends to overestimate the social importance of the journalist. The analysis of Slovene textbooks reinforces this claim.

When dealing with objectivity, Slovene textbooks are homogeneous; they see objectivity as a problematic concept in a sense that it is impossible to achieve, but it still remains a viable ideal. Thus, elements of objectivity such as detachment, balance, non-partisanship, and facticity are 'prescribed' for journalists in these texts. Professionalisation of journalism is seen as an answer to almost all of its problems. Importantly, such a view contributes to the production and reproduction of journalistic authority, and professionalisation has become one of the main journalistic ideologies.

Finally, the analysis revealed that Slovene journalism textbooks are ahistorical; they hardly ever mention the period of socialist journalism. This is important because:

> *[the] representation of journalism history has several consequences: it helps shape the actual content of the news, structures labour relations, and directs students' attention toward specific aspects of the industry and away from the others. (Lester, 1995: 31)*

For all intents and purposes, Slovenia's period of socialism – and the journalism practised during that period – is wiped from journalism's historical ledger.

Conclusion

In the discourses of journalism awards and textbooks, objectivity is the key element of journalists' professional self-perception, and the authority of journalism is based on a (self-)declared capacity to present and reflect a more or less undistorted reality. Through its elements of detachment, balance, non-partisanship, and facticity, objectivity represents the primary part of journalism's self-definition in Slovenia. Detachment and balance are important to this discussion, but most interesting is the definition of non-partisanship; in Slovenia, this means not only excluding political party preferences, but also resisting socialism and any remnants of it. Thus, the journalism community redefines socialism; resistance to it is seen as the most important journalistic value.

These cases highlight a lack of an in-depth critical view of journalism; what prevails is an idealisation of journalism and an uncritical use of problematic concepts. Furthermore, journalists and journalism educators deal with their profession in very similar ways and share similar presumptions of journalism and its role. Finally, analyses of journalism awards and journalism textbooks demonstrate that ethics emerges from the individual, the institutional, and the cultural domains. While the individual domain is highlighted in textbooks, awards deal mainly with institutional and cultural forces that influence journalists' ethical reasoning. Most notable, however, is the influence of democratic journalism ideals – particularly those developed in the United States – on postsocialist journalism.

References

Anderson, Christopher (2008) 'Journalism: Expertise, Authority, and Power in Democratic Life', in D. Hesmondhalgh and J. Toynbee (eds), *The Media and Social Theory* (London: Routledge), 248–64.

Carlson, Matt (2011) 'Where Once Stood Titans: Second-Order Paradigm Repair and the Vanishing US Newspaper', *Journalism*, 13(3): 267–83.

Deuze, Mark (2005) 'What is Journalism? Professional Identity and Ideology of Journalists Reconsidered', *Journalism*, 6(4): 442–64.

Ettema, James S., and Glasser, Theodore L. (1998) *Custodians of Conscience: Investigative Journalism and Public Virtue* (New York: Columbia University Press).

Fiske, John (1989) *Understanding Popular Culture* (Boston: Unwin Hyman).

Hallin, Daniel C. (2000) 'Commercialism and Professionalism in the American News Media', in James Curran and Michael Gurevitch (eds), *Mass Media and Society* (London: Arnold), 218–37.

Hass, Tanni (2006) 'Mainstream News Media Self-Criticism: A Proposal for Future Research', *Critical Studies in Mass Communication*, 23(4): 350–5.

Jontes, Dejan (2010) *Novinarstvo kot kultura: Miti in vrednote* (Ljubljana: Fakulteta za družbene vede).

Košir, Manca (1988) *Nastavki za teorijo novinarskih vrst* (Ljubljana: DZS).

Košir, Manca (1991) 'Svoboda novinarstva je mrtva, živeli svobodni novinarji!', *Naši razgledi*, 40(13): 382–3.

Lester, Elizabeth (1995) 'Discursive Strategies of Exclusion: The Ideological Construction of Newsworkers', in Hanno Hardt and Bonnie Brennen (eds), *Newsworkers: Towards a History of Rank and File* (Minneapolis, MN: University of Minnesota Press), 30–47.

Lule, Jack (1992) 'Journalism and Criticism: The Philadephia Inquirer Norplant Editorial', *Critical Studies in Mass Communication*, 9(1): 91–109.

Thomson, Elizabeth A., White, Peter R., and Kitley, Philip (2008) '"Objectivity" and "Hard News" Reporting across Cultures: Comparing the News Report in English, French, Japanese and Indonesian Journalism', *Journalism Studies*, 9 (2): 212–28.

Trapp, Mary (1978) 'Consequences of an Individualist Theme in American Views of Journalistic Responsibility', *Journal of Communication Inquiry*, 3(13): 13–26.

Vos, Tim P. (2011) '"Homo Journalisticus": Journalism Education's Role in Articulating the Objectivity Norm', *Journalism*, 13(4): 435–49.

Zelizer, Barbie (1993) 'Has Communication Explained Journalism?', *Journal of Communication*, 43(4): 80–8.

Zelizer, Barbie (2004) *Taking Journalism Seriously: News and the Academy* (London: Sage).

Part II

Accountability Mechanisms

7

Journalists, Journalism Ethics, and Media Accountability: A Comparative Survey of 14 European and Arab Countries

Susanne Fengler, Tobias Eberwein, Julia Lönnendonker, and Laura Schneider-Mombaur

The *News of the World* phone hacking scandal in the United Kingdom in 2011 and the subsequent Leveson Inquiry aimed at investigating the 'culture, practices and ethics of the press' clearly reminded us of the fact that democratic societies constantly have to walk a tightrope between ensuring ethical behaviour of the media while safeguarding the freedom of the press. Because of the prominent role that mass media plays in modern societies, a growing number of media scholars in recent years have emphasised the urgent need to hold the media accountable (e.g. Nordenstreng, 1999). Concerned media professionals have echoed this call. Apart from Britain's recent scandal, media fraud cases – for example, Tom Kummer at the German *Süddeutsche Zeitung Magazin* in 2001 and Jayson Blair at the American *New York Times* in 2003 – stress the relevance and urgency of the topic. Societies must have genuine trust in the quality of the information provided to them by the mass media. However, journalists and media organisations often do not live up to the expectations, and 'media can cause serious harm' even 'without violating the law' (Bertrand, 2000: 22; see also Baldi, 2007: 17).

Observers agree that, from a normative point of view, the quality of the media has to be monitored because of the media's unique function in democratic societies. Journalism can be considered a 'public good' (e.g. McQuail, 1992), which – in a moral sense – calls for credibility and responsibility towards society. The media creates a public sphere where controversial arguments regarding political (and other) matters are exchanged. Therefore, evaluating instruments aimed at strengthening the media's quality and soliciting up-to-date feedback on journalists' attitudes towards these instruments are crucial investments in safeguarding free and pluralist media systems that contribute to functioning democracies.

In countries that guarantee freedom of the press and thus forbid state interference into journalism, various 'non-state means' (Bertrand, 2000) have been developed to hold the media accountable. These traditional media accountability instruments – for example, press councils, ombudspersons, and media criticism in trade journals and the popular press – all have the task of monitoring journalists' professional performance and following up on journalistic malpractice. Additionally, 'unwritten laws' – so-called informal institutions – such as codes of ethics and culturally shaped norms and values influence journalists' actions (North, 1990). Furthermore, recent years have seen the emergence of new, mostly online, media accountability instruments. Some of these, such as journalist and newsroom blogs and online ombudspersons, offer journalists web-based forums to discuss journalistic standards and media quality. In addition, new instruments that facilitate audience participation have evolved; among these are users' blogs, comment and complaint applications, webcasts of meetings provided by press councils and media regulators, and, of course, audience criticism voiced via Twitter and Facebook.

Figure 7.1 offers an overview of both established and innovative instruments of media accountability, sorted and classified according to Shoemaker and Reese's (1996) model of spheres of influence on journalism. The figure locates press councils and trade journals – trailblazers of today's wide-ranging accountability instruments – on the media routines level, while the majority of 'responsive' instruments such as ombudspersons and newsroom/journalist blogs reside on the individual and organisational levels.

Needed: Comparative research on media accountability

In recent years, media professionals worldwide have discussed the potential benefits of media self-regulation and accountability for preserving press freedom and media plurality:

- In a report on media pluralism, the Commission of the European

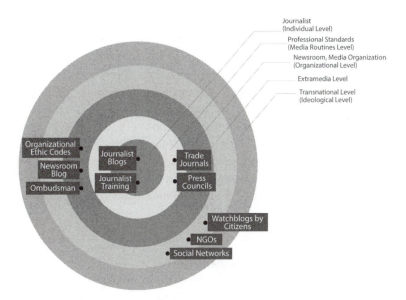

Figure 7.1 Established and innovative media accountability instruments

Source: MediaAcT, adapted from Shoemaker and Reese, 1996

Communities (2007) mentioned 'voluntary or co-regulatory approaches' as potential tools for monitoring media pluralism.

- In resolution 1636, the Parliamentary Assembly of the Council of Europe (2008) counted media self-regulation as one of the indicators for media in a democracy.
- The Organisation for Security and Co-operation in Europe (2008) issued the *Media Self-Regulation Guidebook*, targeting media practitioners in Eastern Europe.

Nevertheless – apart from the study presented here – this red-hot topic has not been seriously discussed by media scholars who do comparative research. Our international survey of almost 1,800 journalists in 14 European and Arab states – 'Media Accountability and Transparency in Europe' (MediaAcT) – helps fill the void. The study seeks to reveal the status of media accountability structures in different countries, to assess the impact of the internet and the social web on self-regulation, and finally to understand journalists' attitudes towards and experiences with media self-regulation and accountability.

Prior to this study, no sound empirical data existed on how journalists themselves – as both subjects of and actors in media self-regulation – perceive the influence of media accountability instruments on journalistic standards. At the same time, little was known about the existence and quality of media accountability instruments in Eastern Europe, where self-regulation mechanisms were only partly established during those countries' political transformations (Thomaß and Tzankoff, 2001). Our study aimed to address both of these issues. The two sections that follow set the conceptual groundwork for the questions posed in our survey. Following that discussion, we report on some of the survey findings and then offer insights and recommendations on the future of media accountability.

Mapping media accountability

In *Comparing Media Systems*, Hallin and Mancini (2004) laid out their well-known model of journalism cultures and media systems in the Western world. An extended model comprising Eastern European, Asian, African, and Arab countries was developed in a more recent volume (Hallin and Mancini, 2012). In their original study, Hallin and Mancini (2004) identified three different journalism cultures and media systems by comparing political and economic features of the countries under study:

- The *liberal model* (e.g. UK, USA) is characterised by highly deregulated media markets, little state interference into the media sector, and a highly developed culture of professionalism among journalists.
- The *democratic corporatist model* (e.g. Scandinavian countries, Germany, Austria) is also associated with high professionalism among journalists but differs from the liberal model with regard to the influential role public broadcasting plays in these countries.
- The *polarised pluralist model* (e.g. Italy, Spain, France) features political actors with strong influences on both private and public news organisations, a weak professional culture among journalists, and a rather marginal role for the print media.

Media accountability instruments played a minor role in Hallin and Mancini's analysis. The authors examined the existence of press councils in the various models as an indicator for journalistic professionalism and detected that no press councils or only weak ones could be found in the countries of the polarised pluralist model. Although Baldi and Hasebrink (2007) used Hallin and Mancini's model in their study of viewer participation in public broadcasting across Europe, no study in the field of media accountability has systematically drawn on the model to identify and explain 'cultures of accountability'.

In analysing the most recent studies on the status quo of media accountability instruments in several European countries, it is striking to see that countries belonging to the liberal model show significant differences in terms of the maturity of their self-regulatory mechanisms. For example, while the UK boasts a large number of media accountability instruments (Jempson and Powell, 2011; Jempson et al., 2011), the USA, which lacks a national press council, now lags behind. It is also questionable whether and how the countless politically motivated media blogs in the USA seek to (and succeed in) positively impact journalistic standards (Domingo, 2011; Fengler, 2008). In terms of established instruments of media accountability, a country like Austria, which Hallin and Mancini locate in the democratic model, displays far more similarities with the media accountability structures in countries such as France or Italy, which belong to the polarised model (Karmasin et al., 2011). What's more, France and Portugal – both of which belong to the polarised model characterised by a traditionally weak accountability culture – have a far higher number of ombudspersons than nearly all other European countries belonging to the liberal and the democratic model (Bettels et al., 2011).

Following Hallin and Mancini's model, one might further assume that the relationship between the media and the public in a country with a high degree of political intervention in the media (e.g. France) might be different from a country with a highly deregulated media system (e.g. the USA). In fact, a meta-analysis of polls on citizens' perception of the media provides hints that trust in journalism varies across journalism cultures and media systems.

Although the aforementioned data are only partially comparable and thus need to be interpreted with prudence, Figure 7.2 shows that the liberal model seems to foster audience distrust in journalism, while trust is rather high in the democratic and pluralist models. The Arab world, with its largely state-controlled media systems, needs separate consideration here (see Pies and Hawatmeh, 2011).

Observations like the ones noted above may serve to weaken the heuristic value of the Hallin and Mancini model for the field of media

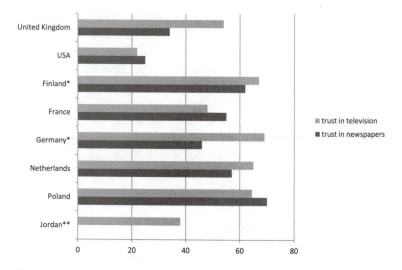

Figure 7.2 Percentage of citizens who consider media outlets to be trustworthy

Sources: UK: Ofcom, 2010; USA: Gallup, 2010; Finland: EVA, 2009; France: TNS, 2010; Germany: MHMK, 2009; Netherlands: Eurobarometer, TNS-Nipo, 2007; Poland: Newsweek Poland, 2003/2011; Jordan: CSS, 2010
*Trust in regional newspapers and in public service TV
** Trust in state TV

accountability. Our study, therefore, seeks to explore whether factors apart from political and economic constraints have an influence on the maturity of media accountability initiatives in different countries.

New perspectives on media accountability

Hallin and Mancini's model distinguishes between governmental/political and professional media regulation. While the liberal model has the lowest degree of state regulation among the three Western models, the polarised model has the highest degree – and the lowest degree of self-regulation. We suggest using Puppis's (2007) model to illustrate the degree of autonomy between media and politics, which Hallin and Mancini use as an indicator for 'professionalised' versus 'politicised' journalism cultures. As Figure 7.3 indicates, Puppis adds the dimension of co-regulation, a joint effort between state and private actors to regulate the media.

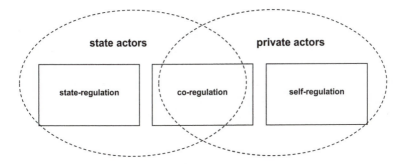

Figure 7.3 Regulation models for the media sector

Source: Puppis, 2007

Because studies have diagnosed severe deficits in the traditional media self-regulation approach, two options seem to be available to solve this dilemma.

Political intervention

One solution is that the state becomes more involved in media accountability by providing incentives to comply with the rules (co-regulation). As a mean between the two poles of self-regulation and state regulation, the model of co-regulation (enforced voluntary regulation or audited self-regulation) seems a reasonable approach to media account-ability, especially in a time of rapid technological change. Private players could develop their own self-regulatory procedures in close cooperation with state actors or on behalf of the state. The main issues concerning this approach are whether and how the state participates, and how the latent danger of government intrusion into media freedom can be mitigated.

Participatory models

A second option is that non-state actors – particularly media users – become more involved in the process of holding the media accountable in the digital age (see Eberwein et al., 2013; Fengler, 2012). In the past, audiences were seen as either not interested or not knowledgeable enough to evaluate journalistic performance; this is likely because media professionals – especially in non-Anglo-Saxon journalism cultures – tend to have a rather negative perception of the public. Moreover, before the advent of the internet, it was costly for unsatisfied audience members to voice their criticism. They could write a letter to the editor, call the newsroom, or, at best, contact the ombudsperson, but all options were time-consuming and often left users frustrated. Additionally, calling an unknown editor in a newsroom required a certain degree of personal stamina. Therefore, before the development of the social web, the vast majority of media consumers were a 'latent group' (Olson, 1971) – people who potentially had an opinion about the quality of journalism but no forum for coordinating their interests.

Today, technological developments have significantly lowered the cost for members of the public to monitor and 'punish' the media. An infinite number of media consumers can now share the burden of media monitoring online, and Web 2.0 provides a plethora of fast, low-cost options for voicing criticism and protest, including email, chats, comment forums, Twitter, Facebook, and others. What's more, much of this can be done anonymously.

In his study of institutional change, North (1990) noted that institutions evolve over time and thus constantly alter the choices available to us. Most often this change is slow. However, given the rapid development of information technology, we are currently observing a concomitant change in the public's options for holding the media accountable. Already, because complaint forms are easily spread via the internet, people can use the web to encourage others to file a complaint. In Germany, for example, the German Press Council received an unprece- dented 240 complaints for a single case. In the UK, an email campaign generated 25,000 complaints to the Press Complaints Commission on a single case (Eberwein et al., 2011). And while the public might not have the expertise to judge journalistic performance from a professional point of view, its knowledge should not be underestimated (Hasebrink et al., 2007). Users of a prominent German media blog frequently cited their interest in the media serving society as a motive for using the blog (Mayer et al., 2008).

The MediaAcT project

Drawing on Hallin and Mancini's model of journalism cultures and the emergence of new perspectives on media accountability, the MediaAcT project explores journalists' evaluations of the impact of traditional and

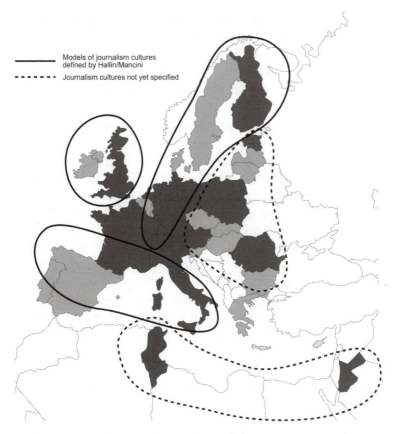

Figure 7.4 Countries included in the MediaAcT study

Austria (A), Estonia (EST), Finland (FIN), France (F), Germany (GER), Italy (I), Jordan (JOR), Netherlands (NL), Poland (PL), Romania (ROM), Spain (E), Switzerland (CH), Tunisia (TN), United Kingdom (UK)

innovative media accountability instruments; it investigates contextual factors that influence that impact; and it provides for an international comparison of accountability cultures, including an examination of whether journalists' attitudes are becoming 'globalised'. Specific research questions for the project include the following:

1. How do journalists across Europe and the Arab world perceive, practise, and evaluate both established and innovative media accountability instruments?

2.   How do journalists' attitudes towards media accountability and transparency differ across journalism cultures and media systems, and what similarities can be found?

3.   What factors enable or discourage media accountability and transparency activities across Europe and the Arab world?

In order to start from common empirical ground, international research partners in all 14 countries included in the MediaAcT study (see Figure 7.4) conducted an audit of media accountability structures in their own country (for further details, see Eberwein et al. (2011)). Based on this information, we then conducted a standardised online survey of journalists in the 14 countries, aimed at gathering insights into their attitudes about media accountability and self-regulation.

The field phase of the survey ran from May 2011 to March 2012. During that time, 1,762 journalists completed the questionnaire. None of the national samples contained fewer than 100 respondents. The following sections highlight initial results of our comparative survey. For this chapter, we focus on the comparison between traditional and innovative media accountability instruments.

General overview: Traditional media accountability instruments

How do journalists across Europe and the Arab world evaluate traditional media accountability instruments? Although media self-regulation and accountability are regarded as a prerequisite for press freedom by media professionals worldwide, our respondents consider the impact of conventional media accountability instruments to be rather low – a result that not only manifested itself in all media segments (daily and weekly newspapers, magazines, private and public broadcasting, news agencies, online news), but also across all investigated media systems (see Figure 7.5).

On average, fewer than one-third of journalists surveyed said that press and media councils have a 'high' or 'very high' impact on journalistic performance. Other traditional instruments of media accountability such as ombudspersons and media criticism in the popular press or in trade journals were judged as even less influential. Among the traditional media accountability instruments, company editorial guidelines, professional codes of ethics, and journalism education were rated the highest in terms of impact. An important variable in this context seems to be the media sector: journalists from news agencies and private media rated organisational codes higher than did print journalists, who mostly rely on professional codes (e.g. journalism associations). External media accountability instruments, however, did not have a discernible impact on the profession (regardless of media sector): while at least one-fifth of the respondents said that academic analyses of the media have an effect on journalistic reporting, viewers' associations and non-governmental organisations or foundations hardly seem to matter.

In contrast, media laws – included as a mechanism of media regulation for the sake of comparison – are considered far more significant than any of the aforementioned instruments. Almost 60% of the journalists reported that laws regulating the media have a high or a very high impact on journalism standards. This result demonstrates that formal institutions such as laws are perceived as considerably more meaningful than informal institutions such as codes of ethics or other media accountability instruments. This is likely because journalists are afraid of potential sanctions that laws can bring, and they expect more drastic punitive measures from laws than from self-regulatory mechanisms.

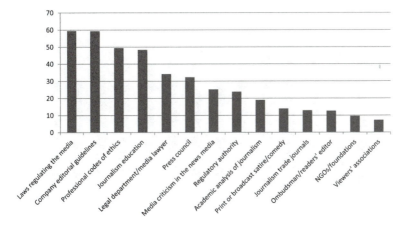

Figure 7.5 Percentage of respondents who said the media accountability instrument has a 'high' impact or 'very high' impact

Source: MediaAcT

Comparative perspectives: Traditional media accountability instruments in different media systems

A closer look at the survey data reveals that attitudes about media accountability and self-regulation vary noticeably in the different journalism cultures studied by the MediaAcT project. This may serve as an early indicator of the existence of heterogeneous 'cultures of accountability' worldwide.

In that respect – as Figure 7.6 shows – company codes are considered to have a higher impact on journalism cultures with a comparatively weak tradition of journalistic professionalism. This includes countries that fit the polarised pluralist model (Italy, France) and those in Eastern Europe (Romania, Estonia, Poland) and the Arab world (Jordan, Tunisia). Particularly in the cases of the Eastern European and Arab countries, this might be explained by their relatively young history of independent journalism and their quickly expanding media sectors. Journalists in countries such as Finland, the UK, and Germany, who have much more experience with a free press and its professional accountability tools, ascribe less influence to codes.

On the other hand, the impact attributed to journalism education seems to correlate with the quality of the country's education. For example, journalism education was cited as an influential or very influential media accountability instrument by almost 62% of the

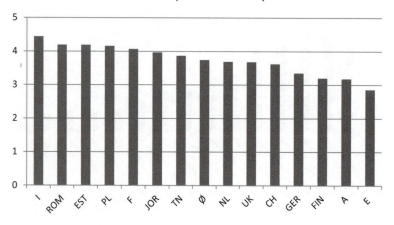

Figure 7.6 Ratings for company editorial codes
(1 = no impact, 5 = very high impact)

Source: MediaAcT

German journalists, while only 21% of them perceived inadequate professional training as a major problem. At the same time, 41% of Spanish journalists criticised the inadequate professional training of journalists, while no more than 22% considered journalism education to be a powerful media accountability instrument.

Having identified the press council as a central pillar of today's wide-ranging accountability instruments, it is interesting to see that fewer than one-third of respondents ascribed a high or very high influence to press councils. These ratings support previous studies that have detected scepticism among media professionals about the impact of press councils (see e.g. Reinemann, 2010). At the high end of the ratings was Finland with its well-respected media council and lively accountability culture. Conversely, the press council in Poland is essentially non-existent, and particularly low ratings from Polish journalists seem to reflect this weakness (see Figure 7.7). Another explanatory factor emerges from the proportion of journalists engaged in trade unions or other professional organisations. Generally speaking, the more journalists are organised in unions, the higher they rate the impact of traditional media accountability instruments. This result demonstrates that the attitude towards codes of ethics, press councils, and other traditional instruments clearly depends on the degree of journalistic professionalism in a particular country.

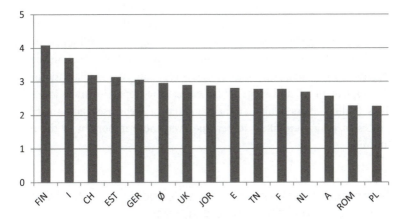

Figure 7.7 Ratings for press councils
(1 = no impact, 5 = very high impact)

Source: MediaAcT

General overview: Innovative media accountability instruments in the digital age

Even though the survey findings leave no doubt that journalists from all analysed countries tend to give more weight to traditional and established media accountability instruments than emerging ones, the data do point to a growing awareness of the importance of innovative and audience-inclusive online accountability tools such as web-based user comments, citizen blogs, and social media-based criticism. Journalist and newsroom blogs already have a measurable impact, although at a modest level (see Figure 7.8). All of these innovative media accountability instruments are characterised by their media-related responsiveness, which can be regarded as an important monitor of accountability processes into the future.

According to the surveyed journalists, online user comments – usually collected with the help of standardised comment forums that appear directly below or next to journalistic texts – are the most effective way for audience members to become involved in the media account-ability processes. More than one-quarter of the respondents said user comments have a 'high' or 'very high' impact on journalists' behaviour. Other influential channels through which to voice audience criticism are social media platforms such as Twitter and Facebook. Online media criticism by journalist bloggers falls in the middle of the spectrum. Less influential are citizen blogs – only 12% of journalists ascribed a noteworthy impact to them – and in-house media blogs.

Taken as a whole, respondents value the influence of new online media accountability instruments nearly as highly as traditional media accountability instruments. For example, journalist blogs are considered equally as influential as traditional media reporting and media criticism in the popular press, and blogs by far exceed the impact of trade journals. This finding offers a hint at the potential of web-based accountability processes, which are likely to become even more important in the near future.

Comparative perspective: Innovative media accountability instruments in different media systems

A comparative view of innovative media accountability instruments reveals slight but visible differences between the participating countries. Journalists from the Arab world – who are working in political systems

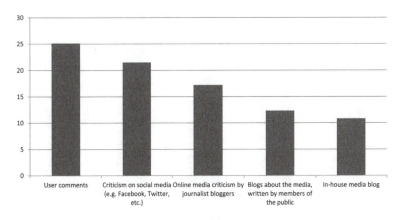

Figure 7.8 Percentage of respondents who reported that the emerging media accountability instrument has a 'high' or 'very high' impact

Source: MediaAcT

transitioning from autocracy to democracy – as well as from Spain value the impact of audience-inclusive media accountability processes via Twitter and Facebook more than practitioners from other European countries (see Figure 7.9). The reasons seem obvious: in Jordan, for example, the digital sphere remains a less tightly controlled arena than the print and broadcasting sectors, even though several attempts have been made by the regime to exert control over online journalism. This might explain why Jordanian journalists rate the impact of web-based media accountability instruments higher than most traditional instruments. Jordan is a country with a state-controlled media system; media criticism is inherently criticism of the ruling elite. Therefore, only online media accountability instruments offer the necessary freedom for critical discussions. Similarly, Spanish journalists were heavily restricted during the Franco regime and consequently lacked any experience with media self-regulation during the decades of politically influenced journalism. Traditional accountability instruments only started to develop in Spain in 1975, which might help explain their relative weakness in comparison to countries with a longer tradition of media self-regulation and a discernible interest in audience-inclusive online instruments.

Regarding the appraisal of online user comments, Finland tops the list (see Figure 7.10). This can be explained by the fact that Finland is one

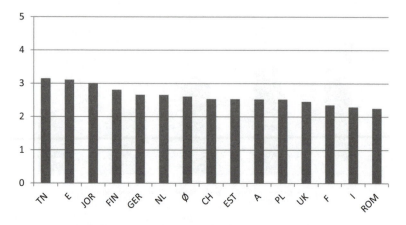

Figure 7.9 Ratings for criticism on social media
(1 = no impact, 5 = very high impact)

Source: MediaAcT

of the world's leading internet countries as measured by hotspots in comparison to inhabitants (sparsely populated area, government funding for a good internet infrastructure). This setting clearly provides for the development of a lively web-based culture of communication that also influences the state of media accountability.

Taken as a whole, however, differences in the analysed countries' perceptions of innovative media accountability instruments are far less compelling than assessments of traditional instruments. This finding may be interpreted as a first indicator of a trend towards transcultural convergence caused by the digitisation of journalistic communication.

Summary and outlook

Our survey data show that the impact of both traditional and new web-based media accountability instruments must be judged as moderate at best. Among the traditional instruments, in-house and professional codes of ethics as well as journalism education are the mechanisms with the highest relevance for journalistic performance. Press councils, media reporting, ombudspersons, professional associations, NGOs, and media research are not expected to have a lasting influence on practical newsroom work. The same is true for most online accountability

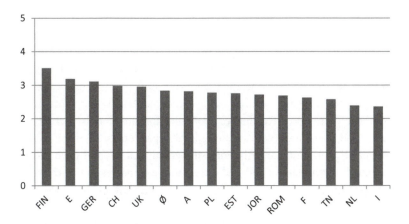

Figure 7.10 Ratings for user comments
(1 = no impact, 5 = very high impact)

Source: MediaAcT

tools although, in many countries, digital innovations such as comment functions and social networking-based media criticism are already described as more influential than traditional media accountability instruments. The highest impact, however, emanates from formal institutions such as the law, which typically has greater power to impose sanctions than self-regulatory and other non-state account-ability tools.

What do these findings mean for the future of media self-regulation and its effect on journalism ethics? In order to make media accountability more effective, do we need the state to get involved by regulating the media's self-regulation efforts? Many of our respondents viewed such prospects with decided scepticism, likely because they are afraid that formal systems of media regulation could be misused for political purposes – a fear that is not unjustified in a country such as Germany where journalists are sensitised both by historical experiences with media control during the Nazi regime and also by experiences in the former GDR. Despite this uneasiness, we believe it is time to think about incentives for media regulation that could well be encouraged by the state. Many interesting examples of this idea can already be found throughout Europe. For instance, Irish newsrooms have legal advantages if they recognise the national press council, while Danish media firms receive fiscal support if they actively engage in self-regulatory practices.

On the other hand, the data also demonstrate that media organisations have an obligation when it comes to upholding the rules of journalistic behaviour. They are in a particularly expedient position to create appreciable incentives for responsible newswork – and impose effective sanctions. As we learned from our survey, journalists calculate very precisely which instruments of media accountability may pose a risk for them personally. The highest potential for sanction is ascribed to media and press laws (with in-house legal departments following closely behind). If journalistic organisations strengthen their support for in-house accountability initiatives and make clear that a transgression of the rules has consequences for the standing of a journalist within the newsroom, those advances would surely leave a mark.

But if journalists view the role of the state in self-regulatory processes with scepticism and if newsrooms still leave a lot to be desired with regard to media accountability, what are other ways forward? Thanks to Web 2.0, if media audiences are willing, they can share their voices much more easily and quickly than they could in the past. Our survey indicates that web-based audience feedback has indeed increased in all of the analysed countries. And at least in some cases, digital accountability tools seem to have a notable impact on journalistic behaviour (see Bichler et al., 2012). On average, however, this impact has been rather mild. In fact, a majority of journalists appear uninterested in user criticism – a clear indication of journalists' resistance to interference from the outside world.

In order to communicate the potential benefits of participatory media regulation and improve the quality of journalistic performance in general, much progress can be made through well-organised educational programmes. Alongside media laws and codes of ethics, our survey respondents rated journalism education as one of the most important factors in influencing journalists' daily routines. Although usually not regarded as a classical instrument of media self-regulation, education must not be underrated. This finding should serve as a further argument to support and advance the varied systems of journalism training in the countries of our study – and worldwide.

Note

All web addresses in this chapter were last accessed in May 2013. For more information on the MediaAcT project, visit www.mediaact.eu. A book that includes the complete study is also forthcoming: *Journalists and Media Accountability; An International Study of News People in the Digital Age* (New York: Peter Lang).

References

Baldi, Paolo (2007) 'Media Accountability in Europe: A Fragmented Picture', in Paolo Baldi and Uwe Hasebrink (eds), *Broadcasters and Citizens in Europe: Trends in Media Accountability and Viewer Participation in Europe* (Bristol and Chicago: Intellect), 17–31.

Baldi, Paolo, and Hasebrink, Uwe (eds) (2007) *Broadcasters and Citizens in Europe: Trends in Media Accountability and Viewer Participation in Europe* (Bristol and Chicago: Intellect).

Bertrand, Claude-Jean (2000) *Media Ethics and Accountability Systems* (New Brunswick, NJ and London: Transaction Publishers).

Bettels, Tina, Fengler, Susanne, Trilling, Mariella, and Sträter, Andreas (2011) *Mogelpackung im WWW? Wie europäische Medien ihr Publikum online an redaktionellen Prozessen teilhaben lassen – Ergebnisse einer international vergleichenden Studie.* European Journalism Observatory: http://de.ejo-online. eu/?p=4783.

Bichler, Klaus, Harro-Loit, Halliki, Karmasin, Matthias, Kraus, Daniela, Lauk, Epp, Loit, Urmas, Fengler, Susanne, and Schneider-Mombaur, Laura (2012) *Best Practice Guidebook*: www.mediaact.eu/strategies.html.

Commission of the European Communities (2007) *Media Pluralism in the Member States of the European Union*, Commission Staff Working Document (Brussels: EC): http://ec.europa.eu/information_society/media_taskforce/doc/ pluralism/media_pluralism_swp_en.pdf.

Domingo, David (2011) *Entrenched in Detachment: Professional Values are the Main Constraint to Accountability in the United States.* MediaAcT working paper: www.mediaact.eu/online.html.

Eberwein, Tobias, Fengler, Susanne, Lauk, Epp, and Leppik-Bork, Tanja (eds) (2011) *Mapping Media Accountability – in Europe and Beyond* (Cologne: Herbert von Halem).

Eberwein, Tobias, Leppik-Bork, Tanja, and Lönnendonker, Julia (2013) 'Participatory Media Regulation: International Perspectives on the Structural Deficits of Media Self-Regulation and the Potentials of Web-Based Accountability Processes', in Manuel Puppis, Matthias Künzler, and Otfried Jarren (eds), *Media Structures and Media Performance* (Vienna: ÖAW), 135–58.

Fengler, Susanne (2008) 'Media Journalism and the Power of Blogging Citizens', in Torbjörn von Krogh (ed.), *Media Accountability Today – and Tomorrow* (Göteborg: Nordicom), 61–8.

Fengler, Susanne (2012) 'From Media Self-Regulation to "Crowd-Criticism": Media Accountability in the Digital Age', *Central European Journal of Communication*, 5(2): 175–89.

Hallin, Daniel, and Mancini, Paolo (2004) *Comparing Media Systems: Three Models of Media and Politics* (Cambridge: Cambridge University Press).

Hallin, Daniel, and Mancini, Paolo (eds) (2012) *Comparing Media Systems Beyond the Western World* (Cambridge: Cambridge University Press).

Hasebrink, Uwe, Herzog, Anja, and Eilders, Christiane (2007) 'Media Users' Participation in Europe from a Civil Society Perspective', in Paolo Baldi and Uwe Hasebrink (eds), *Broadcasters and Citizens in Europe: Trends in Media Accountability and Viewer Participation in Europe* (Bristol and Chicago: Intellect), 75–91.

Jempson, Mike, and Powell, Wayne (2011) 'United Kingdom: From the Gentlemen's Club to the Blogosphere', in Tobias Eberwein, Susanne Fengler, Epp Lauk, and Tanja Leppik-Bork (eds), *Mapping Media Accountability – in Europe and Beyond* (Cologne: Herbert von Halem), 194–216.

Jempson, Mike, Powell, Wayne, and Evers, Huub (2011) *Critical Citizens Online: Adding or Subtracting from Conventional Media Regulation?* MediaAcT working paper: www.mediaact.eu/online.html.

Karmasin, Matthias, Kraus, Daniela, Kaltenbrunner, Andy, and Bichler, Klaus (2011) 'Austria: A Border-Crosser', in Tobias Eberwein, Susanne Fengler, Epp Lauk, and Tanja Leppik-Bork (eds), *Mapping Media Accountability – in Europe and Beyond* (Cologne: Herbert von Halem), 22–35.

Mayer, Florian L., Mehling, Gabriele, Raabe, Johannes, Schmidt, Jan, and Wied, Kristina (2008) 'Watchblogs aus der Sicht der Nutzer: Befunde einer Onlinebefragung zur Nutzung und Bewertung von Bildblog', *Media Perspektiven*, 11: 589–94.

McQuail, Denis (1992) *Media Performance: Mass Communication and the Public Interest* (London: Sage).

Nordenstreng, Kaarle (1999) 'European Landscape of Media Self-Regulation', in OSCE (ed.), *Freedom and Responsibility Yearbook 1989/99* (Vienna: OSCE), 169–85.

North, Douglass C. (1990) *Institutions, Institutional Change and Economic Performance* (Cambridge: Cambridge University Press).

Olson, Mancur (1971) *The Logic of Collective Action: Public Goods and the Theory of Groups* (Cambridge, MA: Harvard University Press).

Organisation for Security and Co-operation in Europe (OSCE) (2008) *Media Self-Regulation Guidebook*: www.osce.org/fom/31497.

Parliamentary Assembly of the Council of Europe (2008) *Resolution 1636 (2008), Indicators for Media in a Democracy*: http://assembly.coe.int/Mainf.asp?link=/ Documents/AdoptedText/ta08/ERES1636.htm.

Pies, Judith, and Hawatmeh, George (2011) 'Jordan: Media Accountability under the Patronage of the Regime', in Tobias Eberwein, Susanne Fengler, Epp Lauk, and Tanja Leppik-Bork (eds), *Mapping Media Accountability – in Europe and Beyond* (Cologne: Herbert von Halem), 101–13.

Puppis, Manuel (2007) 'Media Governance as a Horizontal Extension of Media Regulation: The Importance of Self- and Co-Regulation', *Communications*, 32(3): 383–9.

Reinemann, Carsten (2010) 'Das Versprechen der Selbstkontrolle. Presserat und Pressekodex im Urteil von Journalisten', in Carsten Reinemann and Rudolf Stöber (eds), *Wer die Vergangenheit kennt, hat eine Zukunft: Festschrift für Jürgen Wilke* (Cologne: Herbert von Halem), 236–63.

Shoemaker, Pamela, and Reese, Stephen, D. (1996) *Mediating the Message: Theories of Influences on Mass Media Content* (2nd edn, White Plains, NY: Longman).

Thomaß, Barbara, and Tzankoff, Michaela (2001) 'Medien und Transformation in den postkommunistischen Staaten Osteuropas', in Barbara Thomaß and Michaela Tzankoff (eds), *Medien und Transformation in Osteuropa* (Wiesbaden: Westdeutscher Verlag), 235–52.

8

How News Ombudsmen Help Create Ethical and Responsible News Organisations

Carlos Maciá-Barber

The ombudsman – also referred to as the readers' representative, public editor, or readers' advocate – occupies a unique position at a news organisation. Called on to serve as a liaison between news organisations and news audiences, the ombudsman's task is often associated with the mythical figure of Sisyphus, who was eternally condemned to roll a boulder up a mountain and then watch it roll back down again. For the ombudsman, the task is corrections, and the errors committed by journalists and those in charge of news organisations repeat themselves again and again (Neto, 2000).

The very existence of ombudsmen, however, implies that media institutions are capable of improvement. Depending on the main attribute used to brand the role, the terms used to describe ombudsmen turn out to be strikingly metaphorical: vigilant (*watchdog, policeman*), responsible (*newspaper's conscience*), people's advocate (*lawyer, prosecutor, judge, mediator, devil's advocate, censor, pariah, loner*), company's advocate (*apologist, public relations flack, Pontius Pilate*), and giver of aid to both journalists and the public (*doctor, fireman, priest*). I take the view that all of these sobriquets reflect, to varying degrees, the work of ombudsmen throughout the world. The news ombudsman is not a miraculous cure for the ills afflicting news organisations or the errors committed by their employees. At the same time – when it is used to its fullest potential – the ombudsman function can help achieve more responsible and ethically sustainable news media.

How is this accomplished? Above all, ombudsmen exemplify courage and honesty in the fair and balanced analysis of errors committed by news organisations. Additionally, ombudsmen work by means of sincere, constructive criticism to improve the quality of the product, which, after all, is the ultimate objective. As role models, ombudsmen can also inspire by example. In short, when ombudsmen promote ethics in editorial departments, they help companies protect themselves from their own abuses while, at the same time, protecting society as a whole from media excesses.

Despite its potential, the ombudsman's role must be carefully defined. Ombudsmen must never become censors who limit freedom of expression nor inquisitors who persecute and punish colleagues who act or think in different ways. Nor is the office a platform from which to institutionalise personal preferences or a place to launch one's own career. Even less so should it be a public relations tool for cleaning up an organisation's image or justifying the errors and excesses committed by owners and editors.

Although worldwide the idea of the ombudsman is becoming increasingly popular, different stakeholders have different and even opposing conceptions of the nature, regulation, and organisation of the function. Today, two main models – public and private, each with its own characteristics – can be distinguished. In the public model, found, for example, in Sweden and South Africa, the action of the ombudsman covers either the entire range of media formats or a section of them (press, radio, television, digital); this model also features a clear external institutional influence (parliament, press council, judiciary) and a markedly judicial nature. The private model presupposes the adoption of the ombudsman in a particular private company or corporate group. This system offers three variants: internal, in which the person chosen must be a member of staff; external, in which the ombudsman is hired from outside the organisation or even the profession; and mixed, which uses both options (Maciá-Barber, 2006a).

The structural variety of ombudsman models is related to the different ways in which journalism is conceived and practised in different parts of the world. In Europe alone, three major systems and cultures of journalism can be identified (Hallin and Mancini, 2004): the Mediterranean system (polarised pluralist model), which is practised in France, Italy, Spain, and Portugal; the central and Northern European system (democratic corporatist model), which is practised in Austria,

Germany, Switzerland, the Netherlands, Finland, Denmark, Norway, and Sweden; and the North Atlantic system (liberal model), which is practised in the United Kingdom. Two further models have recently been proposed, although they have not yet been detailed (Eberwein et al., 2011); these include models found in Eastern Europe and in the Mediterranean Arab states (Tunisia and Jordan).

Regardless of the name of the institution, the epithet it receives, or the journalistic culture in which it is exercised, ombudsmen should practise at least eight modes of simultaneous and complementary conduct to help create more ethical and responsible news organisations. The sections that follow explore these modes and offer prescriptions for how ombudsmen can most effectively contribute to ethical journalistic practices.

Ombudsmen should act in an ex-officio capacity

The last decades of the twentieth century showed an increasing lack of respect for the human right to information. This produced a lowering of standards among the general public, many of whom are prepared to exchange their status as citizens for that of mere consumers. The ultimate rationale for the ombudsman function, therefore, is the protection of this right to information. Ombudsmen agree that this task is the most fundamental one, and, in fact, it is underlined in a formal sense in the job descriptions of many. This explains not only the importance but the necessity of ombudsmen acting in an ex-officio capacity as individuals with 'outsider' status – those who are neither audience member nor journalist but someone charged with protecting the right to information.

This ex-officio measure aims to ensure that action is taken in defence of fundamental communication rights, even when audiences themselves – whether from lack of knowledge or passivity – do not take the initiative. One function of ombudsmen, therefore, is to teach audiences – citizens – to fulfil their duties and exercise their rights. Here, even the media benefits from strengthening proactive attitudes on the part of audiences; the ombudsman is, therefore, the media organisation's most critical member, with a solid knowledge of the tasks of the position, the rules of the organisation, and the methods of journalism.

However, when considering the relationship established and maintained between a news organisation and its ombudsman, two different and opposed positions have become entrenched. The first, held by the US editor Robert J. Haiman, contends that the ombudsman is nothing more than an infiltrator among the masses (Lambeth, 1986). This is the case because the ombudsman is selected and paid by the organisation's management, irrespective of the type of contract or the profile of the individual. As a result, the public, who identifies the ombudsman with a cosmetic response to criticism, lacks trust in the system (Day, 1991). The second interpretation tends to see the ombudsman as an intruder in the editorial team – another kind of outsider – both because of the specific remit of the position and because the employment contract or particular regulatory framework in which the ombudsman operates confers a significant degree of autonomy and independence. This is an indispensable condition that allows ombudsmen to fulfil their primary objective: defending the rights of readers, viewers, or listeners. Autonomy and independence are supposed to both prevent higher placed hierarchies (owners, executives, managers) from interfering with ombudsmen as they carry out their tasks and prevent journalists or the public from dictating their activities.

Because of ombudsmen's ex-officio roles, they should be granted the power to investigate any error, deficiency, or presumed violation of professional ethics without having to wait for a complaint. In other words, an ombudsman should not simply be a bureaucrat who processes grievances (Costa, 2006). While this power is often specified in an ombudsman's job description or in regulations, it does not exist in all media organisations. On occasion, ombudsmen are viewed only as a second court of appeals for cases in which complainants view an explanation provided by the company or the professionals involved as unsatisfactory.

The following four practices form the basis of ombudsmen's ex-officio role:

- *Regulations.* Some organisations have regulations that include a statement of principles, the process for selection and appointment, the functions of the ombudsman, the limits of the position's remit, and the characteristics governing the relationships established among the different parties (owners, managers, editorial team, ombudsman, public). The objective here is to prevent arbitrary or discretionary actions by participants in the journalistic process.
- *Limited appointments.* The goal of limiting appointments to a specific term is to prevent both the risk of the ombudsman becoming attached to the position and the dwindling commitment that comes

with the security of having a permanent position. Limited terms – generally between two and six years – have been adopted by virtually all companies.

- *Confidentiality.* Inquiries and investigations undertaken by the ombudsman to establish the cause, motive, and consequences surrounding the publication of a particular item arousing controversy must remain confidential. The same should be true of internal reports. Access to a final report should only be given to outside individuals once that report is ready for distribution, which is sometimes not until its public disclosure. This is intended to prevent any member of the news team or the management from being able to pressure the ombudsman in a way that would change the result of an ongoing inquiry or influence a decision in a way that benefits a particular party. Without doubt, this confidentiality guarantees ombudsmen greater freedom in carrying out their responsibilities.

- *Employment and trade union safeguards.* Obstacles faced by ombudsmen may derive from pressure exerted on their current jobs or a threat of future reprisal, which affect ombudsmen's employment relationship with the organisation when their term expires. This fear has materialised on more than one occasion. To eliminate this risk, organisations can take direct action by, first, guaranteeing that ombudsmen cannot be fired or penalised during their mandate as a result of carrying out their duties. Second, organisations can give an assurance that, if the ombudsman is an employee, that person will be reassigned to his or her previous position at the end of the term. These guarantees resemble those that might be granted and recognised by law for trade union members.

The ex-officio role is essential. First, because it guarantees ombudsmen's independence, allowing them to approach any kind of subject with complete freedom and to initiate an investigation at any time. If, at any time, the public turns out to be passive, its role is taken up by the ombudsman, thus avoiding the risk that the problems remain unaddressed. Second, the ex-officio capacity facilitates the correction of errors: if ombudsmen had to wait for a complaint to be made, this would result in undesirable delays, thus exacerbating the damage caused. Finally, this role proves a valuable indicator for measuring ombudsmen's activity. If an ombudsman ignores a relevant issue, this is undoubtedly evidence of defective work.

Ombudsmen should put their official duties ahead of their own careers

The individuals selected to carry out the ombudsman function – 60–70% of whom are between 50 and 55 years of age – tend to have professional experience of approximately two decades as journalists and one decade as managers (Ettema and Glasser, 1987; Maciá-Barber, 2001; Thomas, 1995). Thanks to their long careers in journalism, it is, therefore, likely that those appointed, even if they belong to the staff, can count on having the initial respect of their colleagues. This is also illustrated by the fact that it is customary for an ombudsman's nomination to be approved by the editorial (or management) committee, regardless of whether these are required. Although Christopher Meyers (2000) and others have argued that this familiarity with the profession automatically makes it impossible to have an objective view of the newsmaking process, I do not agree. Such a profile does not, in principle, suggest that appointees are likely to harbour outlandish professional ambitions for the future, especially when the very nature and purpose of the task entrusted to them is bound to generate disagreements and cause personal relationships to sour. Indeed, anyone accepting this position is assumed for this very reason to possess the high degree of drive and motivation necessary to deal with these future difficulties.

One potential reason for criticising the notion of an ombudsman is that individuals named to the position may have difficulty separating their own personal opinions from general journalistic criteria. The counter to this argument is that owners and managers should appoint candidates who are capable and, quite simply, experienced enough not to confuse these issues. In the event that an ombudsman made such a mistake, management of the organisation would likely point out the error. It is certainly the case that every ombudsman stamps his or her personality, attitude, experience, and rules for action on the office. This phenomenon is not negative; it contributes to the value of the function, demonstrating that its importance and usefulness do not depend exclusively on the merits of the particular person occupying the role at the time.

On occasion, media organisations choose a journalist from outside their staff as ombudsman, believing that the office functions more effectively with this structure (Maciá-Barber, 2006a, 2006b). This practice was used by the *Washington Post* from 1970 to 2013. During those 43 years, the ombudsman's dissociation from the company was a prerequisite, and the ombudsman signed a contract as an independent agent. Appointed individuals were not allowed to be employees of the paper nor, once their mandate had expired, could they take up positions at the *Post*. This approach has two aims. First, it prevents owners or managers of the organisation from being able to pressure or influence the ombudsman; second, it eliminates any temptation that might be felt by the ombudsman to win the organisation's approval in the hope of obtaining a permanent position in the future.

To reinforce the independence of the ombudsman, some even contend that the selected person should come from outside the profession entirely. In Spain and Italy, where such cases exist, judges or university professors have been appointed. Here, the claim is that an absolute lack of ties to and interests in the world of journalism allows ombudsmen complete moral freedom. In other words, the disassociation makes genuine criticism possible. As Meyers (2000) contends, the appointed person ought to be someone with sufficient knowledge of journalism but not conditioned by allegiance to it.

Those who oppose this option rightly point out the inherent risk: ombudsmen may lack needed knowledge about the internal workings of the media and the media's professional practices. No doubt, the ombudsman's role would be effectively diminished if not made impossible in this case. Therefore, to prevent this from occurring, I contend that it is crucial for selected individuals to enter the job with wide-ranging experience and personal relationships with the media.

Ombudsmen should assist with journalists' self-evaluation and self-regulation

Together with others, ombudsmen can serve as an adequate and valuable mechanism for contributing to the professional self-evaluation and self-regulation of journalists (Ettema and Glasser, 1987; Mesquita, 1998). The aim here is to give journalists themselves the responsibility for ensuring that the profession functions within an ethical framework. This does not entail either censorship or self-censorship, but simply a professional conscientiousness focused on being willing to maximise journalism's rigour and integrity.

In his analysis of the introduction and establishment of ombudsmen in the Brazilian press, Mário Vitor Santos (1998), ombudsman at *Folha de*

São Paulo, claims that this unbureaucratic, free, and universal system brought about important innovations in that country. Before the ombudsman system was introduced, readers who wanted to give feedback depended on the willingness, accessibility, and integrity of owners, editors, and journalists. In theory, the presence of an ombudsman means that corrections and clarifications become less dependent on the will of those responsible for the errors and those in charge of the organisations, or even on recourse to legal action.

By facilitating the flow of vertical communication (top-down from the board of directors to employees) and horizontal communication (among the members of each employee group), ombudsmen clearly contribute to the practice of internal democracy within a company. Sharing information about company decisions generally creates mutual trust. However, like other businesses and institutions, transparent communication in news organisations is not always ideal; stakeholders may have mutual distrust, divergent criteria, personal enmities, professional snobbery, a lack of proper channels, professional quarrels, deficient training, or an accumulation of all of these. Ombudsmen are basically a source of information whose authority derives from the fact that they have two types of information at their disposal: information about the wrongs committed by journalists and information about where to go to effect change (Meyer, 1987).

Achieving profit is a legitimate aim of media organisations, but it is neither the primary nor the most substantial one. Indeed, any business has to be ethically sustainable throughout its levels – from its top director through to its most remote supplier. However, in news organisations, the general public interest should be satisfied first and foremost. This is followed by the tastes and demands of the relevant audience, and, finally, by the specific interest of each media corporation. The result is a triad of legitimate and complementary interests. Reversing this order would imply manipulating the public and being underhanded and unclear. The overriding challenge faced by every news ombudsman, then, is ensuring that this order of precedence is observed by those at the organisation.

The ombudsman function can also be distorted if it is viewed as an efficient form of public relations (see e.g. Deuze and Dalen, 2006; Nemeth, 2003). In fact, Abe M. Rosenthal regarded the ombudsman as a ruse for getting the editor out of a jam (Bagdikian, 1974). In 1989, Sir William Wood, ombudsman at the British tabloid the *Daily Mirror*, complained that his appointment appeared to be little more than an exercise in public relations. A crucial question, therefore, remains unanswered: if the ombudsman function is merely an exercise in marketing – attractive for the purposes of improving the image of the news organisation and even beneficial in averting court actions – why wouldn't all media organisations have one?

Constant communication – at any time or in any direction – turns out to be indispensable for ombudsmen. Two observations are pertinent here. First, the ever-increasing efforts of ombudsmen to be active in blogs and social media – in particular Twitter – are deserving of praise. Second, the resulting accessibility and speed of communication allow ombudsmen to show more care and attention to individual complaints offered by readers, viewers, and listeners. A cause for concern, on the other hand, is the lack of wide-ranging and detailed reports on structural weak spots within each company that result from proprietor or shareholder pressures, advertiser interference, political coercion, or deficient professional training. The examination and analysis of individual complaints by ombudsmen is absolutely essential, but it merely shows the cracks caused by systemic failures. Consequently, to be fully effective, ombudsmen must conduct rigorous analyses of the deep-seated causes that underlie organisational and hiring systems, patterns of corporate actions, and editorial decisions in media corporations. Now is the perfect moment for rebuilding from scratch a business model that is experiencing severe crisis, and the ombudsman can clearly help with this process.

Ombudsmen should promote the right to information and citizen participation

The news ombudsman role presupposes a model for social participation. As Article 19 of the Universal Declaration of Human Rights states, 'Everyone has the right to freedom of opinion and expression; this right includes freedom to hold opinions without interference and to seek, receive and impart information and ideas through any media and regardless of frontiers' (United Nations, 1948). This principle includes the postulate that the right to information is an indispensable social right that allows individuals to actively take part in public acts. The powers to seek, receive, and impart information are at the heart of this right, and it is founded on the belief that information means participation. Today's digital and technological revolution has contributed significantly to achieving this right, thanks, in part, to the mediation and actions of ombudsmen.

Ombudsmen represent an accessible and direct means of communication with the audience. Over the long term, active involvement by the public via its relationship with the ombudsman creates identification – an emotional investment – with the principles, efforts, and work of journalists at a news organisation. Therefore, members of the public come to see the organisation as their own (Bailey, 1990). News organisations that introduce ombudsmen are placing their faith in an ethical tool whose success depends to a large extent on the trust of readers, listeners, and viewers. These audience members have an accessible point of contact in an ombudsman – someone who is not only willing but obliged to pay attention to them, provide a channel for their complaints, answer their questions, and listen to their suggestions. This in itself encourages participation (Ettema and Glasser, 1987; Neto, 2000). Moreover, if this involvement is still not forthcoming or is of little significance, ombudsmen can and ought to encourage the audience to become active. We see this in countries such as Spain, Portugal, and Mexico, for example, where audiences are invited to participate in radio and television programmes, whether live or by means of pre-recorded conversations with ombudsmen.

Like other institutions, associations, or groups, ombudsmen face a dearth of citizen involvement. A number of news ombudsmen have complained about the low level of intervention by their audiences. These audiences often forget that they, too, have a duty to monitor the media and contribute to improving the work of news organisations, the professional practice of journalists, and society as a whole. Consequently, with the aim of increasing the public's involvement, ombudsmen pursue diverse expository strategies to stimulate dialogue with consumers. The most common methods include use of the terms *reader, listener,* or *viewer* as direct, individual forms of address; ombudsmen often present themselves as just another member of the audience. Another common tactic is using direct questions. Here, the aim is to stir people's feelings and consciences, thus provoking a reaction. Often, ombudsmen identify members of the public and include their comments and arguments as direct quotations in columns or on radio broadcasts or television programmes. Other valuable strategies aimed at strengthening ties with the community include meetings with community leaders or representatives.

Ombudsmen should foster media literacy

Encouraging mutual understanding between the media and the general public is a primary task of the ombudsman, and an invaluable contribution is made when ombudsmen describe the work they carry out (Costa, 2006; Dvorkin, 2011; Fidalgo, 2004; Mayes, 2007; Neto, 2000; Okrent, 2006). This undoubtedly contributes to improving media literacy.

Clearly, as users of communication media, most consumers do not have complete mastery of the knowledge necessary for making fully informed and conscious decisions. For example, many consumers lack a comprehensive understanding of the nature and purpose of journalism; others aren't aware of the technological or chronological limitations that drive a reporter and determine the journalistic message. One reason for this is the lack of an adequate basic education – as occurs in other areas such as finance or the law – that would allow consumers to make choices based on full knowledge of the issues. However, also evident is a lack of personal interest, ignorance of the media's impact on our daily lives, or limited awareness of the damaging consequences of misinformation.

As the MacBride Report pointed out more than 30 years ago, fostering a critical and questioning frame of mind is a fundamental aspect of the democratisation of information (International Commission for the Study of Communication Problems, 1980). Therefore, through their work, ombudsmen contribute to publicising the principles of professional journalistic ethics to both journalists and the public at large. Ombudsmen also assist in the task of educating individuals in their roles as consumers of all kinds of information – from news to advertising. Ombudsmen educate us about the essence of the journalism profession and the management and working methods of news organisations. They also help explain our rights as they relate to advertising.

Ombudsmen should guard the rights of journalists

In addition to being an educator and advocate for the public, ombudsmen can also serve as employee advocates. They can come to the assistance of journalists by serving as their voice or by defending newsworkers from criticisms that might be unfounded or unjustified (Alix, 1997). In fact, ombudsmen at many organisations are obligated to listen to and report faithfully journalists' versions of events under investigation. This situation, however, is occasionally the source of criticism levelled against ombuds-men on the grounds that the work does no more than defend corporate interests.

Within journalism, a recurrent and not infrequent debate relates to the actions of ombudsmen when a public figure (a politician, business person, or celebrity) or a source (spokesperson, press officer, or witness) presents a complaint. In such cases, someone at the heart of the editorial team is often ready to point out that ombudsmen put themselves at the service of those sources who have an interest in using their complaint to pressure the news organisation or its journalists and to interfere in the investigation with the aim of protecting their own self-interest. Mário Mesquita (1998), pioneering ombudsman – *provedor do leitor* – of the Portuguese newspaper *Diário de Notícias*, does not deny this possibility but rightly points out that complaints originating from the instigators of news stories are just as legitimate as any others and, for this reason, should not be ignored. Yes, Mesquita argues, these complaints might be motivated by self-interest – just as those of the anonymous individual may be – but this does not automatically mean they are unfounded. If sources' concerns were dismissed, the illegitimate pressure would, then, come from the news organisation itself. Similarly, complaints or suggestions from members of staff must also be considered, even though they may be motivated by individual professional interests or attempts to discredit the careers of other journalists.

Ombudsmen should be given the power to ensure that editors meet their obligations

Without doubt, the executive power of an ombudsman neither is nor can be the same as that exercised by the owners and managers of news organisations; even in a best-case scenario, an ombudsman's powers are considerably less than those of a chairman, chief executive, or editor. Because ombudsmen are not granted legitimate power to act and intervene at the editorial heart of the organisation, they lack true and effective executive power (Shipp, 2000). The role is more advisory than executive, and there is no guarantee that ombudsmen will receive a response to requests or positive support and cooperation from colleagues. While ombudsmen can investigate, make recommendations, and exhort, they do not make decisions, nor can they determine a specific journalistic action or guarantee organisational change. Put simply, the remit is representative, not executive.

Ombudsmen *should*, however, be vested with real decision-making and intervention powers, giving them the ability to introduce significant changes in the methods and work of the news organisation. If the position of the ombudsman has no greater authority than moral authority – if it lacks coercive power – perhaps, then, it is preferable that the ombudsman not be equated with safeguarding the principle of press freedom itself.

When James Gannon was editor of the *Des Moines Register*, he contended that it was part of the editor's remit to deal with complaints, not that of someone stuck in a corner and lacking any real power (Tate, 1984). Until the Jayson Blair scandal erupted in 2003, the *New York Times* shared this position. Andrew Rosenthal, one of the paper's most renowned editors, argued in the early 1990s that if someone else took on the duties of dealing with errors committed by the paper, managers would become complacent (McKenna, 1993). A similar view can be found among French editors, who see ombudsmen as intruding on the territory that rightly belongs to them; they also believe the ombudsman's role does not exonerate them from the obligations and duties inherent in their job (Alix, 1997). In Great Britain, when Sir Geoffrey Owen was editor of the *Financial Times*, he refused to sign on to the 1989 Fleet Street agreement to introduce an ombudsman; he believed that readers ought to complain to the editor because that was part of the editor's job. Similarly, Anthony Miles – chairman of the Mirror Group and member of the British Press Council (1975–8) – thought the powers granted to the position really belonged to the editor.

In reviewing perceptions of the ombudsman function, it becomes clear that many journalists have completely changed their opinion. Elissa Papirno, for example, was extremely sceptical when she accepted the post of opinion editor at the *Hartford Courant*, but after five years in the position, she admitted that she had come to appreciate the virtues of her role (Moses, 2000). For other journalists, an intermediate position is the most justifiable. When, for example, the *Sarasota Herald-Tribune* joined the Journalism Credibility Project supported by the American Society of Newspaper Editors (ASNE), it assigned journalists to take turns acting as a readers' advocate.

Whatever the scenario, it is a clear obligation of ombudsmen to work to ensure that all people in positions of responsibility consistently fulfil their duties. What's more, ombudsmen should work in collaboration with others at the organisation to foster an ethically outstanding company that routinely acts well (virtuously), improves individuals' practice, aims for perfection, and contributes to the common good. Limiting an ombudsman's function to ensuring legal compliance, respecting human rights, and abiding by codes of ethics – while commendable – is barely more than a first step.

Ombudsmen should not yield to depression or despair

One distinctive feature of the ombudsman function is that it is a one-person office (with the exception of the Japanese model). This makes the position one with an unmistakable and high degree of personalisation and one that carries with it both advantages and disadvantages. It allows familiarity with journalists and facilitates external recognition and proximity to readers, but it simultaneously lacks the authority of an official collective body. This doesn't mean ombudsmen approach their tasks alone, although the lack of support from qualified assistants is indeed a common complaint. This lack of support can lead to situations of work overload, which can then result in decreased effectiveness. Ombudsmen have considerable obligations: responding to audience members, conducting internal investigations, managing daily tasks, writing columns or producing programmes, participating in conferences, and attending debates, lectures, and visits. This accumulation of tasks results in an extremely demanding role that can cause considerable physical and mental exhaustion. In fact, the heavy workload is one of the most serious drawbacks of the position, and the workload can lead to burnout. Of even greater concern is that the accumulation of tasks can cause a delay in the process of investigating and responding to issues.

Beyond workload issues, the fact that someone is supervising and judging the activity of colleagues can cause serious moral dilemmas. As Ben C. Bradlee has pointed out, ombudsmen are analogous to members of an internal affairs unit of a police department; journalists feel uncomfortable having people constantly poking their noses into their work (cited in McKenna, 1993). The result of this can be apathy; ombudsmen frequently complain about the sluggishness with which requests and complaints are addressed. Ombudsmen also have to get used to the fact that editors are often simply too busy with other concerns.

Some ombudsmen also point out that their moods and states of mind change daily. Ombudsmen are frequently caught in a hostile crossfire between fellow journalists and audience members, which can lead to a sense of isolation. For this reason, Arthur C. Nauman (1994) maintains that the definition of a good ombudsman is someone with strength of character and the ability to cope with the psychological problems that result from a position of isolation at the paper. Claude-Jean Bertrand (2000) rightly emphasises certain virtues that ought to accompany ombudsmen's work, including diplomacy, courage, kindness, firmness, common sense, and patience.

The rise of the news ombudsman is also affecting and influencing the attitudes of journalists (Nelson and Starck, 1974; Pritchard, 1993). Some reporters see this mediation as an obstacle to their direct relationship with the public, and when someone is appointed to represent the interests of audiences, an increase in tensions at the organisation is inevitable (Getlin, 2000). Unfortunately, the ombudsman's dialogue with fellow journalists can sometimes deteriorate into bitter argument.

Nonetheless, the role of ombudsman should not be viewed with excessive pessimism. After all, the very same endeavour – counteracting our errors – is what drives humanity's progress. In the process of searching for truth and improving our world, error invariably appears. We should appreciate ombudsmen for their efforts at leading us forward and helping create more ethical and responsible news organisations.

Note

All web addresses in this chapter were last accessed in June 2013.

References

Alix, François-Xavier (1997) *Une éthique pour l'information: De Gutenberg à Internet* (Paris and Montreal: L'Harmattan).

Bagdikian, Ben H. (1974) 'The Saga of a Newspaper Ombudsman', in Michel C. Emery and Ted C. Smythe (eds), *Readings in Mass Communication: Concepts and Issues in the Mass Media* (Dubuque, IA: Wm C. Brown Publishers), 74–7.

Bailey, Charles W. (1990) 'Newspapers Need Ombudsmen (An Editor's View)', *Washington Journalism Review*, 12(9): 31–4.

Bertrand, Claude-Jean (2000) *La Déontologie des Médias* (Paris: Presses Universitaires de France).

Costa, Caio Túlio (2006) *O Relógio de Pascal: A Experiência do Primeiro Ombudsman da Imprensa Brasileira* (São Paulo: Editora Geração).

Day, Louis A. (1991) *Ethics in Media Communications: Cases and Controversies* (Belmont, CA: Wadsworth).

Deuze, Mark, and Dalen, Arjen van (2006) 'Readers' Advocates or Newspapers' Ambassadors? Newspaper Ombudsmen in the Netherlands', *European Journal of Communication*, 21(4): 457–75.

Dvorkin, Jeffrey A. (2011) *The Modern News Ombudsman: A Users Guide* (Toronto: Organisation of News Ombudsmen).

Eberwein, Tobias, Fengler, Susanne, Lauk, Epp, and Leppik-Bork, Tanja (eds) (2011) *Mapping Media Accountability – in Europe and Beyond* (Cologne: Herbert von Halem).

Ettema, James S., and Glasser, Theodore L. (1987) 'Public Accountability or Public Relations? Newspaper Ombudsmen Define their Role', *Journalism Quarterly*, 64(1): 3–12.

Fidalgo, Joaquim (2004) *Em Nome do Leitor* (Coimbra: Minerva).

Getlin, Joshua (2000) 'The Critics: Ombudsman', *Columbia Journalism Review*, 38 (6): 51–65.

Hallin, Daniel C., and Mancini, Paolo (2004) *Comparing Media Systems: Three Models of Media and Politics* (Cambridge: Cambridge University Press).

International Commission for the Study of Communication Problems (1980) *Many Voices, One World: Towards a New, More Just and More Efficient World Information and Communication Order*, The MacBride Report (Paris: UNESCO; London: Kogan Page; New York: Unipub).

Lambeth, Edmund B. (1986) *Committed Journalism: An Ethic for the Profession* (Bloomington, IN: Indiana University Press).

Maciá-Barber, Carlos (2001) *La participación y los derechos de los públicos en el proceso informativo: La figura del defensor del lector, del lector y del telespectador* (Madrid: Universidad CEU San Pablo).

Maciá-Barber, Carlos (2006a) *La figura del defensor del lector, del oyente y del telespectador: Los paladines contra el periodismo descaminado* (Madrid: Universitas).

Maciá-Barber, Carlos (2006b) 'A Press Ombudsman Model for Improvement of Journalistic Practices in Spain', *Comunicación y Sociedad*, 19(1): 47–66.

Mayes, Ian (2007) *Journalism Right and Wrong: Ethical and Other Issues Raised by Readers in the Guardian's Open Door Column* (London: Guardian Books).

McKenna, Kate (1993) 'The Loneliest Job in the Newsroom', *American Journalism Review*, 15: 41–4.

Mesquita, Mário (1998) 'La médiation solitaire de l'ombudsman de presse', *Recherches en Communication*, 9: 83–92.

Meyer, Philip (1987) *Ethical Journalism: A Guide for Students, Practitioners and Consumers* (Lanham, MD: University Press of America).

Meyers, Christopher (2000) 'Creating an Effective Newspaper Ombudsman Position', *Journal of Mass Media Ethics*, 15(4): 248–56.

Moses, Lucia (2000) 'Is there a Doctor in the House? Increasingly, Newspapers Call on Ombudsmen to Cure What Ails Them', *Editor and Publisher*, 133(1): 27–8.

Nauman, Arthur C. (1994) 'News Ombudsmanship: Its History and Rationale', paper from conference, 1 June, Seoul, on 'Press Regulation: How Far has it Come?'.

Nelson, David R., and Starck, Kenneth (1974) 'The Newspaper Ombudsman as Viewed by the Rest of the Staff', *Journalism Quarterly*, 51(3): 453–7.

Nemeth, Neil (2003) *News Ombudsmen in North America: Assessing an Experiment in Social Responsibility* (Westport, CT: Praeger).

Neto, Lira (2000) *A Herança de Sísifo: Da Arte de Carregar Pedras como Ombudsman na Imprensa* (Fortaleza, Brasil: Edições Demócrito Rocha).

Okrent, Daniel (2006) *Public Editor #1: The Collected Columns (with Reflections, Reconsiderations, and Even a Few Retractions) of the First Ombudsman of the New York Times* (New York: Public Affairs).

Pritchard, David (1993) 'The Impact of Newspaper Ombudsmen on Journalists' Attitudes', *Journalism Quarterly*, 70(1): 77–86.

Santos, Mário Vitor (1998) 'Ombudsman: Conquistas e Impasses', Observatório da Imprensa, 20 Apr.: www.observatoriodaimprensa.com.br/cadernos/cid200498 a.htm.

Shipp, E. R. (2000) 'When it's Not Good', *Washington Post*, 28 May: B06.

Tate, Casandra (1984) 'What Do Ombudsmen Do?', *Columbia Journalism Review*, 23(1): 37–41.

Thomas, Maggie B. (1995) 'News Ombudsman: An Inside View', survey presented at the 1995 International Convention of the Organisation of News Ombudsmen, Fort Worth, TX, 8 May: http://newsombudsmen.org/articles/ articles-about-ombudsmen/news-ombudsmen-an-inside-view.

United Nations (1948) *The Universal Declaration of Human Rights*: www.un.org/ Overview/rights.html.

9

Do Professionalism and Ethics Reduce or Increase Pressure for Legal Accountability?

Robert E. Drechsel

'The First Amendment must be protected from its enemies, but it must be saved from its best friends as well', the legal philosopher Ronald Dworkin warned some 35 years ago (Dworkin, 1980: 57). His concern: the tendency of the American press to argue for its freedom on the basis of policy, not principle – to assert that various extensions of its First Amendment rights are essential not in and of themselves but so the press can serve the public interest by providing the public with information it needs. The great danger, he argued, is that a policy rationale inevitably invites balancing the press's asserted interests against the public interest in whatever the competing interest happens to be; this ends up facilitating other interests that more easily trump the First Amendment. Even when the press wins with a 'policy' argument, Dworkin asserted, the result is First Amendment protection that may be broad but dangerously shallow and fragile.

If Dworkin were right, the implications are sobering. Ethical and professional standards based on journalists' strong commitment to serving the public interest might be as likely to lead to less legal freedom rather than more. Through professionalisation, journalists might unwittingly be creating expectations and standards of conduct for which they could ultimately be held legally, not just morally, responsible.

But was Dworkin right? Could socially responsible professionalism be legally dangerous? This chapter addresses that question by first examining the professionalisation of American journalism that has led it to embrace a moral obligation to serve the public interest, and the concomitant development of First Amendment theory that complements it. Next, the chapter turns to two specific legal contexts to see how conducive law is to transforming professional and ethical standards into legal standards. Finally, the chapter briefly examines recent issues involving social responsibility and press freedom in Canada and the United Kingdom – two countries similar to the United States but without the same First Amendment protections. Even if Dworkin's concerns turn out to be overstated in the United States, perhaps they are valid elsewhere.

Professionalisation

The trajectory of American journalism for at least the last century has been towards an ever-greater embrace of a public service role and a trusteeship obligation to serve the public interest. At both the individual and organisational levels, journalism has bought into an idea that many journalists not so long ago found unacceptable – the idea that they have a moral obligation to serve the public. The ethics code of the Society of Professional Journalists, for example, declares that its members 'believe that public enlightenment is the forerunner of justice and the foundation of democracy' and that the 'duty of the journalist is to further those ends by seeking truth and providing a fair and comprehensive account of events and issues' (Society of Professional Journalists, 1996). The American Society of Newspaper Editors (ASNE) *Statement of Principles* is even more specific:

> *The primary purpose of gathering and distributing news and opinion is to serve the general welfare by informing the people and enabling them to make judgments on the issues of the time. Newspapermen and women who abuse the power of their professional role for selfish motives or unworthy purposes are faithless to that public trust ... These principles are intended to preserve, protect and strengthen the bond of trust and respect between American journalists and the American people, a bond that is essential to sustain the grant of freedom entrusted to both by the nation's founders. (American Society of Newspaper Editors, 1975)*

Such organisations and their codes reflect not only the degree to which the news media have embraced responsibilities that go beyond simple libertarianism, but also the degree to which they have come to see themselves as professional. Whether one believes journalists are, or ever can be, bona fide professionals is far less important than the fact that the occupation's development clearly shows signs of professionalisation.

There appears to be considerable agreement that some or all of the following developments signal that an occupation is professionalising. People begin doing the work full-time and stake out a particular jurisdiction; training schools are established in an effort to reinforce standards, and ultimately training migrates to the university level; occupational organisations are established; ethics codes are established; and legal protection of the occupation's monopolisation of skills is sought. The occupation itself begins to require mastery of an underlying basic body of abstract knowledge and develops a strong commitment to the idea of service. Mechanisms to control and maintain standards are developed, as are methods to control access to the occupation. Two important goals of professionalisation are the achievement of a degree of autonomy for practitioners and the ability of the occupation in general to set its own standards of conduct, often with ultimate enforcement of those standards backed by government (see e.g. Barber, 1965; Elliott, 1972; Goode, 1969; Hughes, 1965; Moore, 1970; Wilensky, 1964). Formal licensing is not a requirement, although it may often be present (Wilensky, 1964: 145).

If journalism hasn't achieved professional status, it hasn't been for lack of effort. Douglas Birkhead concluded that journalism's professionalism movement began in the late nineteenth century (Birkhead, 1984). Already then, Birkhead asserts, professionalisation was driven primarily by a need to resolve a crisis of public confidence in the press (p. 11). Mary Cronin succinctly summarises the roots of journalistic professionalism this way:

> *Editorial associations, schools and courses of journalism, ethics codes and trade publications all began. This new professional drive was evident with the establishment of such news-oriented organisations as the National Newspaper Association in 1885, the American Newspaper Publishers Association in 1887, the increasing number of state press associations and the formation, by college students, of the Society of Professional Journalists. (Cronin, 1992: 24–5; see also Kobre, 1969: 532–6, 725–37)*

In 1912, the first journalism education organisation, the American Association of Teachers of Journalism, was formed. The American Association of Schools and Departments of Journalism was created in

1917, and in 1945 a formal accreditation system for journalism education was implemented (Dressel, 1960).

So fervent was support for professionalisation that some journalists themselves called for licensing (see e.g. Crawford, 1924: 141–3; Flint, 1925: 396–402). Even the renowned Kansas editor William Allen White asserted that:

> *until the people of this country get it well in their heads that journalism is a profession which must be licensed and controlled, as the medical and legal professions are licensed and controlled, there can be no freedom of the press which is not liable to great abuses. ... When the newspaper is socially controlled as medicine and law are, the freedom of our newspaper will be an asset. As it is, our freedom is a liability. (Cited in Flint, 1925: 401, and also in Gibbons, 1926: 61)*

Meanwhile, ethics codes were proliferating, and journalists and journalism educators were calling for journalism organisations to create ethical standards and enforce them internally.

Self-enforcement, however, was controversial. The American Newspaper Publishers Association almost immediately became embroiled in a dispute about whether to expel a member alleged to have received bribes in connection with an oil-leasing scandal. The issue set in motion an intra-organisational dispute over code enforcement that lasted for years before ending in failure for the proponents of enforcement (Hoxie, 1987). Again in 1972, ASNE members overwhelmingly rejected setting up a grievance committee to deal with ethics complaints (Pitts, 1974: 367–8).

More recently, the Society of Professional Journalists has struggled with the question of the enforcement of its ethics code. The society adopted a new code in 1973 that contained a censure clause and, 10 years later, considered adding a code enforcement mechanism that would have culminated with the formation of a National Ethics Council with the power to censure or even expel members for code violations. The proposal, however, was voted down (Bukro, 1985–6).

On the journalism education front, Willard Bleyer, founder of what became the School of Journalism at the University of Wisconsin-Madison, called for enforceable ethics codes (Bronstein and Vaughn, 1998: 22). He preferred self-regulation but saw press freedom as primarily the right of readers, with newspapers' freedom being the freedom to furnish readers with complete, accurate, fair, and unbiased news of current affairs (Hoxie, 1987: 33). Bleyer hoped that 'if regulation (of the press) does come, it should be the result, as it has been in the professions of law and medicine, of the creation of an enlightened public opinion in support of professional standards adopted by journalists themselves (Bleyer, 1930).

Bleyer was not alone. Casper Yost, a driving force in the founding of the ASNE, also saw press freedom from the public's standpoint. The press is the only private institution, he said, that is 'shielded by the mandate of that fundamental law [the First Amendment], and this was due not to any desire to confer a special privilege upon the press for its own benefit, but for the sole purpose of protecting the rights and liberties of the people' (Yost, 1924: 115–16). Journalism professor Nelson Crawford at Kansas State University, in a 1924 book on journalism ethics, even foresaw a day when strong ethical standards could become a basis for some type of licensing. However, 'a professional consciousness and the ethical and social implications flowing from this are necessary before any legal enactment can improve the status of journalism as a profession' (Crawford, 1924: 144).

The argument that the news media invite government regulation if they don't behave responsibly is an old one – and one that has never abated. Nearly a century ago, Walter Lippmann warned:

> There is everywhere an increasingly angry disillusionment about the press, a growing sense of being baffled and misled; and wise publishers will not pooh-pooh these omens . . . If publishers and authors themselves do not face the facts and attempt to deal with them, some day Congress, in a fit of temper, egged on by an outraged public opinion, will operate on the press with an ax. For somehow the community must find a way of making the men who publish news accept responsibility for an honest effort not to misrepresent the facts. (Lippmann, 1920: 75–6)

More than 60 years later, a primary reason for the Society of Professional Journalists' rejection of any organisational enforcement of its ethics code was fear that 'enforcement rules could create legal liabilities and still not guarantee fairness and accuracy' (Bukro, 1985–6: 11–12).

Others have worried that, even if voluntary professional responsibility doesn't lead to less *legal* freedom, it will lead to less press freedom in a more general sense. One especially vocal critic has been John Merrill, who has worried that everything from the concept of a 'people's right to know' to ethics codes, press councils, and ombudsmen represents movement towards a social responsibility/communitarian view of the media – a view he sees as 'neoauthoritarianism' (Merrill et al., 2001: xxi, 170–88).

The idea that the press has a major moral obligation to society may have reached its intellectual zenith in 1947 with the release of the report of the Commission on Freedom of the Press – still the most comprehensive articulation of the social responsibility theory of press freedom. The report proclaimed:

> *Clearly a qualitatively new era of public responsibility for the press has arrived; and it becomes an imperative question whether press performance can any longer be left to the unregulated initiative of the issuers ... The need of the consumer to have adequate and uncontaminated mental food is such that he is under a duty to get it; and, because of this duty, his interest acquires the stature of a right. It becomes legitimate to speak of the moral right of men to the news they can use.*
>
> *Since the consumer is no longer free not to consume, and can get what he requires only through existing press organs, protection of the freedom of the issuer is no longer sufficient to protect automatically either the consumer or the community. The general policy of laissez-faire in this field must be reconsidered. (p. 125)*

The Commission supported continued strong First Amendment protection for the press – the 'issuer', to use the Commission's terminology – but linked such legal protection to an underlying moral right of the public to vital information and the moral duty of the media to provide it. And it predicted that failure to fulfil that duty would lead to government intervention: 'The legal right will stand if the moral right is realized or tolerably approximated. There is a point beyond which failure to realize the moral right will entail encroachment by the state upon the existing legal right' (p. 131).

Several Commission members produced additional volumes expanding on their own views. Perhaps most influential has been philosopher William Ernest Hocking's elaboration of the social responsibility concept (Hocking, 1947). Although insisting he preferred only a 'lightest possible touch' by government (p. 51), he may have gone further than most Commission members in his willingness to permit legal enforcement of the press's moral duties. Steven Bates, after researching the Commission's papers, concluded that Hocking did want to transform moral into legal duties and believed that it was time to correct what he called the 'pernicious impression' that constitutional liberties are unconditional and unalienable. Hocking went so far as to suggest that a codicil should be added to the Bill of Rights to explain that certain liberties should extend only to citizens who exercised them responsibly (Bates, 1995: 13).

Another scholar who delved into the Commission's papers discovered that First Amendment legal scholar Zechariah Chafee, another member of the Commission, found Hocking's views problematic: 'I certainly recognize the moral duty to tell the truth, for example, to tell the truth about the differences with Spain over Cuba in 1898,' Chafee said, 'but do you want to make that a legal duty?' (McIntyre, 1987: 145).

Despite journalism's growing embrace of professionalism, ethics, and service to the public, the Commission's work was met with considerable hostility, perhaps in part because no journalists or journalism educators had been chosen to serve as members. *Chicago Tribune* writer Frank Hughes, in a book devoted to scathing criticism of the Commission, drew a comparison to communism and fascism: 'The new champions of freedom . . . ,' he complained, 'say, for instance, that "freedom" means "accountability," that "right" means "duty," and that people who declare themselves for true, unfettered liberty are "reactionaries"' (Hughes, 1950: 6). Robert Desmond, then president of the American Association of Schools and Departments of Journalism, disparaged the report and predicted that it would be of no enduring value (Desmond, 1947: 192).

Desmond, however, turned out to be utterly wrong; the report has had enduring value. In fact, the Commission's view of journalistic responsibility and public trusteeship has become widely and proudly professed – and not only in ethics codes but in everyday journalistic practice. One of the most influential journalistic professional endeavours in recent years has been the Project for Excellence in Journalism and, in 1997, the formation of the Committee of Concerned Journalists under its umbrella.

Almost immediately, the Committee, troubled by the impact of technological and economic change as well as by strains in journalism's relationship with the public, published a 'Statement of Concern'. It asserted the existence of several 'core principles of journalism', namely:

> those that make journalism a public service central to self-government. They define our profession not as the act of communicating but as a set of responsibilities. Journalism can entertain, amuse and lift our spirits, but news organisations also must cover the matters vital to the well being

131

of our increasingly diverse communities and foster the debate upon which democracy depends. The First Amendment implies obligation as well as freedom. (Committee of Concerned Journalists, 1998: 2)

All of this is not to say that journalists have come to welcome possible legal enforcement of what they acknowledge to be their moral duties. It does, however, suggest that journalists have constructed a foundation of moral/ethical duty to serve the public interest on which corresponding legal duties and limitations could logically be constructed.

Further, just as professionalisation was developing in American journalism, so too was First Amendment jurisprudence and First Amendment theory. One of the first and still most influential First Amendment scholars was the same Zechariah Chafee who was later to serve on the Commission on Freedom of the Press. Chafee's first major work, *Freedom of Speech*, appeared in 1920 and was directed primarily at the issue of freedom of speech in wartime. But it also established Chafee's reputation as a pragmatic balancer of interests, albeit with strong preference for the social interests served by protecting expression and dissent (see also Chafee, 1941).

Later, in a two-volume work for the Commission, *Government and Mass Communications* (1947a, 1947b), Chafee agreed with the Commission's view of the press's obligations:

The press is to be free so that it can give the community the service needed from the press ... [C]onstitutions and courts will not permanently protect the press if it neglects its primary task of furnishing news and opinions in the form which society needs. (Chafee, 1947b: 794–7)

The year after the Commission's report appeared, philosophy professor Alexander Meiklejohn produced what may still be the single most influential theoretical work on the First Amendment – *Free Speech and its Relation to Self-Government* (Meiklejohn, 1948). He asserted that the 'freedom of speech' protected by the First Amendment should be confined to speech pertaining to self-government. Such speech, he insisted, should be absolutely protected by the First Amendment. In other words, the sole rationale for giving speech First Amendment protection was instrumentalist: its role in facilitating self-government.

Meiklejohn's absolutism has gained little traction, but the idea that facilitating self-government lies at the core of the First Amendment for the press has had immense impact. Numerous other theorists have continued to emphasise the need to protect speech (and the press) because of its value in facilitating and sustaining the functioning of a successful democracy (see e.g. Blasi, 1977; Bork, 1971; Emerson, 1970; Graber, 1991; Stewart, 1975; Sunstein, 1993).

Legal theory regarding freedom of speech and the press thus developed in parallel with journalistic professionalisation and its embrace of ethics, high standards, and social responsibility. And legal theory fit comfortably with journalism's professed fealty to serving the public interest and playing a critical role in democratic self-government.

Media professional standards and media law

The relationship between moral and legal responsibility is inherently subject to confusion. As Justice Oliver Wendell Holmes Jr. long ago cautioned: 'The law is full of phraseology drawn from morals, and by the mere force of language continually invites us to pass from one domain to the other' (Holmes, 1897: 459–60). Nevertheless, as United States Chief Justice Earl Warren once noted, 'Law floats on a sea of ethics' (Lind and Ullberg, 1987: 65).

As any number of occupations have professionalised, one of the 'costs' of that process has been legal liability for not performing up to professional standards – that is, malpractice. Such seems clearly to have been the case in medicine (De Ville, 1990; Mohr, 1993; Spiegel and Kavaler, 1997), law (Mallen and Smith, 1989), and accountancy (Carey, 1969), to name but three. Given the trajectory of these three occupations, it would seem logical to expect journalism to feel pressure for the migration of voluntarily developed ethics and standards to legally enforceable ones.

Two relevant legal contexts are illustrative regarding any relationship between media freedom and media accountability: negligence and journalist–source confidentiality.

Negligence

The legal concept of negligence provides an ideal tool for legalising media ethics. A person is negligent if he or she fails to act as a hypothetical reasonable person would have acted under the same circumstances and thus creates an unreasonable risk of harm. If the hypothetical reasonable person – as imagined by a jury – would have done what the defendant did, the defendant is not negligent, no matter how much harm resulted. Conversely, a defendant's conduct could be found negligent even if he or she genuinely believed the conduct would be harmless.

A risk of harm is unreasonable if the magnitude of the risk is found to outweigh the utility of the defendant's conduct (American Law Institute, 1965: §291). The magnitude of the risk depends on such factors as the social value of the endangered interests, how likely the harm is, and the extent of the harm likely to be caused (and/or number of people likely to be affected) (American Law Institute, 1965, §293). On the other side of the balance, utility may depend on the social value of the defendant's actions, the likelihood that the social value will in fact be advanced, and the inefficaciousness or unavailability of less risky courses of action (American Law Institute, 1965, §292).

Underlying the framework of negligence is the equally intangible concept of legal duty. If a defendant had no legal duty to avoid the harm in question, there is no legal remedy no matter how much harm might have occurred. William Prosser, the renowned torts scholar, himself could do no better than say, 'No better general statement can be made, than that the courts will find a duty where, in general, reasonable men would recognise it and agree that it exists' (Prosser and Keeton, 1984: 359).

It is only a short step in logic, then, to see how duties initially recognised purely as moral obligations can evolve into legal duties. The jurist Benjamin Cardozo noted this long ago:

> Duties that had been conceived of as moral only, without other human sanction than the opinion of society, are found to be such that they may effectively and wisely be subjected to another form of sanction, the power of society. The moral norm and the jural have been brought together, and are one. (1928: 43)

Therefore, once a legal duty of some type is recognised, redress for a variety of harms caused by negligence – emotional distress, financial loss, personal injury, or death, among others – becomes possible. And all of these harms can quite plausibly be caused by speech and have been the basis of suits against the media, albeit most of them unsuccessful (see e.g. Drechsel, 1985, 1987; O'Neil, 2001).

Negligence is also a standard of legal fault that can be used as a required element of other torts, the most common example of which is libel. As a result of developments in American libel law since 1964, people suing journalists and journalistic media must establish some degree of legal fault in order to win. For public officials and public figures, the standard is 'actual malice' – publication of defamatory material with either knowledge of its falsity or with reckless disregard for its truth. But for private figures in most states, the standard is negligence (*Gertz v. Robert Welch, Inc.*, 1974; Pember and Calvert, 2013: 199–200).

In determining fault, courts can easily be drawn into considering the defendant's actions relative to recognised occupational standards. And as evidence of those standards, plaintiffs may look to sources, which range from ethics codes and professional standards to textbooks and expert testimony by other journalists and/or journalism teachers (see e.g. *Joseph v. The Scranton Times*, 2008).

Some legal scholars have noted that privacy law is another area in which journalism's professional standards and ethical aspirations are becoming legalised (Gajda, 2009). Others have urged a substantial expansion of the use of media professional standards and ethics in litigation beyond the negligence context (see e.g. Hartman, 1987; Karcher, 2009; Simon, 1984).

Negligence is thus a legal concept seemingly ready-made for importing journalism's ethical principles and professional standards into law. Not surprisingly, any number of scholars have noted the impact the Supreme Court itself might have in affecting journalistic standards, even in cases that seem to be expanding press freedom (see e.g. Bollinger, 1991; Gilles, 2006; Marshall and Gilles, 1994; Murchison et al., 1994; Watson, 2008).

Confidentiality

A second context in which professional standards, ethics, and law have converged is that of the journalist's privilege to withhold confidential sources and unpublished information from legal discovery. In this context, journalists have long asserted a need for legal protection on the instrumental grounds that being able to guarantee confidentiality to sensitive sources is essential for the free flow of important information to the public.

At the Supreme Court, journalists have had little luck, at least when arguing for a privilege based on the First Amendment (*Branzburg v. Hayes*, 1972). Nevertheless, they have been remarkably successful in getting states to provide a privilege statutorily and in getting lower courts to recognise a privilege under common law or even the First Amendment (Pember and Calvert, 2013: 394–404, 415–16). But, in the process, they have made a major concession: permitting government to specify who is and is not a journalist for purposes of the privilege. This isn't licensing, but it does mean that, on a case-by-case basis, journalists will have to be validated as such by the courts. Thus, in this area of law, more than any other, journalists have sought special protection for their occupation much as other occupations have. And they implicitly seek legal validation for ethical and professional standards of source protection.

Then there is the other side of the coin. Suppose a journalist breaks a promise of confidentiality to a source. If the outed source sues for some type of breach of contract, can a journalist deploy the First Amendment as a defence? The Supreme Court has said 'no'. The occasion was a case in which editors overrode reporters' promises of confidentiality to a political operative. The outed source lost his job, and then sued for breach of contract and fraudulent misrepresentation (*Cohen v. Cowles Media*, 1991).

Journalists testified for both sides. Litigants and judges directly cited the literature on journalistic ethics. The Supreme Court sided with the source, concluding that the First Amendment was irrelevant since 'the parties themselves . . . determine the scope of their legal obligations and any restrictions which may be placed on the publication of truthful information are self-imposed' (p. 671).

The Court thus sanctioned legal enforcement of journalism ethics and practices regarding confidentiality. Although the terms of reporter–source agreements are not dictated by government, the courts and contract law are put at sources' disposal to resolve disagreements involving promise-breaking. Many journalists as well were not shy about supporting just such an outcome.

Conclusion

As far as the United States is concerned, Ronald Dworkin may have been theoretically correct in the sense that journalistic ethics and professional standards have become commonly invoked by plaintiffs in efforts to prove legal negligence or to establish new legal duties. By basing their claims to legal protection on their utility in serving the public interest, journalists may indeed have inherently invited plaintiffs to sue when journalists have fallen short and when other social interests can be elevated. But the use of professional ethics and standards can cut both ways; in many instances, journalists can as easily invoke ethics and standards to justify their conduct as plaintiffs can to attack it. And for the most part, efforts to expand negligence liability have been successful only occasionally, in no small part due to the First Amendment. Meanwhile, journalists have been able to use 'policy-based' rationales to expand their right to protect sources, although there are indications that, in the absence of statutory protection, courts may be becoming more sceptical (Pember and Calvert, 2013: 396–7).

But what if there were no First Amendment? Situations in Canada and the United Kingdom are instructive.

The Canadian Charter of Rights and Freedoms includes protection for 'freedom of the press and other media of communication'. But it also declares that this freedom can be subject to 'such reasonable limits prescribed by law as can be demonstrably justified in a free and democratic society' (Canadian Charter, 1982). In the United Kingdom, press freedom is protected not by a written constitution, but most specifically today by the Human Rights Act of 1998, which adopted the language of Article 10 of the European Convention of Human Rights: 'Everyone has the right to freedom of expression'. However, the Act and the Convention explicitly balance freedom with responsibility, declaring that:

> The exercise of these freedoms, since it carries with it duties and responsibilities, may be subject to such formalities, conditions, restrictions or penalties as are prescribed by law and are necessary in a democratic society, in the interests of national security, territorial integrity or public safety, for the prevention of disorder or crime, for the protection of health or morals, for the protection of the reputation or rights of others, for preventing the disclosure of information received in confidence, or for maintaining the authority and impartiality of the judiciary. (Human Rights Act, 1998)

Recent developments in libel law in both Canada and the UK illustrate how responsibility can be legally imposed by holding the press to its own professional standards with judges as the arbiters. In *Grant v. Torstar Corp.* (2009), the Canadian Supreme Court created a new libel defence of 'responsible communication on matters of public interest'. In the process, the court articulated the types of factors relevant to assessing journalistic responsibility, the bulk of which reflect established journalistic practice. Among these factors are the seriousness of the allegation, the public importance of the matter, the urgency of publication, the status/reliability of the source, the need to get both sides of the story, and so on. The Canadian case borrowed heavily from the approach taken in the UK by the House of Lords in *Reynolds v. Times Newspapers Ltd.* (1999) and *Jameel v. Wall Street Journal Europe* (2006). In both cases, the law lords held for media defendants essentially on the grounds that they had acted with professional responsibility, a determination based at least partially by applying the newspapers' voluntary codes of practice. As Lord Hoffmann wrote in *Jameel*:

> [J]ust as the standard of reasonable care in particular areas, such as driving a vehicle, is made more concrete by extra-statutory codes of behaviour like the Highway Code, so the standard of responsible journalism is made more specific by the code of practice which has been adopted by the newspapers and ratified by the Press Complaints Commission. This too, while not binding upon the courts, can provide valuable guidance.

Recently, in *Flood v. Times Newspapers Ltd.* (2012), the Supreme Court of the United Kingdom reiterated the importance of the professional standards approach in determining liability. Again, the result was victory for a newspaper defendant.

Meanwhile, as this chapter was being written, the British media and government were still mulling over the recommendations of the Leveson Inquiry (Leveson, 2012) into the culture, practice, and ethics of the press. Its central recommendation is the creation of a new independent self-regulatory system of press regulation, backed by statute, that would establish a code of responsibility, hear and decide complaints alleging breaches of the code, impose financial sanctions, and order corrections and apologies. The marriage of ethics and law seems inescapable in this context.

Based as they are on concepts of what best serves the public interest and constitutes responsible journalism, the Leveson Inquiry and the Canadian and British approaches to libel would seem to be based squarely on the type of policy rationale that worried Dworkin. The libel cases appear to have expanded media freedom while the Leveson recommendations would limit it. Assessing the risk of using policy arguments for press freedom thus requires keeping in mind that whether freedom has been expanded or contracted depends on one's starting point. The Canadian and British adoption of the 'responsible journalism' defence represents greater protection for press freedom, given the previously plaintiff-friendly state of libel law. On the other hand, if the Leveson Inquiry recommendations are followed, self-regulation by the media will be transformed into a system with far more authority over the press and possible sanctions for failing to follow 'voluntary' standards of conduct. In the USA, a Leveson Inquiry could never have begun without itself being challenged on First Amendment grounds, and the concept of a press regulator would be unthinkable.

Ultimately, it is difficult to comprehend how the press – at least the institutional press – could avoid using or encountering policy-based rationales for its freedom even if it wanted to. The words of Stanley Fish come to mind: '"Free speech" is just the name we give to verbal behaviour that serves the substantive agendas we wish to advance … Speech, in short, is never a value in and of itself but is always produced within the precincts of some assumed conception of the good to which it must yield in the event of conflict' (Fish, 1994: 102, 104).

If Fish is correct – and I believe he is – the question of whether journalism's embrace of ethics and high professional standards puts its legal freedom at risk has no final answer. It will, however, be the subject of endless debate and part of the much larger question of the meaning of liberty itself.

Note

All web addresses in this chapter were last accessed in March 2013.

References

American Law Institute (1965) *Restatement (Second) of Torts* (Washington, DC: American Law Institute).

American Society of Newspaper Editors (1975) *Statement of Principles*: http://asne.org/Article_View/ArticleId/325/ASNEs-Statement-of-Principles.aspx.

Barber, Bernard (1965) 'Some Problems in the Sociology of Professions', in K. S. Lynn (ed.), *The Professions in America* (Boston: Houghton Mifflin), 15–34.

Bates, Stephen (1995) *Realigning Journalism with Democracy: The Hutchins Commission, Its Times and Ours* (Washington, DC: Annenberg Washington Program in Communications Policy Studies of Northwestern University).

Birkhead, Douglas (1984) 'The Power in the Image: Professionalism and the "Communications Revolution"', *American Journalism*, 1(Winter): 1–14.

Blasi, Vincent (1977) 'The Checking Value in First Amendment Theory', *American Bar Foundation Research Journal*, 2(3): 521–649.

Bleyer, Willard G. (1930) 'A Great Need of the Profession', in L. W. Murphy (ed.), *An Introduction to Journalism: Authoritative Views on the Profession* (New York: Thomas Nelson & Sons), 201–3.

Bollinger, Lee G. (1991) *Images of a Free Press* (Chicago: University of Chicago Press).

Bork, Robert (1971) 'Neutral Principles and Some First Amendment Problems', *Indiana Law Journal*, 47(1): 1–35.

Branzburg v. Hayes (1972) 408 U.S. 665.

Bronstein, Carolyn, and Vaughn, Stephen (1998) 'Willard G. Bleyer and the Relevance of Journalism Education', *Journalism and Mass Communication Monographs*, 166: 1–37.

Bukro, Casey (1985–6) 'The SPJ Code's Double-Edged Sword: Accountability, Credibility', *Journal of Mass Media Ethics*, 1(1): 10–13.

Canadian Charter (1982) *Canadian Charter of Rights and Freedoms*: http://laws-lois.justice.gc.ca/eng/Const/page-15.html.

Cardozo, Benjamin N. (1928) *The Paradoxes of Legal Science* (New York: Columbia University Press).

Carey, John L. (1969) *The Rise of the Accounting Profession: From Technician to Professional, 1896–1936* (New York: American Institute of Certified Public Accountants), vol. 1.

Chafee Jr., Zechariah (1920) *Freedom of Speech* (New York: Harcourt, Brace & Howe).

Chafee Jr., Zechariah (1941) *Free Speech in the United States* (Cambridge, MA: Harvard University Press).

Chafee Jr., Zechariah (1947a) *Government and Mass Communications* (Chicago: University of Chicago Press), vol. 1.

Chafee Jr., Zechariah (1947b) *Government and Mass Communications* (Chicago: University of Chicago Press), vol. 2.

Cohen v. Cowles Media (1991) 501 U.S. 663.

Commission on Freedom of the Press (1947) *A Free and Responsible Press* (Chicago: University of Chicago Press).

Committee of Concerned Journalists (1998) 'Statement of Concern: Committee of Concerned Journalists', *IRE Journal*, 21(1): 2.

Crawford, Nelson Antrim (1924) *The Ethics of Journalism* (New York: Alfred A. Knopf).

Cronin, Mary Margaret (1992) 'Profits, Legitimacy and Public Service: The Development of Ethics and Standards in New York City's Newspapers, 1870–1920', PhD dissertation, College of Communication Arts and Sciences, Michigan State University, East Lansing, MI.

De Ville, Kenneth Allen (1990) *Medical Malpractice in Nineteenth-Century America: Origins and Legacy* (New York: New York University Press).

Desmond, Robert W. (1947) 'Of a Free and Responsible Press', *Journalism Quarterly*, 24: 188–92.

Drechsel, Robert E. (1985) 'Mass Media and Negligent Infliction of Emotional Distress', *Journalism Quarterly*, 62(3): 523–7, 539.

Drechsel, Robert E. (1987) 'Media Tort Liability for Physical Harm', *Journalism Quarterly*, 64(1): 99–105, 177.

Dressel, Paul L. (1960) *Liberal Education and Journalism* (New York: Teachers College, Columbia University).

Dworkin, Ronald (1980) 'Is the Press Losing the First Amendment?', *New York Review of Books*, 4 Dec.: 49–57.

Elliott, Philip (1972) *The Sociology of the Professions* (London: Macmillan).

Emerson, Thomas I. (1970) *The System of Freedom of Expression* (New York: Vintage).

FCC v. Fox Television (2009) 129 S.Ct. 1800.

Fish, Stanley (1994) *There's No Such Thing as Free Speech: And It's a Good Thing, Too* (New York: Oxford University Press).

Flint, Leon Nelson (1925) *The Conscience of the Newspaper* (New York: D. Appleton & Co.).

Flood v. Times Newspapers Ltd. (2012) [2012] UKSC 11.

Gajda, A. (2009) 'Judging Journalism: The Turn toward Privacy and Judicial Regulation of the Press', *California Law Review*, 97: 1039–1105.

Gertz v. Robert Welch, Inc. (1974) 418 U.S. 323.

Gibbons, William Futhey (1926) *Newspaper Ethics: A Discussion of Good Practice for Journalists* (Ann Arbor, MI: Edwards Brothers).

Gilles, Susan M. (2006) 'The Image of "Good Journalism" in Privilege, Tort Law, and Constitutional Law', *Ohio Northern University Law Review*, 32: 485–502.

Goode, William J. (1969) 'The Theoretical Limits of Professionalization', in Amitai Etzioni (ed.), *The Semi-Professions and their Organization* (New York: Free Press), 266–313.

Graber, Mark A. (1991) *Transforming Free Speech* (Berkeley, CA: University of California Press).

Grant v. Torstar Corp. (2009) 2009 SCC 61.

Hartman, Lynn W. (1987) 'Standards Governing the News: Their Use, their Character, and their Legal Implications', *Iowa Law Review*, 72: 637–700.

Hocking, William Ernest (1947) *Freedom of the Press: A Framework of Principle* (Chicago: University of Chicago Press).

Holmes, Oliver Wendell (1897) 'The Path of the Law', *Harvard Law Review*, 10(8): 457–78.

Hoxie, Connie M. (1987) 'Ideas of Professional Ethics: Yost, Abbot and the ASNE Canons of Journalism Debate', MA thesis, School of Journalism and Mass Communication, University of Wisconsin-Madison.

Hughes, Everett C. (1965) 'Professions', in K. S. Lynn (ed.), *The Professions in America* (Boston: Houghton Mifflin), 1–14.

Hughes, Frank L. (1950) *Prejudice and the Press* (New York: Devin-Adair Co.).

Human Rights Act of the United Kingdom (1998) Annex E, Article 10(1) and (2): www.legislation.gov.uk/ukpga/1998/42/contents.

Jameel v. Wall Street Journal Europe (2006) 4 All E.R. 1279.

Joseph v. The Scranton Times (2008) 959 A.2d 322 (Super. Ct. Pa.).

Karcher, Richard T. (2009) 'Tort Law and Journalism Ethics', *Loyola University Chicago Law Journal*, 40: 781–845.

Kobre, Sidney (1969) *Development of American Journalism* (Dubuque, IA: Wm C. Brown Co.).

Leveson, Lord Justice Brian (2012) *Leveson Inquiry: Culture, Practice and Ethics of the Press* (London: The Stationery Office).

Lind, Robert C. Jr., and Ullberg, Alan D. (1987) 'Are Professional Codes of Ethics Acquiring the Force of Law?', *ALI-ABA Course Materials Journal*, 11(6): 63–90.

Lippmann, Walter (1920) *Liberty and the News* (New York: Harcourt, Brace & Howe).

Mallen, Ronald E., and Smith, Jeffrey M. (1989) *Legal Malpractice* (3rd edn, St Paul, MN: West Publishing Co.), vol. 1.

Marshall, William P., and Gilles, Susan (1994) 'The Supreme Court, the First Amendment, and Bad Journalism', *Supreme Court Review*, 169–208.

McIntyre, Jerilyn S. (1987) 'Repositioning a Landmark: The Hutchins Commission and Freedom of the Press', *Critical Studies in Mass Communication*, 4: 136–60.

Meiklejohn, Alexander (1948) *Free Speech and its Relation to Self-Government* (New York: Harper & Brothers).

Merrill, John C., Gade, Peter J., and Blevens, Frederick R. (2001) *Twilight of Press Freedom: The Rise of People's Journalism* (Mahwah, NJ: Lawrence Erlbaum Associates).

Mohr, James C. (1993) *Doctors and the Law: Medical Jurisprudence in Nineteenth-Century America* (New York: Oxford University Press).

Moore, Wilbert E. (1970) *The Professions: Roles and Rules* (New York: Russell Sage Foundation).

Murchison, Brian C., Soloski, John, Bezanson, Randall P., Cranberg, Gilbert, and Wissler, Roselle L. (1994) 'Sullivan's Paradox: The Emergence of Judicial Standards of Journalism', *North Carolina Law Review*, 73(1): 7–113.

O'Neil, Robert M. (2001) *The First Amendment and Civil Liability* (Bloomington, IN: Indiana University Press).

Pember, Don R., and Calvert, Clay (2013) *Mass Media Law* (18th edn, New York: McGraw-Hill).

Pitts, Alice Fox (ed.) (1974) *Read All about it! 50 Years of ASNE* (Easton, PA: American Society of Newspaper Editors).

Prosser, William L., and Keeton, W. Page (1984) *Prosser and Keeton on the Law of Torts* (5th edn, St Paul, MN: West Publishing Co.).

Reynolds v. Times Newspapers Ltd. (1999) 4 All E.R. 609.

Simon, T. F. (1984) 'Libel as Malpractice: News Media Ethics and the Standard of Care', *Fordham Law Review*, 53(3): 449–90.

Society of Professional Journalists (1996) *Code of Ethics*: www.spj.org/ethicscode.asp.

Spiegel, Allen D., and Kavaler, Florence (1997) 'America's First Medical Malpractice Crisis: 1835–1865', *Journal of Community Health*, 22(4): 283–308.

Stewart, Potter (1975) 'Or of the Press', *Hastings Law Journal*, 26: 631–7.

Sunstein, Cass R. (1993) *Democracy and the Problem of Free Speech* (New York: Free Press).

Watson, John C. (2008) *Journalism Ethics by Court Decree: The Supreme Court on the Proper Practice of Journalism* (New York: LFB Scholarly Publishing).

Wilensky, Harold (1964) 'The Professionalization of Everyone?', *American Journal of Sociology*, 70(2): 137–58.

Yost, Casper S. (1924) *The Principles of Journalism* (New York: D. Appleton & Co.).

Part III

Intersections: Theory and Practice

10

Ethics and Journalistic Standards: An Examination of the Relationship between Journalism Codes of Ethics and Deontological Moral Theory

Karen L. Slattery

For University of Wisconsin-Madison football fans, it was an exciting victory. The team won 13–10 over the University of Michigan team on a late October afternoon in 1993. As it had been doing for a decade, the university's marching band planned to take the field immediately following the game for the 'Fifth Quarter'. According to tradition, the band would play the victor's fight song followed by UW favourites. The entertainment, in part, served to slow down the rush to the stadium exits as many stayed to enjoy the music and dance in the stadium aisles. But on 31 October, with only seconds left in the game, fans in the student section began shouting 'Let's storm the field'. In the minutes after the game's end, those in the upper rows began bearing down on those below in an effort to get out of the stands. Fans in other sections of the stadium, expecting the traditional post-game celebration, watched in horror as the human wave gathered force, picking up some of the fans and carrying them along while crushing others beneath. In its wake, 69 lay injured, seven critically (Held, 1993). As this tragedy unfolded, a local TV sports photojournalist, on hand to cover the game, had to make split-second decisions about how he should respond.[1]

Events of this sort create a moral dilemma for the journalist because they raise a question about whether the photographer should forgo capturing the images that tell the story to offer assistance to those who need it. Dilemmas exist, according to Kitchener, because 'there are good, but contradictory ethical reasons to take conflicting and incompatible courses of action' (Kitchener, 1984: 43).

The goal of this chapter is to examine the relationship between ethical codes and moral theory in an effort to shed additional light on how journalists might resolve the difficult moral dilemmas they face while gathering and reporting the news. The central argument is that professionals can appeal to deontological moral theory for guidance when codes are unclear or do not extend to the problem at hand. To meet this goal, this chapter first examines the purpose of codes of ethics in relationship to professional behaviour, identifying the strengths and weaknesses of codes. Second, it examines how communication scholars have addressed the problem involving the journalist as Good Samaritan, noting that these scholars have failed to offer an analysis that systematically draws on moral theory. Third, to remedy that shortcoming, the values that underpin the provisions of three professional codes of ethics for US journalists are identified and the relationship between the principles articulated in the provisions and broader deontological norms is explained. The chapter concludes by suggesting that journalists apply deontological moral principles when codes of ethics fail to cover the moral issue in question. The deontological principle of beneficence serves as a framework to critique the actions of the photojournalist in the case described above.

Professions and ethical codes

The concept of a *profession* rests on a foundation of moral responsibility. The definition of the term has often assumed the sociological perspective that links an occupation with a body of knowledge, extensive training, licensing, autonomy, a professional organisation, moral codes, and an element of service to others (Bayles, 1989). Barker (1992), however, drew on codes of ethics as a means to distinguish occupations from professions. He argued that professions in medieval times required practitioners to take an oath to practise in service to others, following an extensive study of related knowledge and skills. A profession's code affords an ethical framework that assures society that the practitioner's skill and knowledge will not be used against the common good (Gardner et al., 2001). He also noted that occupations, unlike professions, are based on contracts that outline expected behaviours, thus putting fewer brakes on the self-interested behaviours of the occupation's members.

Professions, Barker observed, are also based on an implied under-standing between practitioners and society that evolves over time. In exchange for the commitment to this ideal of service, society grants privileges to professions that include autonomy, an ability to set and self-police its standards, and in some instances, 'a degree of monopoly control over entry into the profession' (Barker, 1992: 93). Journalism fits Barker's description of a profession only to some degree; journalism practitioners, for example, are not required to study extensively before entering the field. However, in exchange for serving the interests of the American public, that public – through the United States Constitution – guarantees a free press and, over time, has granted professional journalists such privileges as shield laws and a more robust libel defence than is afforded to other citizens.

In journalism and other professions, codes of ethics are formal, written documents that put forth moral standards to guide members of the profession or organisation (Schwartz, 2002) and point to the morally problematic or expected conflicts professionals will face (Brinkmann, 2002). Codes act as the collective conscience of a profession and 'testimony to the group's recognition of its moral dimension' (Frankel, 1989: 111). Codes reflect a profession's most visible 'enunciation of its professional norms' (Frankel, 1989: 111), and they have the potential to lead to ethical decision-making (L'Etang, 1992). Codes also reflect the most recent thinking of professionals empowered by their profession to articulate problems encountered by practitioners (Bersoff and Koeppl, 1993), and some provisions may be controversial (Jamal and Bowie, 1995). Codes help to structure moral situations, serve as a source of socialisation for newcomers to the profession, and work to deter unethical behaviours (Brinkmann and Ims, 2003). Often designed to satisfy public concern about moral behaviour (Jamal and Bowie, 1995), a code's primary emphasis should be protecting the public it serves (Bersoff and Koeppl, 1993). Codes afford an efficient means of moving a profession towards self-regulation rather than governmental constraint. In addition, codes are divided into provisions that encourage professionals to both avoid moral problems and practise professional courtesy (Starr, 1983).

Despite these strengths, codes of ethics have weaknesses. Contradictions are built into codes (Kitchener, 1984), and codes are 'vague and amorphous, and they are difficult to enforce' (Brinkmann and Ims, 2003: 267). Codes do not cover all contingencies; they often fail to provide explicit direction to the solution of moral problems (Bersoff and Koeppl, 1993). Scholars have argued that the people who need the code the most fail to follow it, while those already engaged in morally correct actions often do not need a code (Brinkmann and Ims, 2003). Some have pointed out that companies or organisations sometimes use codes of ethics as 'a public relations gimmick designed to "show" the public how serious it is about ethics' (Starr, 1983: 99), while others have argued that codes of ethics are designed to protect an organisation economically and, thus, are self-serving (Jamal and Bowie, 1995), narrow in scope (Schwartz, 2002), and potentially coercive (Bersoff and Koeppl, 1993).

Journalism codes of ethics are of little help in solving the dilemma introduced earlier – the one in which the photographer must decide whether to act as a 'Good Samaritan' and provide aid or to act as a journalist and continue taking photographs. Communication scholars who have examined similar dilemmas have pointed out that, while the National Press Photographers Association's (NPPA) ethical code requires members to 'give special consideration to vulnerable subjects and compassion to victims of crime or tragedy' (National Press Photographers Asssociation, 2004), the provision was written in the larger context of journalism objectivity and impartiality (Kim and Kelly, 2010). Thus, the code is not as useful as it might be in this particular instance.

Recognising this shortcoming, communication scholars who have studied the Good Samaritan question as it relates to working journalists have taken a range of approaches to resolving the issue. Marion and Izard (1986) offered a provision to the profession's ethical code after speaking to news professionals about balancing a professional duty to serve as impartial observers against the need to be a good citizen who offers assistance to those in distress; they recommended that journalists who find themselves witnessing life and death circumstances should offer aid to those in need only if there are no rescue workers on the scene or until rescue workers arrive. Kim and Kelly (2010) conducted an experiment to determine how readers reacted to photojournalists' decisions to capture images of subjects experiencing trauma. They concluded that readers recognised that situations were complicated, and the photojournalists' actions depended on circumstances involved. Harless (1990) drew on ideologies of the left and right to further understand the issue of journalist as Good Samaritan.

None of these scholars, however, drew heavily on moral theory to explain their solutions. This chapter serves as a corrective by demonstrating that deontology is a useful theoretical framework for thinking about this and other moral problems in the face of the shortcomings of ethics codes. Put simply, deontological theory can help explain why some moral choices are better than others.

Deontological moral theory

Applied ethics is the arena in which the everyday problems of morality are worked out, and ethics codes are generally situated in this branch of moral philosophy. However, in addition to considering codes of ethics, philosophers have also drawn on theoretical norms and meta-ethical concepts to help resolve problems (Klaidman and Beauchamp, 1987). Philosophers who study meta-ethics examine values, principles, and concepts that comprise moral thought, while philosophers in the area of theoretical normative ethics, unable to arrive at a single moral theory that covers all circumstances, have worked out systems of moral standards used to govern moral conduct (Day, 1991).

While some philosophers have drawn on utilitarian theory, particu- larly rule utilitarianism, as justification for and critiques of codes of ethics (Brinkmann and Ims, 2003; Starr, 1983), others have argued that a stronger relationship exists between ethics codes and deontological theory (L'Etang, 1992). Deontological theory emphasises moral duties and is associated with Immanuel Kant (1984), the eighteenth-century German philosopher who, responding to the role of emotion in morality, argued that moral thinking is based on rationality. Kant assumed that there are universal, a priori moral obligations – that is, objective moral rules – that apply to all individuals, as humans, across time and space. Kant grounded his normative theory in human rationality and conscience, arguing that the distinctly human feature of rationality makes all human beings ends in themselves, rather than means to an end. Kant assumed that, because the moral agent views himself as rational, the moral agent must accord that same view to fellow humans. Therefore, Kant reasoned, universal moral duty requires an unquestioning respect for humans and their dignity. According to Kant, an act is judged right or wrong on the basis of moral duty rather than on consequences. The supreme principle of his moral system is the categorical imperative, which says that an individual must act only on those principles or maxims that he or she could will to become a universal law (Kant, 1984: 188). Respecting duty for its own sake and performing those duties from the standpoint of good will leads to morally correct actions, according to Kant. He said that good will is fostered by reason and tempers the tendency to act out of self-interest or desire (Kant, 1984).

Kant's distinction between types of duties furthers an understanding of how deontological normative theory might help resolve problems when codes fail to offer assistance. According to Kant, duties are either perfect or imperfect. Perfect duties reflect those moral principles that specify behaviour – for example, truth-telling or promise-keeping. Imperfect duties, such as beneficence, require only a commitment to a general principle – in this case, doing good for others. Imperfect duties do not spell out what specifically must be done in a particular instance; circumstances play a role in how the moral agent carries out the commitment to the principle (Baron, 1987).

Kant's version of strict deontology is problematic in that his universal principles sometimes conflict with one another and, as an absolutist, he leaves us little room to negotiate resolutions. The work of W. D. Ross, a Scottish philosopher, helped to resolve that difficulty. Ross (1930) believed that humans have prima facie moral duties. A prima facie duty is obligatory but can be outweighed by another apparent moral duty in a particular instance. He argued that moral obligations vary in importance according to the case at hand; duties generally perceived to be universally binding will assume different levels of priority depending on the nature of the actual moral conflict involved.

Ross articulated a series of prima facie duties that mirrored some of those outlined by Kant. Saying that his list was not necessarily complete, Ross argued that all moral agents have duties of fidelity, reparation, gratitude, justice, beneficence, self-improvement, and non-maleficence. Duties of fidelity are moral claims that emerge as a result of our own actions, and include such obligations as promise-keeping and truth-telling. Duties of reparation, or repairing harm, emerge from actions we have previously committed that were wrong. We owe duties of gratitude for the services that others provide. Duties of justice emerge from the possibility of distribution of pleasure or happiness based on things other than merit. The duty of beneficence directs us to make the lives of others better when and because we can, while duties of self-improvement centre around improving our own virtue and intelligence. Duties of non-maleficence require that we avoid harming or the inclination to harm others.

Ross distinguished between the theoretical prima facie duties and the actual duty that one must choose in a particular circumstance. At times,

Ross said, it will be necessary to violate a prima facie duty. For instance, one might break a promise to meet someone for coffee in order to help someone else who is in distress; however, the moral agent does not lose sight that promise-keeping 'tend[s] to be our duty', while helping someone in distress (beneficence) is the actual duty in that instance (1930: 28). Ross argued that, generally speaking, some of the prima facie duties carry more moral weight than others. He argued that 'a great deal of stringency belongs to the duties of "perfect obligation" – the duties of keeping our promises, of repairing wrongs we have done, and of returning the equivalent of services that we have received' (pp. 41–2).

In summary, deontological moral theory, as originally outlined by Kant and further developed by Ross and others, focuses on the moral obligations all individuals have because we are human beings. The theory argues that the duties are universal and binding and are central to the process of moral decision-making. According to Ross, it is the moral agent's task to determine which duty is the morally right duty – that is, the actual duty, in a given instance.

While Bersoff and Koeppl (1993: 346) have argued that ethics codes 'are formal expressions of normative ethics', they also cautioned that the distinctions drawn between deontological and utilitarian ethics are not always clear, leading them to conclude that neither approach is adequate to address all moral problems. That is likely true. At the same time, the deontological approach is quite helpful for considering the relationship between the journalistic codes of ethics and broader theoretical norms. Both offer principles for moral behaviour; the deontological principles apply to all humans and are, therefore, general in nature, while the principles outlined in codes are particular in that they apply to members of specific professions or groups (Day, 1991). As will be shown next, the principles offered in the codes can be read as specific instances of the broader principles offered by deontological moral theory.

Codes of ethics for journalists

The field of journalism has a number of ethics codes that all point to similar standards. The codes were created by the various professional organisations to which journalists can belong; some of the organisations are specific to the area of journalism practised. For instance, the National Press Photographers Association (2004) (NPPA) has its own code, as does the Radio Television Digital News Association (2000) (RTDNA). The Society of Professional Journalists (1996) (SPJ) has a code aimed at journalists in general, rather than those who practise in a particular medium. Other professional codes exist, but an analysis of all of them is beyond the scope of this chapter. The purpose here is to draw on the codes mentioned to point to a direct relationship between professional codes of ethics and the moral principles outlined by deontologists.

In an effort to understand codes' attributes, scholars have analysed professional codes from a variety of perspectives (Farrell and Farrell, 1998; Frankel, 1989; Wiley, 2000). This study draws on a classification system outlined by Gaumnitz and Lere (2004). Three categories are of interest here: a code's thematic content, its focus, and its shape. Using a deontological lens to examine code provisions, it is possible to identify those themes that dovetail with the prima facie duties outlined by Ross (1930). An examination of the themes also allows us to determine whether the statements reflect commitments to many or only a few of the duties outlined by Ross and whether the code's shape is broad or narrow; a narrow code reflects fewer themes or topics, while a broad code covers a larger number of themes. Gaumnitz and Lere also argued that the nature of the themes offers insight into how the codes are focused – in particular whether they are horizontal or vertical. A vertical, or more narrowly focused, code consists of statements that are slightly different versions of rules that reflect the same moral principles; a horizontal code, or more broadly focused code, reflects fewer statements related to a larger number of principles. Taken together, these concepts help identify what the profession takes to be its most important duties and also help reveal a code's shortcomings. Professionals, in turn, can appeal to deontological moral theory for help in those areas that the codes do not cover.

Each of the three codes – NPPA, RTDNA, and SPJ – begins with a preamble that speaks to the goals of the profession and reflects the values on which the subsequent principles rest. While the terms *values* and *principles* are often substituted for one another, they are distinct concepts (Schwartz, 2002). Principles are guidelines for behaviour, while values underpin that behaviour. A value is defined as a thing we hold dear – that is, a value is our belief or understanding of how something should be (Goldwaith, 1996). Understanding the underlying values furthers an identification of the profession's focus.

According to their code's preambles, all three organisations ground the journalist's role in public enlightenment. The RTDNA and NPPA preambles directly state that journalists are 'trustees of the public' while the SPJ preamble states that public enlightenment is necessary for a democratic and just society; to that end, journalists must be faithful to the field and the professional code. Taken together, the preambles suggest that the goal of the journalist is to pursue truth in the public's interest and, subsequently, in the service of democracy.

The ethics codes vary in length; the SPJ code contains 37 provisions, the RTDNA code contains 41 provisions, and the NPPA code contains 16. At least two-thirds of the provisions of each code revolve around duties of truth-telling, loyalty, and avoiding harm. Code provisions related to truth-telling and loyalty are reflective of the broader prima facie duty that Ross (1930) identified as fidelity, while the code provisions related to avoiding harm reflect the duty of non-maleficence. Specific provisions that are reflective of the prima facie duties of beneficence, justice, and self-improvement, as will be shown, receive minimal attention.

Truth-telling and loyalty are reflective of the prima facie duty of fidelity. Being truthful, according to Ross (1930: 21) rests on a promise 'not to tell lies'. While truth is a meta-ethical concept – philosophers are still debating its meaning – the ethics codes offer insight into how the profession understands the problem of truth as a practical matter. According to the codes, truthful information is accurate, complete, and free of distortion. More specifically, in its accuracy and completeness, truth reflects the diversity of people and their ideas. It is free of manipulation, deception, and is transparent. For instance, the RTDNA code tells members to 'clearly disclose the origin of information and label all material provided by outsiders'. The journalist's opinions are kept out of truth-telling; advocacy is labelled as such.

The code provisions indicate that a journalist has obligations of loyalty to the public, to the ideal of truth, and to the profession. To be in service to those ideals, the journalist must remain independent and trustworthy; journalists must not accept gifts or favours, or let sponsorship, ownership, or peer pressure influence editorial content. Journalists must avoid conflicts of interest, real or perceived, or disclose those that exist. According to the SPJ code, for instance, journalists must 'remain free of associations and activities that may compromise integrity or damage credibility'. The NPPA code cautions the journalist against paying news sources or 'reward[ing] them materially for information or participation', because payment could compromise the quality of information.

Engagement in such behaviour points to wavering loyalties to the public and truth-telling.

According to the three codes, loyalties to the public, to the ideal of truth-telling, and to the profession remain ahead of loyalties to the self, owners of news organisations, advertisers, and others. The RTDNA code, for instance, encourages members to 'refuse to allow the interests of ownership or management to influence news judgment and content inappropriately'. To make certain that the journalist remains committed to the public's interest, journalists are encouraged to hold 'those with power accountable' (SPJ) and to 'strive to ensure that the public's business is conducted in public' (NPPA). Further, members are required to defend press freedom, 'recognizing that any professional or government licensing of journalists is a violation of that freedom' (RTDNA).

Each code also contains a series of provisions that reflect the duty to avoid harm – that is, the prima facie duty of non-maleficence. First, journalists are encouraged to respect the dignity of all persons involved in stories. The SPJ code, for example, says journalists should 'recognize that gathering and reporting information may cause harm or discomfort'. According to the SPJ code, journalists must pay particular attention to the dignity of children and victims of sex crimes; in the RTDNA code, they are told not to contact subjects involved in dangerous situations while those events are unfolding.

The codes also encourage journalists to behave in ways that prevent damage to the profession. They are encouraged to avoid unethical journalistic practices (SPJ), including the intentional sabotage of 'the efforts of other journalists' (NPPA). They are also told to foster an atmosphere of ethics in the newsroom. The RTDNA code, for example, cautions members to 'refrain from ordering or encouraging courses of action that would force employees to commit an unethical act'. According to all three codes, journalists should be accountable for their work by listening to the public's grievances, admitting mistakes, and explaining practices that are related to covering controversial stories.

Receiving far less attention in these codes are the prima facie duties of justice, the obligation to keep promises (which can be viewed as a form of fidelity), beneficence, and self-improvement. The three codes offer few specific guidelines directly related to the principle of justice. The RTDNA code encourages journalists to respect the need for fair trials, as does the SPJ code, which cautions journalists to 'balance a criminal suspect's fair trial rights with the public's right to be informed'. Further, that code tells journalists to seek out those accused of wrongdoing for their responses, and to give 'voice to the voiceless'. All three codes contain one provision that reflects the duty to honour promises. Specifically, they encourage journalists to keep promises of confidentiality to story sources.

At the same time, the codes make only passing references to the principle of beneficence. They, for example, encourage journalists to be compassionate to victims of crime or tragedy, and those suffering grief or those inexperienced in the process of news coverage, but none of the codes specifically addresses the issue of offering aid to those experiencing distress – that is, of acting as a Good Samaritan. Finally, only the NPPA code overtly encourages journalists to engage in a duty of self-improvement. The visual journalist is encouraged to 'think proactively, as a student of psychology, sociology, politics and art to develop a unique vision and presentation'. The NPPA code also encourages journalists to 'strive to be unobtrusive and humble in dealing with subjects'.

The themes embedded in the provisions of the journalists' ethics codes map nicely to the deontological moral duties. Some obligations do receive more emphasis in the codes than others, which is not surprising given the expectation that responsible journalists act in ways that serve the public's interest first and foremost. This narrow focus suggests that journalists' ethics codes are more vertical than horizontal.

However, vertical codes are not particularly helpful when journalists face moral conflicts involving duties to which the codes direct very little attention. Thus, the argument can be made that working journalists need to be able to draw on both normative moral theory, in this case deontology, and codes of ethics in order to work their way through moral dilemmas. The codes alone will not inform journalists in every instance. Where codes fall short, therefore, journalists can appeal to deontological moral theory; this provides a useful way of both understanding and working through a moral conflict.

Truth-telling and beneficence

The case outlined at the beginning of this chapter offers an opportunity to articulate how an understanding of deontological theory – particularly through the lens of Ross's prima facie duties – can be of help when ethical codes fail to cover the problem under consideration. In this instance, the dilemma that emerged with the photojournalist covering the football game revolved around two conflicting obligations: truth-telling and beneficence. According to journalists' codes of ethics, the duty of truth-telling is of the highest importance. As the RTDNA code prescribes, a professional journalist, working in society's interest, should gather and disseminate news without 'fear or favor'. Clearly, the story about fans rushing the football field falls into the category of telling citizens news that they genuinely need to know. The second obligation in this case – beneficence – relates to an obligation to do good; this obligation came into focus when the fans who stormed the field were either injured or injured others in the incident. However, as noted earlier, the codes do not address the obligation of beneficence in a meaningful way. While the NPPA code requires photojournalists to take care when covering victims of a tragedy, the provision offers little assistance in answering the question posed in this instance: should the photojournalist record the news as it unfolds, or should he put down his camera and do good for those who need help? Therefore, it is useful to explore how philosophers' work around the prima facie duty of beneficence can help inform the decision.

According to Ross (1930), the duty of beneficence – that is, the duty to do good – is an imperfect duty. The moral agent decides how and under what circumstances to execute the obligation (Smith, 1990: 21–2). Thus, despite what the code does or does not say, the photojournalist as a human being has the imperfect duty of beneficence – that is, he or she has the general obligation to do good for others. But the fact that the duty is an imperfect duty means that, in this instance, the photojournalist has a choice about whether to help and under what circumstances. That takes us only a short distance towards answering the question in this case; the imperfect duty does not direct the photojournalist to behave in one way over another. However, the work of scholars who have who examined the obligation of beneficence takes us further towards a reasoned solution to this dilemma.

Philosophers have situated the problem of helping another in distress – that is, being a Good Samaritan – in the category of beneficence rather than in the category of repairing or avoiding harm because the harm in cases involving Good Samaritans is not of the moral agent's making. Scholars also argue that, in the case of Good Samaritanism, the imperfect duty of beneficence rests on an assumption that humans – by virtue of living in relation to others, each with his or her own shortcomings – are dependent on one another and, as a result, share a duty of mutual aid. Herman (1984) posited that the duty of beneficence reflects the need to preserve and support fellow humans in their roles as rational moral agents. Stohr (2011) drew on Herman's thinking to identify and reconcile two conflicting claims related to beneficence. On one hand, she contended, beneficence is an imperfect duty that affords the moral agent a choice; he or she must adopt the principle of beneficence but can decide when and how to apply it. On the other hand, some beneficent acts fall into the category of obligatory, particularly in instances when persons are in true need. To that end, according to Stohr, the duty of beneficence should be considered a moral requirement with two parts. First, it offers discretion to the moral agent to decide whether to give help in a specific instance. Second, it requires a narrow duty of respect for others as ends in themselves. Refusing to help someone in true need would 'express indifference' to a rational human being and would violate the principle of beneficence (Stohr, 2011: 61). Further, it would violate Kant's claim that universal moral duties require a moral agent to recognise and respect another's human dignity.

Working within this framework, then, the photojournalist in our example would be expected to work back and forth between the obligations of truth-telling and the dual requirements of the duty of beneficence. Naturally, the photojournalist would be expected to realise that a significant news story was playing out in front of his eyes and that he was obliged to tell that story. He would also be expected to recognise that injuries were in the making as the scene unfolded and that he, as a moral agent, must decide whether to execute his imperfect duty of beneficence at that particular moment. Following Stohr's reasoning, rendering aid was the photojournalist's moral duty because the injured fans were in desperate need of help; ignoring the injured would constitute an expression of indifference to the true needs of fellow humans on the part of the photojournalist. If the photojournalist failed to put down the camera and offer help, he might rightly be accused of using the injured fans as a means to an end – the news story – rather than as ends in themselves. The photojournalist could have claimed he did not cause the harm, but that argument would not absolve him of the duty to offer aid. In cases of Good Samaritanism, deontologists have cast the 'non-doing' of a helpful act (i.e. offering aid) as an act of omission and as morally wrong; the 'harm threatened or already suffered [was] exacerbated, when it need not have been' (Kleinig, 1976). Therefore, while the photographer might not have caused the harm, his lack of immediate assistance could be viewed as a causal factor in the ongoing harm.

Might the moral agent ever be justified in choosing not to put down the camera and offer aid? The latitude afforded by the duty of beneficence does allow the moral agent to make decisions about if and when to help people in need; in this instance, if he observed that others nearby – for example, police and trained rescue personnel normally on hand for football games – were offering victims the necessary aid, he would be morally justified in deciding to put his particular duty of truth-telling ahead of his moral obligation of beneficence. In other words, he wouldn't be morally required to be a Good Samaritan. This reasoning is in keeping with Ross's argument that a moral agent's actual duty in a given situation depends on specific circumstances; this circumstance clearly alters the moral equation.

In the case that we are exploring here, the photographer appeared to have considered the dual obligations of beneficence and truth-telling. His news director at the time, Jill Geisler, conducted a debriefing following the incident and reported that the photojournalist observed on-site police and rescue personnel immediately offering assistance to those suffering injuries. Knowing that the injured were being cared for by professionals, he chose to capture the images of the scene rather than offer aid.[2] In doing so, he foregrounded his journalistic duty to tell the truth and backgrounded his prima facie duty of beneficence. Further, his actions in covering the event also offered evidence that he followed the NPPA code guideline that he take special care with the injured. Geisler, who is now at the Poynter Institute, said the photographer considered the likeliness that his video would go to the network unedited, and he would lose control of the finished piece. Therefore, he carefully avoided shooting the faces of the injured – some of whom were near death – lest their families learn of their plight via the news. Instead, he trained his camera on the faces of the rescuers. His news director contended that the photojournalist acted responsibly in both choosing to cover the story and in the way he covered it.[3] Scholars whose claims about the moral duty of beneficence have been presented here would, in all likelihood, agree.

As noted earlier, journalists often find themselves in situations that demand they make a decision between whether to do good or to get the story. Examining this case through a moral lens, with an emphasis on deontology, reinforces the point that moral theory is able to offer general guidelines for action when a code does not. Actual situations in which journalists find themselves will vary in complexity and demand; the point here is that deontological moral theory affords room for the more complicated and nuanced thinking required for resolving moral dilemmas than the application of codes of ethics allows. Further, moral theory enables us to put a finer point on the rationale for choosing one principle over another than an ethical code alone might permit. Finally, drawing on one's own intuition, while helpful, does not require a reasoned justification for responding one way and not another; theory, on the other hand, does.

In summary, the particular standards expressed in the journalistic codes of ethics reflect the general moral duties articulated by deontologists. The number of provisions related to truth, harm, and loyalty in each code suggests that the codes are vertical, with a primary focus on the duty of truth-telling. The loyalty-related duties in the codes largely operate to serve the ideal of truth, while the harm-related provisions signal the potential for moral conflicts. The overall thrust of the codes seems to be this: tell the truth to citizens and try to avoid harming story subjects and the profession in the process. Ross's prima facie duties help journalists move beyond the codes when necessary and explain actions by drawing on theoretical norms. Those norms – in this case, beneficence – also offer us a means of critiquing the moral decision-making of the photojournalist shooting the images in the case examined here.

Conclusion

The goal of this chapter was to explain how the journalistic codes of ethics are related to moral theory. The case has been made that provisions of the codes reflect prima facie duties articulated by deontological thinkers. The analysis described here suggests that, overall, the codes of the journalism profession seem to be narrowly focused. Reading the codes through a deontological lens suggests that they are most useful when dilemmas involve principles of truth-telling, loyalty, and harm. But when journalists face moral dilemmas that involve principles of beneficence, justice, and self-improvement, the codes are less likely to be of use. When those matters arise, journalists might be better served by looking to Ross's prima facie duties for assistance in thinking through the particular problems. As demonstrated in the case involving the photojournalist and Good Samaritanism, work done by philosophers on the prima facie duty of beneficence serves as a valuable resource for understanding how the journalist resolved this particular conflict and how journalists might think about such events in the future. The theoretical work done by philosophers on general moral obligations, together with professional ethical codes, offers a more reasoned and systematic way of working through moral dilemmas than professional codes alone might provide.

Even in areas where codes speak to specific moral obligations, much work is still to be done to understand professional responsibilities. As just one example, while the codes described above reflect duties of loyalty, they are silent on matters related to the pursuit of truth when the nation is at war. What are the duties of loyalty for a journalist covering a conflict involving his or her nation? How about when his or her country's soldiers violate international laws of war? Patriotism, after all, is a form of loyalty, a prima facie duty. Because the codes say nothing about what a journalist ought to do in an instance when loyalties to truth and to the nation conflict, we might turn to deontological normative theory for guidance in finding a way out of that moral thicket.

In addition to understanding the deontological theory that underpins journalists' professional codes of ethics, a deeper understanding of other meta-ethical concepts in play in moral dilemmas is also needed. A more thorough knowledge of the dimensions of harm, truth, loyalty, beneficence, and other concepts can take us a great distance in developing more careful and nuanced answers to the difficult moral problems that unfold in the field.

Note

1 Jill Geisler, personal communication, 5 Sept. 2012.
2 Ibid.
3 Ibid.

References

Barker, Stephen F. (1992) 'What is a Profession?', *Professional Ethics*, 1: 73–99.

Baron, Marcia (1987) 'Kantian Ethics and Supererogation', *Journal of Philosophy*, 84(5): 237–362.

Bayles, Michael (1989) *Professional Ethics* (Belmont, CA: Wadsworth).

Bersoff, Donald N., and Koeppl, Peter M. (1993) 'The Relation between Ethical Codes and Moral Principles', *Ethics and Behavior*, 3(3–4): 345–57.

Brinkmann, Johannes (2002) 'Marketing Ethics as Professional Ethics: Concepts, Approaches and Typologies', *Journal of Business Ethics*, 41: 159–77.

Brinkmann, Johannes, and Ims, Knut (2003) 'Good Intentions Aside: Drafting a Functionalist Look at Codes of Ethics', *Business Ethics: A European Review*, 12(3): 265–74.

Day, Louis A. (1991) *Ethics in Media Communications: Cases and Controversies* (Belmont, CA: Wadsworth Publishing Co.).

Farrell, Helen, and Farrell, Brian (1998) 'The Language of Business Codes of Ethics: Implications of Knowledge and Power', *Journal of Business Ethics*, 17(6): 587–601.

Frankel, Mark S. (1989) 'Professional Codes: Why, How and with What Impact?', *Journal of Business Ethics*, 8(2–3): 109–15.

Gardner, Howard, Csikszentmihalyi, Mihaly, and Damon, William (2001) *Good Work: When Excellence and Ethics Meet* (New York: Basic Books).

Gaumnitz, Bruce R., and Lere, John C. (2004) 'A Classification Scheme for Codes of Business Ethics', *Journal of Business Ethics*, 49: 329–35.

Goldwaith, John T. (1996) *Values: What They are and How we Know Them* (New York: Prometheus Books).

Harless, James D. (1990) 'Media Ethics, Ideology, and Personal Constructs: Mapping Professional Enigmas', *Journal of Mass Media Ethics*, 5(4): 217–32.

Held, T. (1993) 'Woman Nearly Killed in Crush', *Milwaukee Sentinel*, 1 Nov.

Herman, Barbara (1984) 'Mutual Aid and Respect for Persons', *Ethics*, 94(4): 577–602.

Jamal, Karim, and Bowie, Norman E. (1995) 'Theoretical Considerations for a Meaningful Code of Professional Ethics', *Journal of Business Ethics*, 14(9): 703–14.

Kant, Immanuel (1984) 'Duty and Reason', in Ethel M. Albert, Theodore C. Denise, and Sheldon P. Peterfund (eds), *Great Traditions in Ethics* (Belmont, CA: Wadsworth), 178–97.

Kim, Yung Soo, and Kelly, James D. (2010) 'Public Reactions toward an Ethical Dilemma Faced by Photojournalists: Examining the Conflict between Acting as a Dispassionate Observer and Acting as a "Good Samaritan"', *Journalism and Mass Communication Quarterly*, 87(1): 23–40.

Kitchener, Karen S. (1984) 'Intuition, Critical Evaluation and Ethical Principles: The Foundation for Ethical Decisions in Counseling Psychology', *The Counseling Psychologist*, 12: 43–55.

Klaidman, Stephen, and Beauchamp, Tom L. (1987) *The Virtuous Journalist* (Oxford: Oxford University Press).

Kleinig, John (1976) 'Good Samaritanism', *Philosophy and Public Affairs*, 5(4): 382–407.

L'Etang, Jacquie (1992) 'A Kantian Approach to Codes of Ethics', *Journal of Business Ethics*, 11: 734–44.

Marion, Gail, and Izard, Ralph (1986) 'The Journalist in Life-Saving Situations: Detached Observer or Good Samaritan?', *Journal of Mass Media Ethics*, 1(2): 61–7.

National Press Photographers Association (2004) *NPPA Code of Ethics*: http://nppa.org/professional_development/business_practices/ethics.html.

Radio Television Digital News Association (2000) *Code of Ethics and Professional Conduct*: www.rtdna.org/content/rtdna_code_of_ethics.

Ross, W. D. (1930) *The Right and the Good* (Oxford: Clarendon Press).

Schwartz, Mark S. (2002) 'A Code of Ethics for Corporate Codes of Ethics', *Journal of Business Ethics*, 41: 27–43.

Smith, Patricia (1990) 'The Duty to Rescue and the Slippery Slope Problem', *Social Theory and Practice*, 16(1): 19–41.

Society of Professional Journalists (1996) *SPJ Code of Ethics*: www.spj.org/ethicscode.asp.

Starr, William C. (1983) 'Codes of Ethics: Towards a Rule-Utilitarian Justification', *Journal of Business Ethics*, 2: 99–106.

Stohr, Karen (2011) 'Kantian Beneficence and the Problem of Obligatory Aid', *Journal of Moral Philosophy*, 8: 45–67.

Wiley, Carolyn (2000) 'Ethical Standards for Human Resource Management Professionals: A Comparative Analysis of Five Major Codes', *Journal of Business Ethics*, 25(2): 93–114.

11

The Language of Virtue: What Can We Learn from Early Journalism Codes of Ethics?

Thomas H. Bivins

> To describe a language is to describe a way of life. (Ludwig Wittgenstein)
>
> What I am . . . is in key part what I inherit, a specific past that is present in some degree in my present. (Alasdair MacIntyre)

The 1920s was a watershed decade for American press ethics. Journalism had been under fire since the turn of the century, for although the 'yellow journalism' of the 1890s had passed, sensationalism was still bread and butter as journalists sought more readers. What was needed, many argued, was a press with 'high moral integrity'. It would not be easy.

The culprit, many thought, was propaganda. The massive campaign that was mounted as the United States entered World War I in 1917 seemed an impregnable barrier to truthful reporting and a harbinger of the emerging field's persuasive power. By the war's end, the public was beginning to view even news as potentially propaganda, aided by the rise of public relations as a champion of business and industry. By the early 1920s, states were enacting privacy laws to hinder over-eager reporters. Other laws sought to prevent dishonest advertising (prolific in newspapers). Some states and their press associations even suggested the licensing of journalists (Cronin and McPherson, 1992: n. 7; Keeler et al., 2002: 49). The *practice* of journalism desperately needed to become the *profession* of journalism.

Strides had been made in the late nineteenth century as professional associations, professional publications, and specialised 'beats' emerged.

However, these weren't enough to shield journalism from some of its most serious critics – journalists themselves. Insiders such as Walter Lippmann and Will Irwin decried reporters' lack of training, their laxity in fact-finding, and recurring sensationalism in even the most respected newspapers. The movement towards professionalism had apparently stalled. Ironically, at roughly the same time, the earliest schools of journalism began to appear in the United States, signifying an academic (thus, more professional) approach to the practice. The University of Missouri was the first, in 1908, followed by Columbia University in 1912, and the University of Oregon in 1916. The impetus towards profession-alism was being renewed, and journalism gained new credibility through its association with higher education even as it was under attack for unprofessional conduct.

Short of licensing, ethics codes are often considered a first step from practice to profession (McLeod and Howley, 1964; Wilensky, 1964). Although ethics codes, or at least guidelines, had been around since the middle of the nineteenth century (Banning, 1999; Dicken-Garcia, 1989), it wasn't until the twentieth century that they took full form. In 1910, the Kansas Editorial Association approved the earliest code of ethics adopted by a journalist's association (Crawford, 1924).

Following the Kansas adoption, a spate of ethics codes appeared: Missouri and Texas in 1921, South Dakota and Oregon in 1922, Massachusetts and Washington in 1923, and Iowa and New Jersey in 1924 (Cronin and McPherson, 1992). By 1930, 13 state ethics codes had been adopted. Notably, in 1923, the first national code of ethics was adopted by the newly formed American Society of Newspaper Editors (ASNE). And by 1926, the Society of Professional Journalists (SPJ), which had been formed in 1909 as Sigma Delta Chi (SDX), had officially adopted the ASNE code; it remained intact until it was rewritten specifically for SPJ in 1973. These early codes reflected a traditional libertarian press theory, stressing truth-telling and public service. Most dealt with advertising, especially ads masquerading as news, and excessive editorialising reflecting a possible conflict of interest (Keeler et al., 2002: 49). Because most of these codes followed closely on the heels of World War I, they also tended to deal with propaganda and the burgeoning influence of public relations. In the late 1960s, when Weigle and Clark looked back on the period, these codes often seemed 'quaint' and 'Victorian' in both their writing style and the sentiments they portrayed (Weigle and Clark, 1969: 44).

But, are they really? *Are* they too time-bound, too archaic, a bit too Victorian, a bit too naive? Can anything valuable be drawn today, almost 100 years later, from the language and conventions of early twentieth-century journalism codes? Moral ideas are constructed by language itself. But as language changes, does the morality it refers to also change? As Scottish philosopher Alasdair MacIntyre observed, it is exactly at the level of language that the moral inadequacies and corruptions of our own age are most evident (Hauerwas, 2007: 4).

MacIntyre is most notable for resurrecting the notion of virtue (as described by Aristotle) as a tool for reuniting moral language with moral acts – in the form of historical narrative embodied in a moral tradition. In *After Virtue* (1984), he proposes that 'the forms of practical rationality that guide ethical decision-making are intimately linked to the various moral traditions from which they spring' (cited in Lambeth, 1990: 76). Humans, MacIntyre says, are natural storytellers, and they seek to pass on the 'truth' – as it relates to their lives and roles – via their narratives. As Donahue (1990) points out:

> *An ethics of narrative provides a way in which the norms and principles that constitute a moral tradition can derive their substance and meaning. Stories make principles come alive. (p. 233)*

> *To use narrative in ethical decision-making means to locate moral choices within the context of a 'unified life story.' It is to try to assess in what ways a particular choice is connected to the developing story, to show how a choice 'flows out of' or 'fits into' the history of a person or community. (p. 239)*

MacIntyre (cited in Cain, 2008: 10) suggests that:

> *the concepts distinctive of a particular historically embedded moral system are embodied in and draw meaning from particular forms of social practice. Practices in turn find their meanings and their developments in an on-going narrative of stability and transformation within the history of a particular society. It is precisely the process of handing on these practices and narratives that constitutes a tradition.*

These practices and narratives are tied by that tradition to the past, yet with an obligation to the future to continue to provide excellence so that the tradition will be passed on in 'good order to those who will practice it in the future' (Clayton, 2005: section 6, para. 8). As Slingerland (2001)

167

notes, 'Being initiated into a social practice requires accepting the authority of the teacher, as well as the standards of excellence handed down by the practice tradition' (p. 106).

The narrative integral to the passing on of tradition is composed of words, and words should relate directly to the concepts that they seek to describe, embodied in the tradition of which they are a part. MacIntyre's linking of moral traditions, moral language, and social practice is particularly relevant to the 'practice' of journalism. Many of the journalism codes of the early twentieth century used moral language in a way that bore an actual relationship to the beliefs of their creators and to the normative guidelines those beliefs engendered. I argue that, today, this is no longer true. My premise is that the relationship between belief, language, and action can and should be revitalised. The language and sentiments we take as archaic and out-of-touch today might yet inform us. In this modern age, we seem to have lost contact with what is morally important in journalism – a loss that is nowhere more obvious than in our codes.

Using several codes from the early twentieth century and applying a MacIntyrean analysis, I will attempt to determine whether the reaction to the world in which these journalists lived, as presented within their codes, can provide us with a more commonsense and, perhaps, more elegant approach to the ethics of modern journalistic practices. At the same time, I will highlight a resurgence of both Aristotelian and MacIntyrean concepts newly applied to journalism today – a resurgence that resonates surprisingly with one code in particular from nearly 100 years ago.

MacIntyre's project

To understand MacIntyre, we must begin with Aristotle. Aristotle's virtues are community-centred; they contribute to the betterment of society, not just the individual. However, it is *within* the virtuous actor that morality lies, not in the action itself or the output produced by the actor. A virtuous person will produce a good product. The Aristotelian tradition aligned the virtues with the practical and moral excellence produced within a society, the ultimate goal of which is 'human flourishing' (*eudemonia*). This is the *telos* (end) to which all humans should subscribe, and it is this *telos* that MacIntyre says is missing from the world we now live in.

Teleology is the belief that final causes (goals, purposes) exist not only in nature, but also in human beings. Humans have, or should have, a goal, which is to flourish through the development of a good character, leading to good action. According to MacIntyre, the philosophers of the Enlightenment rejected Aristotle's teleological explanation for human behaviour and substituted approaches privileging either vaguely specified ends with varying outcomes (utilitarianism) or human intuition guided by intent and an innate sense of obligation, resulting in unalterable rules (deontology). MacIntyre sees the current state of morality in disarray because humans lack a clear sense of what they should aspire to, which is to be good – not 'happy', not self-sufficient, not self-indulged – but good within the framework of a society whose members share the goal and benefit of virtuous action. Aristotle's teleology assumed a relationship between moral words, moral acts, and moral ends. MacIntyre thus holds that if we reject Aristotle's teleology, we reject that relationship. Words become untethered from their attendant associations of acts and ends.

MacIntyre suggests that Aristotle's belief in a *telos* common to human endeavour led to a formulation of language as part of the carrier of moral understanding. Thus, the language that has come down to us as a descriptor of moral action is that which describes the path that leads to achieving that *telos*. Therefore, 'good' becomes a designation of effectiveness in carrying out a task, or fulfilling a purpose, leading to a goal. How effectively that purpose is realised will determine the 'goodness' or 'badness' of the act and the person's character. Moral language, thus, has a direct connection to moral action. MacIntyre believes that modernity, and specifically Enlightenment philosophy, has severed the link between the language used to describe morality and the moral act itself.

Starting from his premise that morality has lost any grounding – and is based not on reason but on 'shrill' disagreements that can never be settled – MacIntyre attempts to rebuild, from an Aristotelian platform, a social concept that ties *telos* to virtuous action through practices, links life to a narrative order that includes practices, and links that narrative order to a moral tradition that can be passed on.

Virtues, practices, and traditions

As MacIntyre notes, any area of human endeavour, such as professions, in which standards of excellence guide the production of societal goods is an 'appropriate locus for the exercise of the virtues, and the virtues are those qualities that allow practitioners to excel in their roles' (cited in Levy, 2004: 111). He calls these endeavours 'practices'.

According to MacIntyre, a practice is a unique environment in which people may apply their virtues to their work, and by so doing, help establish and further standards of excellence within that practice. As part of this pursuit of excellence, the activity must produce both 'internal goods' and 'external goods'. Internal goods are those produced through excellent performance resulting in an excellent product, one that serves not only the practice, but also the community as a whole. External goods are those such as money, power, and fame, the acquisition of which by an individual or a practice is self-serving and often runs counter to or even interferes with the production of internal goods. Values that drive excellence often proceed from virtues or character. For example, a belief in truth-telling derives from the virtue of honesty (i.e. having an honest character). The employment of values such as these within a practice results in excellence of internal goods. In turn, MacIntyre's definition of a virtue stems from his definition of a practice. A virtue is 'an acquired human quality the possession and exercise of which tends to enable us to achieve those goods which are internal to practices and the lack of which effectively prevents us from achieving any such goods' (MacIntyre, 1984: 191). He identifies the following three basic virtues that are common to most endeavours:

- *Justice*, which demands that we recognise the skills, knowledge, and expertise of other practitioners, and that we learn from those who know more and have greater experience than we do.
- *Courage*, which requires that we take self-endangering risks, push ourselves to the limits of our capacities, and are prepared to challenge existing practice in the interest of extending the practice, despite institutional pressures against such critique.
- *Honesty*, which asks us to be able to accept criticism and to learn from our errors and mistakes.

Justice, especially, points out the Aristotelian focus on learning from our predecessors. These virtues and resulting standards of excellence are thus passed on via the language of historical narrative.

The practice and virtues of journalism

Although MacIntyre's examples of practices are limited, several scholars have noted that journalism has the potential to fit rather neatly into this category. In 1987, Klaidman and Beauchamp coined the phrase the 'virtuous journalist'. Lambeth (1990, 1992) also explored the application of MacIntyre's ideas to journalism and identified its internal goods: serving the public interest; fairness; clear, vivid, and precise prose; keeping the reader squarely in mind; and preserving First Amendment rights to free expression. These goods, he says, 'derive from the heart of the practice of journalism', benefiting both society and the practice (Lambeth, 1992: 73).

The journalistic virtues required for excellence in practice are listed by Lambeth (1992) as 'principles'. These include truth-telling, humaneness, justice, freedom, and stewardship of free expression (p. 80). In a more recent, in-depth study of MacIntyre's approach, Borden (2007: 80) lists the following journalistic virtues and their functions:

- *Courage and ingenuity*: defending against corruption by external goods.
- *Stewardship*: sustaining institutional bearers of the practice.
- *Justice, courage, honesty* (MacIntyre's key virtues): maintaining relationships needed to achieve the practice's goals through a discipline of verification.
- *Integrity, sense of legacy*: preserving the practice's link to tradition.
- *Accountability, modesty*: supporting the practice's regenerative capabilities through a discipline of confirmation.

Borden cautions, however, that 'it is not just that individual virtues are necessary to achieve the practice's internal goods; they also make possible the conditions that enable practices themselves to flourish' (2007: 80).

For others, the key benefit of virtue ethics as it applies to the practice of journalism is that it supports democracy. As Cohen (2004: 268) says:

> *Within a democracy, the virtues of journalists include character traits that are conducive to the stated end of journalistic practice . . . [T]hese character traits can be defined as habits or dispositions to act in manners that advance the end of a democratic press. These habits involve dedication to principles of conduct that follow from the journalistic end of serving democracy. Insofar as this end is a moral end, these virtues and their corresponding principles are also moral.*

Cohen suggests that virtues such as responsibility, loyalty, fairness, impartiality, honesty, and courage in reporting news are all part of 'what it means to be a competent journalist' (p. 269).

Quinn (2007: 172) proposes that ethical decisions are best made when internally derived (as from the elements of good character) rather than externally derived (as from rules or guidelines). Following Aristotle, Quinn suggests that character is best provided by education and life experience. Quinn also suggests that journalists develop an ideal 'standard by which one ought to judge one's actions both in a general sense – what it is to be a good journalist – or in a particular circumstance, how ought a journalist to act in this situation, right now' (p. 172). This requires internalising a standard of conduct and a conception of excellence by which to guide one's motivations and judge one's own actions. Quinn says that the process of developing this internalised standard allows journalists to bolster certain key virtues, such as justice and integrity, while continually testing and adjusting their actions. The novice may require constant comparison of the ideal against the impulse. The seasoned journalist, on the other hand, may have reached a point of character development in which the right action has become second nature. This is completely in line with Aristotle's notion that the 'golden mean' is always the obvious choice.

This, however, does raise a question. If character ought to be the focus of action and if it is derived, at least in part, from tradition, then why do we need a code of ethics at all? Why not rely simply on tradition and the historical narrative by which it is passed on?

The relationship of codes to character

One of the strongest reasons for belonging to a profession is that certain behaviours, peculiar to that occupation, are spelled out and either encouraged or discouraged by its code. For many, a formal code of ethics provides a first line of defence against proposed unethical actions. It is a reference point for the profession as a whole and a sounding board against which to test options for action. Ethicist Richard Johannesen states, 'For some people, formal codes are a necessary mark of a true profession' (1988: 59). He offers a list of how professional codes function as useful guidelines for practitioners, among them that 'codes should be seen as having a function not just of serving as rules of behaviour, but primarily as *establishing expectations for character*. In other words, codes reflect a wide range of character traits necessary for someone to be a professional' (Johannesen, 2002: 184).

This last point is extremely instructional if we are to understand why something normally expected to be rule-bound can also serve a different function. Johannesen (1988) points out that a code should declare the moral bases on which it is founded, and he strongly suggests that codes should be seen as having a function not just of serving as rules of behaviour, but primarily as establishing expectations for *character* – to depict the ideal character of the professional for whom the code is written. In the words of Karen Lebacqz (1985: 71), a 'professional is called not simply to *do* something but to *be* something'. This goes beyond the common view of a code as simply a set of guidelines for professionals to follow. This speaks directly to character.

Lebacqz cites several key virtues, or character traits, that go to the core of what professionals value most: justice, beneficence, non-injury, honesty, and fidelity. These are not always stated directly in codes, but rather appear in code provisions that, in essence, paint a picture of the professional as a person of moral character (Lebacqz, 1985: 68). In fact, Lebacqz points out that such codes describe the virtuous professional as one 'bound by certain ethical principles and as incorporating those principles into his or her very character' (p. 70). Ultimately, 'when we act, we not only do something, we also shape our own character . . . And so each choice about what to do is also a choice about whom to be – or more accurately, whom to become' (p. 83).

Comparing codes and their use of moral language

Scholarly research into early press codes has been somewhat spotty but on the rise since the 1980s. Dicken-Garcia's 1989 book explored nineteenth-century precursors to twentieth-century codes. Cronin and McPherson (1992) covered the early twentieth-century codes in a detailed comparison. Most recently, Wilkins and Brennen (2004) contrasted two codes from the early part of the twentieth century with a modern code from the *New York Times*. They viewed journalism codes of ethics from a cultural materialist perspective, noting that, as such, codes may be seen as 'cultural practices existing within an on-going social process' (p. 298). As they note, 'Ethics codes are explicit forms of practical communication created in a historically specific society and produced under particular social, economic, and political conditions' (p. 298).

Wilkins and Brennen draw from this perspective the suggestion that what is found missing in codes (especially when compared across time) 'provides insights into the larger issues associated with the incorporation of specific journalistic ethics codes' (2004: 298). Although they recognise the shifting social landscape as being an active change agent in the type of responses evident in codes over time, they also point out that codes are 'within the domain of ethics and moral philosophy', which allows them to 'articulate both a set of rules for "normal journalistic practice" as well as an inspiration to the highest ideals in the profession' (p. 302).

Wilkins and Brennen's study supports their thesis that time, ideology, and social–political–economic pressures dictate the focus of the codes. They point out that the early codes reflect 'an era of classical realism, in which texts are thought to represent the truth non-problematically' (2004: 208). Importantly, they also suggest that such ideals as public trust, history, and culture may, in today's environment, succumb to the reality of economic competition. Their study highlights the problems that those involved in a practice such as journalism encounter when the acquisition of external goods overrides the production of internal goods. As MacIntyre (1984: 196) warns:

> *The cultivation of truthfulness, justice and courage will often, the world being what it contingently is, bar us from being rich or famous or powerful. Thus although we may hope that we can not only achieve the standards of excellence and the internal goods of certain practices by possessing the virtues and become rich, famous and powerful, the virtues are always a potential stumbling block to this comfortable ambition. We would therefore expect that, if in a particular society the pursuit of external goods were to become dominant, the concept of the virtues might first suffer attrition and then perhaps something near total effacement, although simulacra might abound.*

Lambeth (1992) lists such external goods as wealth, fame, prestige, and position – the pursuit of which 'can corrupt practices such as journalism' (p. 19). Or, as Aucoin (1993) says:

> *If the making of profit is recognized as a mark of excellence in a practice such as journalism, there would be incongruity between the standard of excellence and the internal values of the activity, which would include such things as telling the whole story, providing a representative view of society and telling the truth. (p. 19)*

It is interesting to note that a piece in the *St Louis Journalism Review* (2004) featuring the Wilkins and Brennen study was titled 'Evolving

Ethics may be Eroding Journalism'. One of the authors of the study is quoted as saying:

> If the recent Jayson Blair incident is any indication, management's financial concerns – as articulated in the [New York Times] ethics code – have their parallels in real life. The emphasis reveals something central about the profession: concerns about financial profitability do remain on an equal footing with journalistic duty and service. (para. 14)

The Review's piece also notes that 'Jayson Blair and Stephen Glass may thus be the result of an evolving marketplace that has largely *bypassed journalism's early traditions*' (para. 13, emphasis added).

These 'early traditions' were themselves the product of a narrative that had existed at the turn of the twentieth century and before (Dicken-Garcia, 1989). Those precursors to the codes of the 1920s had laid the moral groundwork with phrases that, though fraught with Victorian sensibilities, nonetheless spoke the language of character. 'The newspaper should be a gentleman', Will Irwin wrote in 1911 (Weigle and Clark, 1969: 44).

Locating language in time tells us something about that time and the people who spoke those words, but as Brewer (2007: para. 14) observed:

> [W]ords tend to change in meaning as time passes. This need not matter if words have an arbitrary relationship with the things or concepts to which they refer, for in this case change in language can be seen as a form of natural development (or even progress). But if words are linked, for example by their etymology, to some fixed and independent meaning, then the more words diverge from their original form, the more corrupt ... language becomes.

It is my thesis that the words used to describe morality, especially in early codes of ethics, *did* relate to a 'fixed and independent meaning', and that those same words, and the sentiments they portray, have diverged so far from their original meaning that the moral standing of modern codes has become corrupted.

What's in a word?

A recent study by Kesebir and Kesebir (2012) tracked the appearance of words related to moral character and virtue in American books from 1901 to 2000. The results show a drastic decline in the use of concepts such as decency, dignity, morality, and virtue. In addition, words denoting virtues (honesty, honour, kindness, courage, mercy, etc.) also significantly declined throughout the twentieth century. Kesebir and Kesebir conclude that, 'in keeping with the larger trends in the moral landscape of the United States ... the attention paid to concepts of moral character and virtue has declined over the course of the twentieth century' (p. 12). The authors note 'People simply do not think/talk/write about morality and virtue as much anymore. The vocabulary for talking about issues of good and bad, right and wrong thus seems to be shrinking' (cited in Doll, 2012: para. 6).

> [M]oral values and virtues require a supportive sociocultural environ-ment to flourish ... A lexicon of morality and virtue concepts is an integral part of this supportive structure, and its fading from public arena may thus inflict personal and societal costs ... We believe that a virtue-salient culture would provide a more fertile ground for individual and societal flourishing than one where concepts of moral excellence are at the fringes of public conversation. (Kesebir and Kesebir, 2012: 14)

Most of the codes developed in the 1920s included broad-stroke preambles followed by more specific advice on how to accomplish the traditional goals of journalism. The typical approach at the time included paeans to journalism's watchdog role, its growing professionalism, its purveyance of strict editorial standards, its role as a provider of truth, and its independent voice free from the pressures of advertisers and others. Importantly, the codes varied in philosophical grounding and in the language they used to present their cause. 'Some of the codes [from this era] are long and utilitarian, others short, grandiloquent and vague, with most combining both flowery language and practical direction' (Cronin and McPherson, 1992: 357–8). Among those that consistently cite the virtues of both journalism and journalists are the South Dakota code (1922), the American Society of Newspaper Editors (ASNE) code (1923), and, especially, the Oregon code (1922). All of these codes may be found packaged conveniently by Nelson Crawford in his 1924 volume on the ethics of journalism.

The Oregon journalism code

On 14 January 1922, the *Code of Ethics for Journalism* was adopted unanimously by the Oregon State Editorial Association (OSEA) at its annual convention (Crawford, 1924: 187–94). It was written by Colin V.

Dyment, a faculty member in the School of Journalism and Dean of the College of Literature, Science and the Arts at the University of Oregon. Dyment had worked as a newspaper reporter and editor for a number of years, and it was the combination of practical experience and a scholarly mind that led to his appointment to the Oregon faculty in 1913. The head of the department, later Dean of the School, Eric Allen, was himself a graduate in philosophy. He and Dyment were of accord in believing in a strong, liberal arts education for young journalists-to-be and a solid, philosophical foundation in ethics (Turnbull, 1965: 17–25). According to Cronin and McPherson (1992), journalism professors such as Dyment and Allen were in the forefront of the campaign for ethics codes: 'Professors served as the trade's conscience, exhorting journalists to follow the lead of lawyers and doctors by heightening the requirements for admission to practice journalism as well as encouraging the adoption of codes of ethics' (p. 356).

Dyment was commissioned by the OSEA convention 'to take charge of drawing up a code which should lay the emphasis not upon such matters as the maintenance of rates, etc., but upon the ethical relation of the newspaper to the public' (Allen, 1922: 177). Importantly, Allen noted that the code was 'chary of either prescribing or condemning concrete practices', recognising that practices would often differ, because individual editors would apply the principles differently (p. 178). Allen and Dyment both realised that 'beyond the making clear of causes and results, ethics, as a science, does not go. From that point good will and clean intent must take hold; if these do not exist society is in a parlous state' (Allen, 1922: 176). In the foreword to the volume from which Allen is quoted here (devoted entirely to professional ethics), R. M. MacIver, a professor of political economy, echoed Allen's sentiments – and Aristotle's:

> Ethics cannot be summed up into a series of inviolate rules or commandments which can be applied everywhere and always without regard of circumstances, thought of consequences, or comprehension of the ends to be attained. What is universal is the good in view, and ethical rules are but the generally approved ways of preserving it. The rules may clash with one another, and then the only way out is to look for guidance to the ideal. (MacIver, 1922: 8)

This belief was also emphasised more recently by Klaidman and Beauchamp (1987: 19) when they noted that 'by cultivating moral virtues, doing what is right … can become a matter of course rather than a conflicted debate over how to interpret rules whose meaning and application may be less than clear'.

Virtue versus rules

What makes the Oregon code important is its focus on the Aristotelian idea of a *telos* for journalism. Allen (1922: 173) saw the code as at 'minimum the best practices of the profession, and as the optimum the state of perfect knowledge, perfect good will and perfect courage'. He stressed the Aristotelian ideal of a morally mature person capable of using both learned education and life experience to make moral decisions:

> *The editor's belief as to what constitutes 'public and social interest' can be affected only by the gradual moralization and rationalization of all society, by education of the young newspapermen and by logical criticism. For his informed judgment no written rule can be substituted. (p. 176)*

The preamble to the Oregon code opens with a quote from Aristotle, reflecting the scholarly depth and interests of its author: 'Not only all arts and sciences but all actions directed by choice aim at some good.' As Johannesen (1988) suggested, a code should declare the moral bases on which it is founded. The Oregon preamble (emphasis added throughout) is sprinkled with hints of its Aristotelian roots:

- We believe in the teaching of the great ethicists that a general state of happiness and well-being is attainable throughout the world; and that this state is *the chief end-in-view of society*.
- We recognize an instinct in every good man that his utterances and his deeds should make a reasonable and continuous contribution towards *this ultimate state*, in the possibility of which we reiterate our belief, however remote it may now seem.
- All the agencies and instrumentalities employed by men, singly or collectively, should be based upon the best ethical practice of the time, so that *the end-in-view* of society may thereby be hastened.

In addition to the preamble, four of the seven articles of the code begin with a set of virtues: sincerity, truth, care, competency, thoroughness, justice, mercy, kindliness, moderation, conservatism, and proportion. The remaining three articles deal with the specific concerns of partisanship and propaganda, public service and social policy, and advertising and circulation – topics common to nearly all codes written during this period.

Most importantly, Article VI flatly states that a newspaper and its journalists should be moral exemplars – an attitude that supports both Aristotle's and MacIntyre's insistence on moral leadership as a teaching tool for those exploring the path to a virtuous character:

> We dispute the maxim sometimes heard that a newspaper should follow its constituency in public morals and policy rather than try to lead it. ... It is not true that a newspaper should be only as advanced in its ethical atmosphere as it conceives the average of its readers to be. No man who is not in ethical advance of the average of his community should be in the profession of journalism.

The Oregon code was not the only code that made use of the language of virtue (although it was the only one to overtly refer to its philosophical roots). The South Dakota code noted that it was founded on the 'basic principle of truth and justice and it embodied 'those ideals of service and that sense of propriety and honour which should imbue the motives and guide the actions of all who enter upon this profession'. This preamble is followed, like Oregon's code, with a series of articles headed by virtues such as truth and honesty, fairness and accuracy, sincerity and decency, honour and respect (Crawford, 1924: 195–8).

Likewise, the ASNE code, adopted the year after the Oregon and South Dakota codes, references a set of journalistic virtues: sincerity, truthfulness, accuracy, impartiality, fair play, and decency (see Crawford, 1924: 183–5). Its preamble also notes, in a very Aristotelian manner, that 'Journalism ... demands of its practitioners the widest range of intelligence, or knowledge, and of experience, as well as natural and trained powers of observation and reasoning.' It also cites its obligations as 'teacher and interpreter'.

What all of these early codes of ethics had in common, regardless of their philosophical or practical approaches, was that they relied on already existing press traditions and, 'therefore, were useful in publicizing the standards, ideals and values that many journalists considered professional' (Cronin and McPherson, 1992: 371).

A return to the language of tradition

As noted earlier, MacIntyre (1984: 2) warns that all we have left today, both linguistically and philosophically, are 'simulacra of morality', and we have 'lost our comprehension, both theoretical and practical, of morality' itself. Or as the *St Louis Journalism Review* (2004) opined – in reference to the 2004 Wilkins and Brennen study – perhaps today's 'evolving marketplace ... has largely bypassed journalism's early traditions' (para. 13). However, this is the easy explanation for what has happened to the tone of journalism codes over the past 100 years. The question posed at the beginning of this chapter was whether anything valuable can be drawn today from the language and conventions of early twentieth-century journalism codes, or whether we are simply being forced to react to a moral complexity that we see as unique to our present time – thus justifying our rejection of a moral language we now find a bit too naive.

Do codes, as Wilkins and Brennan suggest, simply reflect the exigencies of the times in which they are written, or is there a larger tradition that may inform journalism outside of time and socially constituted pressures? Journalism *has* changed. Today's concerns and the effect of those concerns on the practice are surely a reaction to pressures that in some ways are unique to the twenty-first century; however, journalism of the early twentieth century was also reacting to enormous changes and pressures. Although times have changed, the challenges that face modern journalism bear a remarkable resemblance to those of nearly 100 years ago when, in 1922, Eric Allen noted that 'economic laws are behind most of the tendencies of present day journalism' (p. 175). This is clearly a statement that could have been made today.

The 1920s brought complex challenges to a practice already in flux. Journalism was changing then as it is changing now, and that earlier change brought about an introspection that questioned journalism's place within the paradigm of a democratic society. In many cases, the response was reflexive, resulting in codes – not unlike the modern-day *New York Times* code explicated by Wilkins and Brennen (2004) – that dealt with the specific threats and challenges facing newspapers of the day. Journalists then were worried about the effects and pressures of advertising and propaganda and how to distinguish in the minds of their constituents the true value of news from those other loud and demanding messages. As Cronin and McPherson (1995: 890) note:

> *From the outset, ethics codes have been more than philosophical statements of virtuous practices. They provide situational guidelines as well. Editors recognize that new reporters do not enter newsrooms with an understanding of news ethics. Ethics must be taught: often through*

> *compiling lists of norms considered ethical. This duality of purpose helps*
> *explain why ethics codes are often ignored within a few years of adoption*
> *– situational concerns can become out-dated quickly.*

However, many of these codes went beyond a simple listing of issues. The best of them presented journalism with a philosophical framework that would allow individual newspapers and editors the leeway to make their own decisions without having to resort to rules. Instead, they were asked to rely on education, and life and professional experience.

These codes also invoked the tradition of journalism – a tradition stressing public service within a practice based on the expected virtues of its members. And 60 years before MacIntyre built his theory of practices and warned of the tension between the creation of internal and external goods, Eric Allen was declaiming: 'conscience is alive in the newspaper profession; the writer knows many, many newspapers which sacrifice and have sacrificed profits to principle; and the establishment of a code is a step in the already active mobilization of the constructive ethical forces in journalism' (1922: 10). Codes of the time emphasised the virtues of sincerity, truth, care, competency, thoroughness, justice, mercy, kindliness, moderation, conservatism, and proportion. These virtues, their writers believed, would result in a journalism whose actions were, as Aristotle urged, 'directed by choice' and aimed 'at some good' – not just for journalism, but for society as a whole.

Yes, times *have* changed. As Dicken-Garcia (1989) points out, the contemporary discussion of journalistic ethics tends to 'proceed from the practical', concentrating on the everyday activities of journalists, especially decision-making. Nineteenth- and early twentieth-century discussions tended to focus on the broader effects of the press. Dicken-Garcia notes: 'Present-day interest in decision-making processes leads to an emphasis on the concrete, the realm of standards, and confusion of standards with the higher-level abstraction of ethics – at the expense of studying ethics in the larger social context' (p. 235). And, as Cronin and McPherson (1995: 897) contend, practical concerns 'have continually kept ethics codes from being a central concern to press members'.

In a prescient warning, Eric Allen pointed out in 1922 that differentiating between a simple listing of rules and a flexible and intellectually useful philosophical grounding illustrated 'some of the difficulties that await the future author of a code which shall be explicit as to practices and which will not, like the Oregon Code, rest content with principles' (p. 179). Although he couldn't have foreseen the complexities of modern society and its effects on journalism, he was certainly aware of the forces, contemporary and potential, that affected the journalism of his day – forces not entirely alien to today's purveyors of news. The big questions that consume journalism today aren't that much different than they were then: how to survive in a challenging economic climate, how to differentiate between news and everything else, how to serve the public interest, how to remain a vital component of a working democracy, and, most importantly, how to articulate the principles that you stand for. Then, as now, we have only words. And, as playwright Tom Stoppard (1984: 53) said: 'Words are sacred; they deserve respect.'

Note

All web addresses in this chapter were last accessed in May 2013.

References

Allen, Eric W. (1922) 'The Social Value of a Code of Ethics for Journalists', *Annals of the American Academy of Political and Social Science*, 101: 170–9.

Aucoin, James L. (1993) 'Professionals or Practitioners? The Macintyrean Social Practice Paradigm and the study of Journalism Development', paper at conference of Association for Education in Journalism and Mass Communication, Communication Theory and Methodology Division.

Banning, Stephen E. (1999) 'Truth is our Ultimate Goal: A Mid-19th Century Concern for Journalism Ethics', *Journal of Media History*, 16(1): 17–39.

Borden, Sandra L. (2007) *Journalism as Practice: MacIntyre, Virtue Ethics and the Press* (Aldershot: Ashgate Publishing).

Brewer, Charlotte (2007) 'Language and Morality', in *Examining the OED*, Academic Research Project, Hertford College, Oxford: http://oed.hertford.ox.ac.uk/main/content/view/117/278.

Cain, Richard (2008) Alasdair MacIntyre's Critique of Contemporary Ethics: Can the Towering Figure of 20th-Century Ethics have it Both Ways?', *Cardinal Perspectives*, Wheeling Jesuit University: www.wju.edu/faculty/cardinal perspectives/winners_0708.asp.

Clayton, Ted (2005) 'Political Philosophy of Alasdair MacIntyre', *Internet Encyclopedia of Philosophy*: www.iep.utm.edu/p-macint/#H6ß.

Cohen, Elliot (2004) 'What would Cronkite do? Journalistic Virtue, Corporate News, and the Demise of the Fourth Estate', *Journal of Mass Media Ethics*, 19 (3–4): 268.

Crawford, Nelson A. (1924) *The Ethics of Journalism* (New York: Alfred A. Knopf).

Cronin, Mary M., and McPherson, James B. (1992) 'Reaching for Professionalism and Respectability: The Development of Ethics Codes in the 1920s', paper at conference of American Journalism Historians Association.

Cronin, Mary M., and McPherson, James B. (1995) 'Pronouncements and Denunciations: An Analysis of State Press Association Ethics Codes from the 1920s', *Journalism and Mass Communication Quarterly*, 72(4): 890–901.

Dicken-Garcia, Hazel (1989) *Journalistic Standards in Nineteenth-Century America* (Madison, WI: University of Wisconsin Press).

Doll, Jen (2012) 'The Moral Decline in the Words we Use', *Atlantic Wire*, 24 Aug.: www.theatlanticwire.com/entertainment/2012/08/moral-decline-words-we-use/56142.

Donahue, James A. (1990) 'The Use of Virtue and Character in Applied Ethics', *Horizons*, 17(2): 228–43.

Hauerwas, Stanley (2007) 'The Virtues of Alasdair MacIntyre', *First Things*: www.firstthings.com/article/2007/09/004-the-virtues-of-alasdair-macintyre-6.

Johannesen, Richard L. (1988) 'What should we Teach about Formal Codes of Communication Ethics?', *Journal of Mass Media Ethics*, 3(1): 59–64.

Johannesen, Richard L. (2002) *Ethics in Human Communication* (4th edn, Prospect Heights, IL: Waveland Press).

Keeler, John D., Brown, William, and Tarpley, Douglas (2002) 'Ethics', in W. D. Sloan and L. M. Parcell (eds), *American Journalism: History, Principles, Practices* (Jefferson, NC: McFarland & Co.), 44–55.

Kesebir, Pelin, and Kesebir, Selin (2012) 'The Cultural Salience of Moral Character and Virtue Declined in Twentieth Century America', *Journal of Positive Psychology*: http://ssrn.com/abstract=2120724.

Klaidman, Stephen, and Beauchamp, Tom L. (1987) *The Virtuous Journalist* (New York: Oxford University Press).

Lambeth, Edmund B. (1990) 'Waiting for a New St. Benedict: Alasdair Macintyre and the Theory and Practice of Journalism', *Journal of Mass Media Ethics*, 5(2): 75–87.

Lambeth, Edmund B. (1992) *Committed Journalism: An Ethic for the Profession* (Bloomington, IN: Indiana University Press).

Lebacqz, Karen (1985) *Professional Ethics: Power and Paradox* (Nashville, TN: Abingdon).

Levy, Neil (2004) 'Good Character: Too Little, Too Late', *Journal of Mass Media Ethics*, 19(2): 108–18.

MacIntyre, Alasdair (1984) *After Virtue* (2nd edn, Notre Dame, IN: University of Notre Dame Press).

MacIver, Robert M. (1922) 'The Social Significance of Professional Ethics', *Annals of the American Academy of Political and Social Science*, 101: 5–14.

McLeod, Jack M., and Howley, Searle E., Jr. (1964) 'Professionalism among Newsmen', *Journalism Quarterly*, 41(4): 529–39.

Quinn, Aaron (2007) 'Moral Virtues for Journalists', *Journal of Mass Media Ethics*, 22(2–3): 168–86.

Slingerland, Edward (2001) 'Virtue Ethics, the Analects, and the Problem of Commensurability', *Journal of Religious Ethics*, 29(1): 97–125.

St Louis Journalism Review (2004) 'Evolving Ethics may be Eroding Journalism': www.weeklyscientist.com/ws/articles/sjrethics.htm.

Stoppard, Tom (1984) *The Real Thing: A Play* (London: Faber & Faber).

Turnbull, George S. (1965) *Journalists in the Making; A History of the School of Journalism at the University of Oregon* (Eugene, OR: School of Journalism, University of Oregon).

Weigle, Clifford, and Clark, David G. (1969) *The American Newspaper by Will Irwin: A Series First Appearing in Colliers, January–July 1911* (Ames: Iowa State University Press).

Wilensky, Harold L. (1964) 'The Professionalization of Everyone', *American Journal of Sociology*, 70(2): 137–58.

Wilkins, Lee, and Brennen, Bonnie (2004) 'Conflicted Interests, Contested Terrain: Journalism Ethics Codes Then and Now', *Journalism Studies*, 5(3): 297–309.

12

The Media and Democracy: Using Democratic Theory in Journalism Ethics

David S. Allen and Elizabeth Blanks Hindman

It seems beyond dispute that the freedoms granted to the press are often linked to its role in safeguarding democracy. Journalists, researchers, and the courts use the democratic role of the media as a way to frame discussions of media freedoms and responsibilities, often treating democracy as a unified set of ideas. Democracy, in reality, is far more complex. Democratic theory ranges from elitist models built on traditional liberal values to participatory models grounded in communitarian ideals (Held, 1987).

This project suggests that the importance of democratic theory to the study of journalistic ethics has long been marginalised. Traditionally, discussion about ethics and the mass media has tended to focus primarily on individual human action, positing that if the individual can develop her or his reasoning skills, practice will improve because the media will be staffed by more ethical practitioners. Ethical theory that focuses on individual practice has a difficult time, however, answering questions such as what role the press – as an institution within a democratic system – ought to play in society. Most of what has come to be called ethical theory in the communication field is not set up to answer normative questions at the systemic level.

Opposite to studies that make the individual the focus of attention are those inquiries that view the press as part of and embedded in a larger societal network. However, these works are often not linked explicitly to democratic theory. Some studies also shy away from normative claims, preferring to offer empirical observations that are intended to be more of an influence on policy than on the ethical practice of journalists and journalism (Hallin and Mancini, 2004). Other studies that do offer normative assessments tend to focus on the press's institutional role, offering little guidance on how democratic theory might influence the practice of individual journalists (Christians et al., 2009).

This chapter hopes to spark a discussion about bringing democratic theory into the centre of journalism ethics at both the systemic and individual level. Democratic theory not only articulates how society ought to be structured, but also what role various groups, institutions, and individuals ought to play in society to achieve that desired end. Here we focus on – and apply to questions of journalism ethics – three broad perspectives on democratic theory: elitist, discourse, and communitarian. We argue that for those interested in the ethical practice of journalism, these theories not only assist in understanding current practices of the press in society, but they also direct journalists in the reform of those practices to better serve democracy. While admittedly these theories do not begin to cover all possible societal roles that the press and its practitioners play, we offer these as a way to begin thinking about the importance of democratic theory to journalism ethics.

Elitist perspectives: Efficiency and expertise

Theorists have long been perplexed by the idea of participation in democratic society. On one hand, some theorists bemoan the apathy that exists within most democratic societies. Conversely, others warn of too much participation, fearing inefficiencies will threaten the survival of societies (Pateman, 1970: 3). Rather than articulate solutions to that intractable dilemma, democratic elitists have instead theorised about democracy in different ways. These conceptions of democracy, as Michael Margolis explained, focus on institutions rather than citizens (1983: 117). In elitist theories, we can find the recognition that social forces have become so strong, so overwhelming, that they leave little chance for citizen political participation. They tell of a time when political participation amounted to little more than 'choosing decision-makers and curbing their excesses' (Held, 1987: 143). Elitist theories of democracy thus attempt to retain the idea of democracy while overcoming its deficiencies. Theorists in this area tend to worry about the impractical nature of democracy and popular rule. In their view, classical democratic theory, with its romantic view of participatory democracy, has always been unrealistic.

Democratic elitism

At the root of elitist theories is Max Weber's critique of society. Influenced by the work of Karl Marx as well as liberal theorists, Weber argues that, as modern society has progressed, life has increasingly been rationalised, with democracy being turned over to scientific procedures that emphasise the role of experts and technology (Held, 1987: 143–5).

Weber's idea of formal rationalisation suggests that, as bureaucracies develop, they tend to emphasise values that are important to these bureaucracies – efficiency, predictability, and technology – rather than human labour (Kalberg, 1980: 1158). The growth of bureaucracy, especially as it has spread beyond government to industry and political parties, has had dire consequences for citizens (Allen, 2005). Agreeing with Marx, Weber found bureaucracy to be inherently undemocratic because bureaucrats were no longer responsible to the electorate (Held, 1987: 147–8; Weber, 1958: 139). The result was that citizens found themselves in an iron cage where rationalisation processes inherently become irrational, where they become trapped by their own bureaucratic structures to the point that they could no longer control their world. In fact, attempts to control the world led to citizens losing control of their world. Weber believed that, in modern society, the best that could be accomplished by people was the election of powerful, wise leaders working within an efficient and expert-driven system. For Weber, the only choice was between 'leadership democracy with a "machine" and leaderless democracy' (Weber, 1958: 113).

While Weber can be viewed as being more concerned with the study of modern life than the creation of a theory of democracy, his work had a wide-ranging influence on Joseph Schumpeter (1947), who pulled many of Weber's ideas together into an actual theory of democracy. The Austrian-born economist popularised many of Weber's ideas, and Schumpeter's writings provided the foundation for many studies by social scientists in the post-World War II years (Held, 1987: 164–5). Schumpeter set out to put aside once and for all the idea that democracy means that 'the people' rule. The only real meaning of democracy for Schumpeter was 'that people have the opportunity of accepting or refusing the men who are to rule them' (Schumpeter, 1947: 284–5). Schumpeter's theory was built around a pessimistic view of the individual citizen, noting that people have proven themselves to be bad judges of their own interests (Schumpeter, 1947: 260–1). Echoing earlier ideas articulated by Walter Lippmann, political questions have no reality with most of the electorate, and, therefore, decisions about those questions are not taken seriously (Lippmann, 1922).

Without a reason for 'immediate responsibility', there was little society could do. Education will not help, Schumpeter wrote, because 'people cannot be carried up the ladder' (Schumpeter, 1947: 262). In fact, when people decide to enter the field of political discussion, they drop 'to a lower level of mental performance' (p. 264). They yield to 'extra-rational or irrational' (p. 264) impulses, which do not lead to the creation of a general public will, but to a manufactured will that is the creation of a special-interest group. The idea that people will discover the truth may be true in the long run, but in the short run, they are being fooled into doing 'something they do not really want' (p. 264). Therefore, for Schumpeter, democracy is reduced to little more than citizens deciding who will govern them. It is through voting – and the competition for votes between political elites – that government generates its legitimacy. His theory calls for high-calibre politicians, a well-trained bureaucracy, competition between rival leaders and parties, and a society that will support differences in opinion (Held, 1987: 176).

Schumpeter's formulation of democratic theory, in the words of political theorist Carole Pateman, 'became almost universally accepted' (1970: 5). In creating a democracy without citizens, Weber and Schumpeter paint a less-than-romantic picture of democracy. Citizens struggle to fulfil their civic responsibilities, and it is left to powerful institutions to meet societal needs.

Applying democratic elitism to journalistic practice

Democratic elitism is reflected in many ideas about journalism and its role in democratic societies. One of its earliest articulations was the social responsibility theory of the press, an outgrowth of the work done by the US Commission on Freedom of the Press (1947) – also known as the Hutchins Commission. The Commission's writings contain the idea that society has become far too complex for citizens to act. In response, a professional press will discover truth for citizens (Baker, 2002; Gerald, 1963; Hocking, 1947; Siebert et al., 1956: 73–104). In short, the press will attempt to relieve citizens of doing some of the difficult work of democracy. Elitist theories are also at the heart of one of the central tenets of journalism – that the press should serve as a watchdog on government. Vincent Blasi draws on Schumpeter in his articulation of the watchdog theory of the press (1977: 542). As Blasi acknowledges, this role for the press is based on a pessimistic view of humanity, where citizens have little role to play in democracy other than holding veto power 'when the decisions of officials pass certain bounds' (p. 542).

While many have criticised traditional journalism for its emphasis on routines – from the way news is gathered to the way it is presented – democratic elitism justifies this highly rationalised process through the efficiencies it produces. In important ways, rationalised news processes not only routinise news, but help reinforce the importance of dominant institutions, establishing order and efficiency. As Todd Gitlin notes, 'by going about their business in a professional way, [journalists] systematically frame the news to be compatible with the main institutional arrangements of the society' (1980: 269). Critics have attacked the idea of normalisation (see Bennett, 2003), but for elitists it remains a core ideal for realising the potential of democratic societies. Led by writers such as Lippmann (1922) and Bernays (1947), ideas about news and its role in society were transformed. In the words of Stuart Ewen, 'If news had once been understood as something out there, waiting to be covered, now it was seen as product to be manufactured, something designed and transmitted to bring about a visceral public response' (1996: 171).

In the end, the political theory of democratic elitism articulates an ethical framework between citizens and the institutional press. It justifies not only a strong institutional press and a strong cadre of journalists embedded in a professional class, but also what might be called an informed public – a group of people who are isolated and relatively inactive in civic life, but who are connected to each other through dominant institutions such as the press (Allen, 1995). And, as a result, democratic elitism instils within the press and journalists a responsibility to lead society in the right direction. It is this worldview upon which much of modern journalism is constructed.

Discourse democracy

While elitist theories struggle with ways to retain the notion of democracy, democratic theories that revolve around discourse offer an alternative framework. The goal of discourse theories of democracy is not replacing the work of citizens with institutions, but finding ways to allow those institutions to help create conditions in which discourse will thrive and prosper.

The idea that discourse is central to democratic life has enjoyed popularity of late, primarily with writers working in the tradition of Jürgen Habermas. However, the recent attention is less a new trajectory of political/ethical theory and more a rediscovery of ideas central to American pragmatist thought. Discourse – referred to generally as conversation or communication by many pragmatist thinkers – is seen as the primary way of tying society together. From the early pragmatists to the more recent writings of Habermas, the idea that individuals are the products of society is an idea shared by proponents of the discursive approach.

The importance of discourse to the idea of pragmatism can be traced back to Charles Peirce, who observed that reality was little more than what people – a community of inquirers – happened to agree on at a particular moment in time (Bernstein, 2010: 36; Peirce, 1972: 155). While Peirce was primarily concerned with putting forward a critique of science, the political implications of pragmatism were left to others, most prominently John Dewey (Festenstein, 1997: 21). But what would a democratic theory built on pragmatism – on the idea that there are many competing values and ideas that are equally good – look like? And how might that democratic theory shape the moral life of the individual, the community, and institutions within that community?

Dewey began with an idea about ethics and how to resolve conflicts within society. Rather than formulating a set of principles or laws to guide behaviour, Dewey sought an ethical life through the lived experience. The end that Dewey sought was self-realisation or growth of the individual, but this was not simply for the benefit of the individual. As Dewey noted, 'growth involves becoming responsible, that is, responsive, to the needs and claims of others' (as cited in Festenstein, 1997: 55). Found in Dewey's political theory is freedom for individuals to do what they would like, but that freedom is built on the larger ethical framework that individual actions ought to, in some way, benefit the larger common good. Giving individuals freedom encourages more public deliberation about the common good; democracy, therefore, is a community of critical inquiry. For Dewey, debate and participation in democratic society was vital, as it helped establish 'bonds of trust and sympathy' between individuals and their community (Festenstein, 1997: 88).

Habermas takes seriously the pragmatists' contributions to political theory. However, while many of the pragmatists offered their work as a critique of the work of Immanuel Kant, Habermas seeks to redeem Kantian philosophy. As a result, Richard Bernstein has labelled Habermas's work 'Kantian pragmatism' (2010: 168). Central to this move is Habermas's desire to retain from Kant the idea of universal standards; to get there, discourse becomes central. Continuing with the idea that individualism is created through and by society, Habermas sees the purpose of communicative action – a particular form of discourse – as a way of reaching understanding, not as a way of obtaining success in an argument (Habermas, 1989: 52). Habermas argues that inherent in any speech act is the recognition or acknowledgement that the two sides can come to an understanding or agreement. He argues that, unless two sides have that basic understanding, conversation would not take place; there would be no reason for people to enter into a discussion. Perhaps more importantly, Habermas believes he can link reason with communication. In discourse, Habermas contends, is the understanding that, through the logic of the best argument, consensus will be achieved (Habermas, 1981: 307). Habermas would agree with the pragmatists in seeing that there is a 'plurality of ethical orientations' to ideas about the good life (Habermas, 1981). However, he breaks from them by suggesting that moral norms are standards that can be applied to all people. It is in the search for moral norms where discourse plays a vital role for Habermas.

If deliberative citizenship is built on the notion that people enter discourse with a desire to use reason to attain a consensus, how is that consensus achieved, and what role does it play in ethical, deliberative citizenship? Part of the answer to that question lies in how citizens ought to interact with each other. Habermas's belief in the ability of people to reach understanding through communication is at the heart of two ideas that remain central to his project: the ideal speech situation and discourse ethics. For Habermas, the ideal speech situation is more or less taken for granted in the domain of discourse. It calls for allowing citizens to participate in discourse, letting citizens challenge and introduce new ideas based on their own values and beliefs, and doing so without compulsion (Solum, 1989: 96–7). As Thomas McCarthy explains, it is a goal that speakers seldom achieve but an assumption that is made 'whenever we enter into discourse with the intention of arriving at rational agreement about truth claims' (McCarthy, 1988: 309). Closely related to the ideal speech situation is Habermas's idea of discourse ethics. It is here that moral principles serve as a guide for interpreters and actors engaged in practical discourse. More importantly, it is through this discourse guided by these ethical standards that citizens go about turning particular (individual) interests into generalisable (universal) interests. The transformation of particular interests into generalisable interests follows the rules of discourse ethics. In short, discourse ethics will only consider a norm to be valid if all who would be affected have consented to it, after considering potential consequences and side effects, and if it is valid universally (Habermas, 1990).

While Habermas's ethical theory points the way to significant political/institutional reform, at its core is an often-overlooked call for citizens to approach public life and other citizens in a vastly different way. Democracy, in the end, ought to be less about domination and winning and more about the search for consensus and understanding that is central to democratic life.

Applying discourse democracy to journalistic practice

What role, then, does journalism play in achieving that discourse? Discourse democracy points journalistic practice in the direction of thinking about the role of journalism and journalists in promoting active citizens. While democratic elitism favours an informed public, discourse democracy favours an active citizenry. An active public has developed – or is in the process of developing – avenues that will make a sense of community a reality (Allen, 1995). Journalistic projects that follow a discourse model can lead to structural changes within the industry, perhaps best represented by the public or civic journalism movement in the United States. Such movements call for journalists to break away from traditional, elitist sources to discover what people are really thinking through tactics such as listening sessions and 'crowdsourcing'. At times, it is incumbent upon the press to take actions – such as aiding the formation of neighbourhood salons and community forums – that will promote discourse within the community (Charity, 1995). While journalists following the traditional, elitist function worry about breaking from standards of objectivity through such actions, discourse theory recognises the importance of finding ways to institutionally support the promotion of discourse.

But we would suggest that equally important to structural change is the ethical attitude that individual journalists bring to the work that they do. Underlying discourse theories are the belief in the fallibility of human beings in the search for truth and the need for citizens to remain open to new ideas. From Dewey's ideas about the development of character to Habermas's notions about seeking understanding, citizens are called on to be open to new ideas. Such an attitude challenges journalists – if not all citizens – to refrain from the hyper-politicised and opinionated discourse that dominates much of the media world today. As Habermas teaches us, the goal of public discourse is not winning or dominating; rather it is, or at least ought to be, understanding. The question, therefore, that discourse theory poses for journalism is this: how can the press and individual journalists help citizens work towards understanding?

Discourse theory challenges journalists to think less about what they do as providing an authoritative truth and instead to think about how they – and the institutions they work for – contribute to a discursive search for truth. This is not to say that journalism must surrender its information-providing function, but discourse theory recognises that providing information is merely a means to a much larger end: the end of creating an active public.

Communitarian democracy

Like the discourse approach, communitarianism as a theory of democracy arises at least in part from the work of the American pragmatist John Dewey. For Dewey, community is a – perhaps the – key element in democracy, and democracy 'is the idea of community life itself' (Dewey, 1927: 148). In his classic exploration of the connection between democracy and community, Dewey suggests that both individuals and their collective groups play a critical role:

> From the standpoint of the individual, [the democratic idea] consists in having a responsible share according to capacity in forming and directing the activities of the groups to which one belongs and in participating according to need in the values which the groups sustain. From the standpoint of the groups, it demands liberation of the potentialities of

> *members of a group in harmony with the interests and goods which are*
> *common. (p. 147)*

Finding the balance

More recent communitarians continue to explicate the connection between the individual and community, while maintaining that they are correcting the flaws of liberalism, at least as that philosophy has developed in the United States. Mary Ann Glendon has suggested that, both in its early formation and throughout its history, the United States adopted John Locke's view of liberalism – one that focuses almost entirely on the individual and individual rights – to the near-total exclusion of any sense of individual responsibility. She suggests that Americans should instead look to Rousseau, who, while outlining a conception of liberalism, focuses more on human interdependence and our inherent obligations to others (Glendon, 1991). Americans have taken the concept of individualism and individual rights – particularly property rights – to an extreme, Glendon suggests, leaving 'a near silence concerning responsibility, and a tendency to envision the rights-bearer as a lone autonomous individual' (p. 45).

The '[tilt] toward excessive individualism' of American culture and politics has led, communitarians suggest, to a belief that each person should be free to determine 'the good' for him- or herself (Etzioni, 1995: 21). This in turn diminishes individual obligation to both local communities and to the larger society. Communitarians' concern arises from what they see as the failure of both libertarian liberalism, which they argue has led to moral relativism, and welfare-state liberalism, which in their view has created individuals who have lost the need to care for themselves and thus any sense of their own responsibilities. As Thomas Spragens suggests, contemporary 'liberalism ... is divided into competing ideological wings and is largely divorced from its original moral culture' (1995: 42). The welfare state in twentieth-century Britain and the United States created entire classes of people dependent upon the government and societies complicit in the 'erosion of support for traditional conceptions of good conduct and personal responsibility' (Selznick, 2002: 9).

While modern communitarians are concerned with the erosion of personal responsibility arising from welfare liberalism, they reserve most of their criticism for libertarian liberalism. For Spragens (1995), libertarian (or free-market) liberalism today – at least as practised in the United

States – has perverted Locke's acknowledgement of what Spragens calls the importance of 'complementary obligations, deriving from communal attachments and responsibilities' and has elevated rights to entitlements to be protected by the state at all costs (p. 43). Clifford Christians notes that many communitarian scholars suggest that the 'doctrine of individual rights makes "the good" extrinsic', thus removing individuals from responsibility for their own lives (2006: 5, 16). Philip Selznick sees the result of modern libertarian thinking in the focus of the Reagan and Thatcher eras on market – rather than government or community – solutions to social problems in the United States and Britain, respectively. In both countries, he argues, government – and democratic philosophy – 'sounded a full retreat from social responsibility' (2002: 5).

In addition, the current libertarian conception of liberalism has disallowed a view of what constitutes morality or virtue, at least on a broad scale. We can see this clearly in philosophical and legal discussions regarding freedom of speech and press in the United States, which are based on Milton's and Mill's exhortations to protect all points of view, all voices, all perspectives, on the logic that over time the 'right' ones will prevail (Mill, 1863; Milton, 1644). This metaphorical 'marketplace of ideas' requires that government in all its forms be removed from discussion of what constitutes good and bad speech. For example, in a case determining whether burning an American flag is protected political speech, the US Supreme Court noted that 'if there is a bedrock principle underlying the First Amendment, it is that the Government may not prohibit the expression of an idea simply because society finds the idea itself offensive or disagreeable' (*Texas v. Johnson*, 1988: 414). While protection of 'offensive or disagreeable' (for their era) ideas defended the speech of civil rights (*Brown v. Louisiana*, 1966) and anti-war activists (*Cohen v. California*, 1971), it also led to a moral relativism where nearly any speech or opinion is considered worthy of protection, as in cases protecting neo-Nazi parades (*Collin v. Smith*, 1978) and Ku Klux Klan cross burnings (*Black v. Virginia*, 2003).

Communitarians acknowledge that free speech is important for the development of the individual and of society but remain concerned that free speech without a sense of responsibility will do more harm than good. Nevertheless, American communitarians seem unwilling to advocate legal sanctions against those who 'misuse' free speech and acknowledge that protection of minority viewpoints (be those viewpoints 'good' or 'bad') is necessary (Abramson and Bussiere, 1995). Rather than a government solution (limiting harmful speech), the onus is on society to encourage healthy speech. As Abramson and Bussiere explain, society should 'consider the social as well as private purposes of free speech and free press in a democracy' (1995: 222).

Communitarians have built a critique of modern liberalism, both in its welfare-state and libertarian formations. What remains is to determine the communitarian vision for society and how that vision gives rise to normative expectations of journalism ethics.

Community as a value

Clifford Christians (2006) succinctly summarises communitarianism's concept of community with the phrase 'humans-in-relation'. Within the framework of democratic philosophy, communitarians wish to find a balance between individual-rights-at-all-cost on one side and welfare-state dependency on the other; they want to find a way to honour both rights and responsibilities. Those balances, communitarians believe, can be achieved with a renewed focus on community, which in turn requires individuals to 'learn respect for others as well as self-respect; ... [to appreciate] our own rights and the rights of others; [to] develop the skills of self-government as well as the habit of governing ourselves, and learn to serve others – not just self' (Communitarian Network, 2010).

Even for communitarians, the term community is a bit amorphous. Community is not necessarily geographical or based on interests or shared values. Instead, community is a creation in progress, a space (for lack of a better word) in which citizens can join for the general purpose of creating a good, or moral, society in which each person has a say. Communitarians value a 'strong democracy' – to use Barber's term – valuing citizen participation and bottom-up policy-making (as much as is possible) over representative, top-down democracy (Barber, 1984). Communities should take into account the genuine needs of all members and should provide a locus for moral systems. While communitarians claim they do not want to dictate specific morality, they suggest that moral systems will have certain commonalities. The moral values of any community should be 'nondiscriminatory and applied equally to all members' and should be based 'on a common definition of justice'; in addition, these values 'must incorporate the full range of legitimate needs and values rather than focusing on any one category, be it individualism, autonomy, inter-personal caring or social justice' (Communitarian Network, 2010). Not all communities are moral, but all moral communities will value a responsible citizenry, and their values will withstand the scrutiny of those outside the community.

Communitarians walk a fine line between promoting the freedom of a community to decide its own values and suggesting that some values should be basic to all communities (see Etzioni, 2011). As Amitai Etzioni writes, 'No society can flourish without some shared formulation of the common good' (2004: 2). Even within today's libertarian–liberal political milieu, communitarians argue, Americans share some core values, such as human dignity, tolerance, peace, truth-telling, democracy, hard work, and individual responsibility (Communitarian Network, 2010).

Applying communitarian democracy to journalistic practice

In determining normative expectations of journalism ethics based on communitarian democracy, it is useful to examine those expectations for both individuals and for institutional journalism, recognising that there will be some overlap.

Individual journalists should, first and foremost, demonstrate a commitment to the values of the local community and the society at large (for American journalists, the general values are listed above). They can do this in a number of ways, both in their professional and personal lives. Story choice and treatment should be guided by values, though, of course, news stories should remain as accurate as possible. Journalists should treat their colleagues, sources, and community members with respect, doing their best to treat all as people of value. They should also be as transparent as possible and avoid harming individuals needlessly.

Under a communitarian perspective, the long-standing concept of objectivity would hold less value; journalists would be expected to be active and involved in the life of their communities, to participate in civic and religious organisations, schools, and so on. In addition, they should acknowledge this participation, which would allow them to report more richly on the community. Similarly, individual journalists should support the community and its values (assuming those values are healthy) but should avoid boosterism. Journalists should be free to constructively criticise local institutions, with the goal of assisting their ability to create community.

Normative expectations for the institution are similar. First and foremost, the news media should serve an educational function, helping citizens themselves create and communicate local and social values. The institution and its individual news organisations should offer clear descriptions of policy issues important to the community so that citizens have access to necessary facts. This would mean a lessened emphasis on gossip and meaningless minutiae. Instead, news media should focus on individual and collective responsibility. Additionally, they should provide space for citizen participation in news, through web forums, access to newspaper pages and airwaves, and a right of reply similar to the now defunct 'personal attack rule' of the US Federal Communications Commission.

Finally, news media organisations should be able and willing to take a stand against immoral activities and beliefs – those which go against the values of the community and the society. This, in particular, challenges the libertarian liberalism concept that all ideas should be heard. Under a communitarian concept, not all ideas are worthy of equal time and weight; not all perspectives are healthy and contribute to society. News media should operate like other social institutions in this way and consider this part of their core educational mission.

Communitarians, then, provide a foundation for morality and reject the 'moral relativism' they see in US culture today. Morality is found and defined primarily in community, and the role of the citizen is key in determining the values of the local and broader society. Journalists and their organisations are expected to contribute to the creation and care of those communities – in James Carey's words, to contribute to the 'maintenance of society in time ... [and] the representation of shared beliefs' (1989: 15).

Conclusion: The ethical challenge of multiple democracies

Any discussion of normative press ethics – what the responsibilities of the press and individual journalists should be – must first rest on an understanding of the role of the press within any particular society. In Western democracies, and specifically in the United States, the press has been granted substantial freedom to go about its business. That freedom, though, has been predicated on the press's perceived function in democracy – even though generally the US Supreme Court has been hesitant to hold the press legally accountable for violations of that function (see Hindman, 1997). While there seems to be general agreement that the press has a role in democracy, what one considers that role to be depends in important ways upon one's conception of democracy. Therefore, if we are to have a single normative conception of journalism ethics, we must first come to a common understanding of democracy itself.

We propose, however, that the goal of a single theoretical conception in a diverse society is not only unrealistic but also unnecessary. Instead, we argue that there is room for multiple conceptions of democracy along with multiple roles and responsibilities for journalism. The three theories we have outlined each suggest different purposes and, therefore, different expectations – expectations we believe can be served through a multiplicity of media forms.

First, under elitist conceptions, the press is fairly powerful; the people, on the other hand, are relatively passive in their civic lives but are connected through institutions like the media. In an elitist democracy, the news media can be expected to lead the public, to be a watchdog of the government, and to reinforce the importance of other dominant social institutions. We might assign this role to what some call the legacy media – national newspapers and broadcast networks and their various online partners – which would have both the tradition and resources to undertake this role.

Second, discourse approaches to democracy demonstrate a different view of journalism's purposes. Under discourse democracy, the press is expected to provide a space (literal or metaphorical) for citizens to deliberate thoughtfully and to come to consensus on important issues. In this view, citizens are more active, and the press acts, among other things, as a facilitator of democracy. This role might be fulfilled well by local-level news organisations, which should provide space for discussion of, and action upon, local policy issues.

Finally, communitarian democracy values a return to both individual and institutional responsibility and acknowledges the interconnectedness of society. Here, the press has a role in creating, articulating, and promoting common values, in part through journalists' (and their organisations') participation in their communities. Here we see a role for alternative news organisations – those directed towards specific populations or niche groups. Free from the constraints of objectivity and with the expectation of community involvement, communitarian journalists would, along with other citizens, participate in the creation and continuation of their communities (see Hindman, 1998).

While these theories of democracy share some key concepts (freedom of the press and the citizenry, for example) in relation to journalism ethics, they offer different conceptions of the good and different roles for the press to play in achieving that good. Having said that, this chapter is less concerned with advocating a particular theory. Instead, we suggest that the press does and ought to fill a variety of roles in society – roles that cannot be captured or linked to a particular theory of democracy. In doing so, we join with C. Edwin Baker, who has suggested that the press follows the normative path of what he calls 'complex democracy' where different types of media play different roles with different normative assumptions. As Baker argues, 'a common media serving society as a whole likely will not suffice' (2002: 148). 'Non-segmented' national media have the resources to challenge institutional power while also working towards agreement on the common good, and 'segmented' partisan media assist groups in achieving a fair distribution of social resources (Baker, 2002: 149).

Therefore, we argue that normative theories of the press rarely reflect an easy either/or choice made by an institution or an individual. An ethics guided by democratic theory requires journalists to think about their role in democracy, to understand their institutional place within the realisation of democracy, and to grasp what citizens need from those institutions. For some journalistic institutions, they can play no greater role than serving as a check on the powerful, allowing that information to secondarily be used as part of the democratic discourse within society. However, just as valuable to democracy is a press that is less concerned about fulfilling an elitist role and is more concerned about promoting discourse and community.

Journalistic ethics, examined through the lens of democratic theory, helps practitioners and citizens understand press responsibilities and roles. In addition to moving the examination of journalism ethics away from the individual, it ties journalistic practice to the realisation of democracy and to the varied roles that the press plays in that realisation.

Note

All web addresses in this chapter were last accessed in March 2013.

References

Abramson, Jeffrey, and Bussiere, Elizabeth (1995) 'Free Speech and Free Press: A Communitarian Perspective', in Amitai Etzioni (ed.), *New Communitarian Thinking: Persons, Virtues, Institutions, and Communities* (Charlottesville, VA: University Press of Virginia), 218–29.

Allen, David S. (1995) 'The Creation of an (In)active Public Sphere', in David S. Allen and Robert Jensen (eds), *Freeing the First Amendment* (New York: New York University Press), 93–113.

Allen, David S. (2005) *Democracy, Inc.: The Press and Law in the Corporate Rationalization of the Public Sphere* (Urbana, IL: University of Illinois Press).

Baker, C. Edwin (2002) *Media, Markets and Democracy* (Cambridge: Cambridge University Press).

Barber, Benjamin R. (1984) *Strong Democracy: Participatory Politics for a New Age* (Berkeley, CA: University of California Press).

Bennett, W. Lance (2003) *News: The Politics of Illusion* (5th edn, New York: Longman).

Bernays, Edward L. (1947) 'Engineering of Consent', *Annals of the American Academy of Political and Social Science*, 250(Mar.): 113–20.

Bernstein, Richard (2010) *The Pragmatic Turn* (Malden, MA: Polity Press).

Black v. Virginia (2003) 538 U.S. 343.

Blasi, Vincent (1977) 'The Checking Value in First Amendment Theory', *American Bar Foundation Research Journal*, 2(3): 521–649.

Brown v. Louisiana (1966) 383 U.S. 131.

Carey, James (1989) *Communication as Culture: Essays on Media and Society* (Boston: Unwin Hyman).

Charity, Arthur (1995) *Doing Public Journalism* (New York: Guilford Press).

Christians, Clifford (2006) 'Communitarianism: A Third Way', *Media Ethics*, 17 (2): 5, 16.

Christians, Clifford G., Glasser, Theodore L., McQuail, Denis, Nordenstreng, Kaarle, and White, Robert A. (2009) *Normative Theories of the Media: Journalism in Democratic Societies* (Urbana, IL: University of Illinois Press).

Cohen v. California (1971) 403 U.S. 15.

Collin v. Smith (1978) 7th Cir. 578 F. 2d 1197.

Commission on Freedom of the Press (1947) *A Free and Responsible Press* (Chicago: University of Chicago Press).

Communitarian Network (2010) *Responsive Communitarian Platform*: http://communitariannetwork.org/about-communitarianism/responsive-communitarian-platform.

Dewey, John (1927) *The Public and its Problems* (New York: Henry Holt & Co.).

Etzioni, Amitai (1995) 'Old Chestnuts and New Spurs', in Amitai Etzioni (ed.), *New Communitarian Thinking: Persons, Virtues, Institutions, and Communities* (Charlottesville, VA: University Press of Virginia), 16–36.

Etzioni, Amitai (2004) *The Common Good* (Malden, MA: Polity Press).

Etzioni, Amitai (2011) 'Should we Support Illiberal Religious Democracies?', *Political Quarterly*, 82(4): 567–73.

Ewen, Stuart (1996) *PR! A Social History of Spin* (New York: Basic Books).

Festenstein, Matthew (1997) *Pragmatism and Political Theory: From Dewey to Rorty* (Chicago: University of Chicago Press).

Gerald, J. Edward (1963) *The Social Responsibility Theory of the Press* (Minneapolis, MN: University of Minnesota Press).

Gitlin, Todd (1980) *The Whole World is Watching* (Berkeley, CA: University of California Press).

Glendon, Mary Ann (1991) *Rights Talk: The Impoverishment of Political Discourse* (New York: Free Press).

Habermas, Jürgen (1981) *The Theory of Communicative Action*, tr. Thomas McCarthy (Boston: Beacon Press), vol. 1.

Habermas, Jürgen (1989) *The Theory of Communicative Action*, tr. Thomas McCarthy (Boston: Beacon Press), vol. 2.

Habermas, Jürgen (1990) 'Morality and Ethical Life', in *Moral Consciousness and Communicative Action*, tr. Christian Lenhardt and Shierry Weber Nicholson (Cambridge, MA: MIT Press), 195–215.

Hallin, Daniel C., and Mancini, Paolo (2004) *Comparing Media Systems: Three Models of Media and Politics* (Cambridge: Cambridge University Press).

Held, David (1987) *Models of Democracy* (Stanford, CA: Stanford University Press).

Hindman, Elizabeth Blanks (1997) *Rights vs. Responsibilities: The Supreme Court and the Media* (Westport, CT: Greenwood Press).

Hindman, Elizabeth Blanks (1998) 'Community, Democracy, and Neighborhood News', *Journal of Communication*, 48(2): 27–39.

Hocking, William E. (1947) *Freedom of the Press: A Framework of Principle* (Chicago: University of Chicago Press).

Kalberg, Stephen (1980). 'Max Weber's Types of Rationality: Cornerstones for the Analysis of Rationalization Processes in History', *American Journal of Sociology*, 85: 1145–79.

Lippmann, Walter (1922) *Public Opinion* (New York: Free Press).

Margolis, Michael (1983) 'Democracy: American Style', in Graeme Duncan (ed.), *Democratic Theory and Practice* (Cambridge: Cambridge University Press), 115–32.

McCarthy, Thomas (1988) *The Critical Theory of Jürgen Habermas* (Cambridge, MA: MIT Press).

Mill, John Stuart (1863) *On Liberty* (Boston: Ticknor & Fields).

Milton, John (1644) *Areopagitica: A Speech for the Liberty of Unlicensed Printing to the Parliament of England*: www.gutenberg.org/catalog/world/readfile?fk_files=3273999.

Pateman, Carole (1970) *Participation and Democratic Theory* (Cambridge: Cambridge University Press).

Peirce, Charles (1972) 'Illustrations of the Logic of Science', in Edward C. Moore (ed.), *Charles S. Peirce: The Essential Writings* (New York: Harper & Row), 119–57.

Schumpeter, Joseph A. (1947) *Capitalism, Socialism, and Democracy* (2nd edn, New York: Harper & Brothers Publishers).

Selznick, Philip (2002) *The Communitarian Persuasion* (Washington, DC: Woodrow Wilson Center Press).

Siebert, Fredrick S., Peterson, Theodore, and Schramm, Wilbur (1956) *Four Theories of the Press* (Urbana, IL: University of Illinois Press).

Solum, Lawrence Byard (1989) 'Freedom of Communicative Action: A Theory of the First Amendment Freedom of Speech', *Northwestern Law Review*, 83(Fall/Winter): 54–135.

Spragens, Thomas A., Jr. (1995) 'Communitarian Liberalism', in Amitai Etzioni (ed.), *New Communitarian Thinking: Persons, Virtues, Institutions, and Communities* (Charlottesville, VA: University Press of Virginia), 37–51.

Texas v. Johnson (1988) 491 U.S. 397.

Weber, Max (1958) 'Science as a Vocation', in H. H. Gerth and C. Wright Mills (eds), *From Max Weber: Essays in Sociology* (New York: Oxford University Press), 129–56.

Part IV

Emerging Issues in a Global, Digital Age

13

Towards Knowledge-Centred Newswork: The Ethics of Newsroom Collaboration in the Digital Era

Yael de Haan, Annemarie Landman, and Jan Lauren Boyles

Professional journalists working within newsrooms have historically acted as one of society's autonomous manufacturers of knowledge (Kovach and Rosenstiel, 2010; Park, 1940). Such knowledge production is vital in that the dissemination of news meets the broader informational needs of civic society, enabling citizens to make informed decisions as part of democratic life (Carey, 1993; Gans, 2003). While this process of newsmaking appears straightforward on the surface, technological shifts have recently upended the traditional manner in which journalistic institutions operate in their service of the public. The entry of digital technology acts as one of the most significant factors changing the ethical practice of journalism today – a transition that both journalists and media organisations cannot ignore (Cassidy, 2007; Chung et al., 2007; Hermida, 2010, 2012; Witschge and Nygren, 2009). At the same time, structural changes in the media landscape (including media concentration, commercialisation, competition, and audience fragmentation) are demanding reconceptions of both news thinking and news working.

Because of these developments, modern newsworkers no longer serve as an absolute gatekeeper for the information that ultimately reaches audiences (Bruns, 2008; Gillmor, 2004). Social and citizen media content platforms now provide citizens the opportunity to gather information outside of traditional media (Ahmad, 2010; Hermida, 2012; Lasorsa, 2012; Mitchelstein and Boczkowski, 2009). This content, which includes submissions from Facebook and Twitter, is used not only by the audience to gather and spread information but is also employed by journalists to filter news and to assess a story's relative importance (Hermida, 2012; Lasorsa, 2012). Increasingly, news organisations are incorporating expertise from insightful crowds of citizens (Bruns, 2005, 2008, 2010; Gillmor, 2004; Robinson, 2011).

While the fruits of such emergent, collaborative newswork may yield rich returns, the act of audience engagement has created numerous ethical dilemmas relating to journalistic skills in the daily practice and newswork routines of craft practitioners. The speed by which user-generated content floods into the modern networked newsroom, for example, can challenge long-standing first principles of the craft, including ethical precepts of verification and accuracy (Bruno, 2011; Hermida, 2012; Lasorsa, 2012). This cyclical influx of digital citizen submissions also makes the task of distinguishing credible content more difficult for trained journalists. Additionally, this overload of external submissions by untrained news practitioners appears to diminish journalistic authority (de Haan, 2011).

Besides dilemmas relating to skills and ethics, new technologies have also had an effect on the structure of media organisations. Terms such as *multimediality* and *convergence* are increasingly seen as the solution to deal with the entry of digital technologies into the newsroom. However, potential collaboration between newsroom practitioners of various media platforms has also caused logistical and organisational drawbacks while, at the same time, raising new ethical questions (Achtenhagen and Raviola, 2009; Tameling and Broersma, 2013).

This chapter therefore examines how journalists are coping with two prominent challenges in newsrooms today – internal convergence and external collaboration – both of which have been precipitated by technological change and have subsequent consequences for journalism ethics. The chapter begins with a review of the literature, which articulates recent forces in media technology that have altered the broader media architecture – impacts that are subsequently metamorphosing day-to-day practitioner roles and duties. Next, as evidence of this claim, the chapter incorporates empirical findings, drawn from a survey and in-depth interviews with journalists in the Netherlands. The data illustrate the on-the-ground ethical struggles that newsworkers encounter as part of digital production. The chapter concludes with suggestions on how media practitioners can, perhaps, meet these challenges through adoption of knowledge-centred newswork – a conception that encourages open lines of engagement with informative audience members as well as with colleagues in the newsroom.

Theoretical overview

External collaboration

As a partial result of understaffed and overworked newsrooms, professional journalists have increasingly turned towards citizens in the process of news production. Particularly at the local level – where newsroom layoffs and buyouts have been the most dramatic – citizens can expand the organisation's ability to gather information during times of breaking news and beyond (St John and Johnson, 2012).

New media researcher Axel Bruns (2008: 215) heralds the promise of collaborative news production routines when he notes that 'broad, community based approaches to the mapping of knowledge ... are by necessity the only available tools for dealing with the vast bulk of the knowledge iceberg'. In our times, the 'knowledge iceberg' of networked data is ubiquitous: the current digital universe is estimated at 35 trillion gigabytes of raw inputs – a number likely to grow exponentially (Rainie and Wellman, 2012). With this explosion in big data, academics argue for 'new filtering routines that don't rely on forcing the ocean of information through one little kitchen strainer' (Weinberger, 2011: 12). Citizen contributors, therefore, forward bits of knowledge through converged mainstream channels primarily because the practice of journalism remains a resource-driven endeavour (Downie and Schudson, 2011).

Proponents of participatory journalism argue that its practice will broaden engagement in the once-insular process of professional news-making (Bruns, 2008; Gillmor, 2004; Paulussen and Ugille, 2008; Paulussen etal. 2008), while concurrently enhancing democratic discussion of news in the public sphere (Joyce, 2007; Lasica, 2003). However, prior research also demonstrates that professional news organisations are cautious in letting the public become co-authors of content because journalists believe that the quality of users' contributions does not comport with the deeply socialised ethical norms of journalistic objectivity and neutrality (Bakker and Paterson, 2011; Brants and de Haan, 2010; Mitchelstein and Boczkowski, 2009; Paulussen and Ugille, 2008;

Thurman, 2008). Underlying these reasons, journalists feel that audience engagement can challenge professional autonomy and authority (de Haan, 2011).

This co-production of newswork introduces further conundrums for journalists in their day-to-day work. Professional newsworkers must, increasingly, wade through citizen submissions. This task, in some cases, produces information overload (Hermida, 2012; Sakaki et al., 2010). Journalists must also carefully assess the credibility of such submissions – a time-consuming task (Castillo et al., 2011; Hermida, 2011; Lasorsa, 2012; Lewis et al., 2010; Muthukumaraswamy, 2010; Newman, 2009). As journalists must respond swiftly in today's accelerated 24-hour news cycle, the balance between being first and being accurate is once again challenged (Gowing, 2009; Hermida, 2011, 2012; Newman, 2009). In the end, while citizen contributions have the potential to open up journalism practice, the entry of user-generated content concurrently questions long-standing ethical principles of the journalistic craft.

Internal convergence

Scholars have shown that the emergence of digital technologies has not only influenced the news production process and journalists' professional skills, but it has also challenged current internal organisational structures. Concepts such as multimediality and convergence – both of which reference the organisational integration of journalistic production across platforms of print, broadcast, and online news – are now everyday parlance for news practitioners (Deuze, 2008; Mitchelstein and Boczkowski, 2009; Quinn, 2005). In fact, Deuze (2008) speaks of a 'convergence culture', which he defines as the ongoing merger of media enterprises as well as the unification of media production and consumption practices.

Prior research, which has sought to more clearly delineate this culture, has identified several positive externalities for journalists working in converged newsrooms. Some studies have argued that news practitioners' ability to publish content across platforms has allowed them to more easily migrate between media genres – a move that enables greater career mobility (Singer, 2004a). A journalist who used to write for a newspaper, for instance, can now become a television reporter, or vice versa. Other studies of converged media outlets have illustrated greater collegiality between competitors from other media (Deuze, 2004; Tameling and Broersma, 2012).

When the organisational integration of print, broadcast, and online activities is viewed through a business lens, convergence can be attractive to publishers and editorial managers. News leaders perceive that multi-skilled journalists can toil for a wider range of platforms, thereby augmenting the amount of news produced for the same or little additional cost. In this sense, convergence is often viewed as a cost-containment strategy; media organisations can trim expenses through increased worker productivity (Quinn, 2005).

While 'multi-skilling' may benefit the bottom line for the news organisation, the strategy also increases burdens placed upon individual newsworkers. With the pressure of an increasing workload due to multi-platform publishing, journalists have less time to search for stories. As a result, media practitioners spend more time behind their computers (Dupagne and Garrison, 2006; Tameling and Broersma, 2012). In addition, the stress of navigating news in the converged environment often forces journalists to sacrifice veracity for speed – even though accurately informing the audience has persisted as the primary ethical virtue of newswork among professional journalists (Deuze, 2004, 2008; Mitchelstein and Boczkowski, 2009; Singer, 2004b). Given these constraints, journalists say their work is less challenging and less creative (Deuze, 2004; Tameling and Broersma, 2012).

Prior research also indicates that the trend towards convergence has not been uniform across organisations, industries, and countries because of differences in merging old and new media logics (Deuze, 2008; Mitchelstein and Boczkowski, 2009; Tameling and Broersma, 2012). This trend towards convergence has thus not only challenged the organisational structure, but has also placed significant ethical constraints on reliability and source dependency. Nevertheless, a majority of scholars (as well as media professionals) is convinced that an integrated and convergent newsroom is the only way to deal with the entry of new technologies (Tameling and Broersma, 2012).

Clearly, journalists face a pair of challenges, both of which are wrought by technological advances that have disrupted the news industry. Externally, journalists are encountering obstacles to integrating raw materials from audience engagement. Internally, journalists are finding pressures to embrace multi-skilling in converged newsrooms. Consequently, these adaptations to daily practice, when taken together, are reshaping journalistic roles for the digital age.

Shifts in journalistic roles

New technologies are impacting journalists' daily practice at both the organisational and individual levels. These changes to daily newsgathering routines are forcing a re-examination of professional roles (McQuail, 2005; Weaver et al., 2006; Witschge and Nygren, 2009). As journalism became increasingly professionalised as an occupation, newsgatherers acquired shared notions of ethical conduct (Davis, 2010; Krause, 2011; Merrill, 1974; Ward, 2004). The adoption and persistence of the ethical precepts undergirding newswork fostered the legitimacy of journalism as a profession, including the adoption of journalistic roles (Davis, 2010; Krause, 2011; Shirky, 2008).

Scholars have identified four key roles that journalists hold: interpreters, disseminators, adversaries, and populist mobilisers (Johnstone et al., 1976; Weaver and Wilhoit, 1986; Weaver et al., 2006). Cross-cultural surveys of journalists' self-perceptions have revealed that most newsworkers subscribe first to the interpretative role, which gives broadest influence to investigating the validity of governmental claims, providing analysis and interpretation of complex problems, and discussing the implications of national policy. In close second, journalists cite their preferred role as disseminators, deeply valuing their ability to share information with the public quickly, to report factual information, and to provide entertainment (Cassidy, 2005; Deuze and Dimoudi, 2002; Weaver and Wilhoit, 1986; Weaver et al., 2006).

Yet migration towards internal convergence and external collaboration appears to be altering how journalists prioritise their duty to society (Cassidy, 2007; Deuze and Dimoudi, 2002; Deuze and Paulussen, 2002; Hermida, 2012; Weaver et al., 2006). According to Cassidy (2007), differences between online and traditional journalists' role conceptions can be explained by the fact that online news embodies a 24-hour process; online journalists, therefore, prioritise disseminating the news as quickly as possible. Scholars also contend that the activation of the public in news production stands as another significant reason for transitions in modern practitioner role conceptions (Bakker and Paterson, 2011; Boczkowski, 2004; Cassidy; 2007; Deuze and Paulussen, 2002; Hermida, 2012; Mitchelstein and Boczkowski, 2009; Paulussen and Ugille, 2008). Given the diminished centrality of journalists within the participatory media environment, Deuze and Paulussen (2002: 243) find that 'the more traditional [journalistic] roles, like gatekeeping and agenda-setting, are becoming less important'.

Examining journalistic practice: A Dutch case study

Both external and internal challenges, mainly instigated by technological shifts, seem to question journalists' professional roles. To better understand how new technologies are affecting the ethics of daily journalistic practice, an in-depth look at journalistic routines and journalistic attitudes is needed. To do this, we chose a case-study approach, which allows for a profound understanding of a media organisation (Gerring, 2007; Yin, 1989). One of the largest broadcasting organisations in the Netherlands provided the case. This particular organisation was chosen because it is a national news organisation that reaches a large audience on a daily basis through a variety of platforms. Moreover, like many others across Europe and North America, this particular organisation continuously struggles to respond to the digitisation process (Domingo, 2008; Singer, 2004a; Tameling and Broersma, 2013). The case thus brings forth numerous ethical debates and new ethical considerations that emerge as part of daily journalistic practice in the digital age. Finally, the editor-in-chief of the chosen organisation has a particular concern for the ethical dilemmas around technological innovation. Therefore, the case provided an opportunity to better understand the impacts of external collaboration and internal convergence upon daily journalistic practice.

Within this case study, we used two methods: a survey and in-depth interviews. The online survey provided an overall idea of how journalists are coping with specific online issues and to what extent new technological developments are influencing daily practices and ethical routines. Included were questions related to how journalists use online sources, how they relate to the public, how they perceive their professional roles, and how they approach internal collaboration. The survey instrument was fielded in December 2011. Out of the 120 journalists working for the news organisation, 110 participated in the survey, yielding a response rate of nearly 92%.

In addition, we conducted 17 interviews with journalists from different editorial desks, including the domestic news desk, economy news desk, internet news desk, and research news desk. These conversations enabled us to expand upon salient points from the survey data (Gubrium and Holstein, 2002). Topics encompassed in interviews included the use of online sources, the challenges of audience engagement, the features of multimedia newswork, the role of the organisation's website, the characteristics of the internet news desk, the nature of collaboration between editorial news desks, and the role conceptions of journalists.

Findings

The study's findings illustrate that the dual forces of internal convergence and external collaboration have led newsworkers to partner more closely with other journalists in the newsroom while, at the same time, incorporating citizen contributors into the process of news production. In short, journalism is no longer a closed profession of insular practitioners. Yet as journalistic practices become more open, additional constraints are being placed upon traditional journalistic skills and ethical principles – demands that are also producing changes in the organisational structure of newsrooms.

External collaboration: 'Balancing out' speed and source reliability

Journalists agreed that web-based sources of information have greatly assisted their reporting efforts as news practitioners. According to these newsworkers, user-generated content – particularly submissions sent via Twitter – can be particularly instructive in times of breaking news when journalists are monitoring events in real-time. In the survey, 81.5% of journalists say that online platforms enhance interactivity, making journalism more accessible for the public. More than half of those surveyed (63.1%) believe that the general public expects news organisations to be interactive. Overall, journalists agree that the role of the public as a journalistic source cannot be ignored and that user-generated content can be a valuable extra source of information.

Despite these largely positive opinions towards online engagement, journalists are grappling with the reliability and representativeness of their citizen-based sources, as well as how to interactively engage the audience. Social media use among journalists appears to be a double-edged sword.

While the information may help journalists better understand the landscape of a news event as it occurs, journalists in the study expressed several hesitations about engaging with Twitter and other citizen-driven platforms. News practitioners, in particular, questioned whether Tweets are truly representative of the larger population served. All journalists agreed that Twitter and other social media should only be consulted as an additional source of information. However, in daily practice, the speed with which news is generated obliges journalists to make quick decisions, many of which have ethical implications. As a result, journalists, particularly from the internet desk, do not always have time to check whether social media conversations represent a large body of opinion within the population or even whether the facts are correct.

The adoption of social media as a reporting tool among journalists seems to be uneven. Some newsroom opinion leaders use Twitter frequently and actively. But the majority of editors with whom we spoke view social media as an additional channel for engaging external sources, rather than as a conduit for disseminating information directly from individual journalists to the public. For internet journalists, in particular, restricted time and limited staff present a difficulty in starting an interactive and constructive dialogue through social media.

The final, and perhaps most crucial, dilemma centres upon using audience members as a reliable source of information. In an era when journalism's trustworthiness is increasingly questioned, established news organisations want to hold tightly to this first principle of ethics as an expression of quality. However, in the digital environment, the speed of information and increasingly fierce competition demands a faster production process, which does not sit easily with the trustworthiness of news. Within the newsroom, overall pressure exists to produce news as fast as possible. As an internet desk journalist said: 'We sometimes have no choice than to use Tweets because we have to go "live" every hour with something new.' However, journalists said they compensate by revealing the origin of the sources. 'As long as we tell the viewer that this information originates from Twitter, then the viewer is aware that the information might not be complete,' an interviewee said. 'But they are informed of what is being said.'

Differing ethical norms between television and internet journalists – a result of different temporal cycles of news production – create tension within the newsroom. Nevertheless, all interviewees agree that, in the digital era, the speed of news and the reliability of the news are not necessarily opposing factors. As a final editor said: 'Nowadays we cannot claim that trustworthiness is superior to the speed of news. That is very old-fashioned. Of course, we need to be as fast as possible to bring out the news. It is now a matter of balancing out.'

Despite the influx of user-generated content, journalists have not readily shifted their emphasis as gatekeepers of the news or as watchdogs of society. Nearly nine out of ten journalists surveyed (89%) value the democratic function of monitoring governmental affairs, while more than two-thirds (67%) emphasise that news should keep a watchful eye over industry. Of the journalists surveyed, 88% believe that reporters still have a key role to fill as interpreters and explainers of news. At the same time, nearly three-quarters of respondents (73.9%) prioritise the improvement of internal collaboration within the newsroom to be able to better fulfil their journalistic role.

Internal collaboration: From isolated islands to bundled expertise

While a vast majority of journalists surveyed agree that the digital era demands better collaboration between different news desks, they largely disagree as to how newswork can be better synthesised.

Disagreement is caused by differences in hierarchies, mindsets, and time pressures. The isolation of the internet desk (those primarily responsible for publishing news online) stands as a particularly salient informational bottleneck. In many cases, online journalists were initially sequestered into obscure corners of the newsroom. Yet even placing these employees centrally did not diminish the antagonism of other reporters, particularly television journalists – who were quite vocal in expressing dissatisfaction with the internet desk. Many television reporters perceived their web-based colleagues as mere processors of the news, lacking the specialisation to fully comprehend complex newsroom beats, such as economics or politics. (It should be noted that most internet desk employees included in this sample were young, entry-level hires without extensive experience in other media.) For instance, one television journalist said: 'The internet journalists have a more facilitating role. They are like a conveyor belt machine, producing articles non-stop.' Ironically, while television journalists would like more involvement from the internet journalists, too much interference is felt to hinder their work. A television journalist said 'It will also create problems if they [internet journalists] would all start to help us out and think with us.' This attitude came as no surprise to the internet journalists, who were aware that their television colleagues held negative conceptions of their work.

Such internal rancour can also be traced back to conflicting visions of what the news organisation's online presence should be. Of the journalists surveyed and interviewed, each had divergent ideas about the purpose of the news organisation's website. Some believed it should be a platform to circulate the latest news; others believed it should have a pure commercial purpose of attracting site visits; and still others believed it should complement news bulletins by providing additional, unique information. The journalists did agree on one thing, however: management had communicated hardly any vision regarding the organisation's online presence. As one journalist said: 'I don't even know what the management wants to achieve with this website.'

While employees within converged newsrooms are encouraged to tell time-sensitive stories across a myriad of platforms, the very speed of the news cycle may inhibit collaboration between newsroom employees. A television journalist said he always thinks of the internet desk when constructing pieces, but in practice, collaborating is not very easy: 'When I am working on a story, and I provide input for the website, they [the internet journalists] often finished that news story hours ago. In the meantime, they have written dozens of other stories. This makes it very difficult to work together.'

As a response, some news desks at the organisation have tried to force collaboration between desks, which are commonly referred to as 'islands'. For example, leaders of one newsroom desk asked internet journalists to rotate sitting at the domestic news department, so all newsgatherers could be more in the 'heat of the moment' where the news buzz is. Journalists of all platforms have reacted positively to this experiment. However, while this initiative creates more understanding of each other's work, it does not solve the underlying differences between news desks.

The accelerated pace of newsgathering within converged newsrooms also means that journalists must make split-second ethical decisions to incorporate content, often without thoroughly vetting the veracity of the raw material. Especially with the use of live blogs, many agree that being the first to report the story overrules possessing accurate information. Internet journalists did not express as many apprehensions on this matter; instead, they pointed to the ability to make quick corrections or

217

adjustments on the fly. Television journalists, on the other hand, do not have such easy opportunities for revisions once an error has been broadcast. As one television journalist said: 'What we air on prime time television just has to be correct. We just cannot afford to make any kind of mistakes.'

Even though news management is increasingly focused on building a 24/7 newsroom where the emphasis should be on the internet, in practice we found another story. Robust collaboration is hindered not only by the speed at which news is produced, but also by differences in hierarchy. Moreover, as one journalist made clear, 'We think fundamentally differently about journalism than our television colleagues,' referring to attitudes about ethical principles that relate to reliability, representativeness, and corrections. Conflicting mindsets and the current organisational structure still lead to many news desks working on their own islands.

Towards a notion of knowledge-centred newswork

News organisations are, by nature, conservative in their decision-making processes and often resistant to change (Lowrey, 2011) – particularly when different subgroups within an organisation cling to different work routines and standards (Lowrey, 2002). However, as a matter of survival, the forces of industry disruption are requiring innovative responses (Christensen et al., 2012). While cultural and structural impediments in the newsroom may currently limit robust levels of engagement both internally and externally, this research shows that journalists feel the need to adapt their work routines and look for forms of collaboration in order to adequately respond to changing news consumption.

As this research has shown, the turbulent and disruptive nature of the current media ecosystem – driven by shifts in technology – has forced the upending of several core characteristics of day-to-day journalistic practice, including newsgathering routines and roles. Yet, at the same time, journalists of the modern era have equally stressed the value of returning to the craft's first principles of ethics in times of chaos. The overwhelming majority of newsgatherers still see accuracy, in particular, as the ethical lodestar by which to orient their work. Yet the information overload of the digital age creates new ethical dilemmas within the newsroom, making the verification role and the employment of ethical tenets even more important. As Bill Kovach and Tom Rosenstiel contend, 'Since the press is no longer the only source of news, its authority must come from how it gathers and authenticates its facts' (2010: 185). And it is exactly this new information-gathering and authentication process that calls for more collaboration among the different groups of newsroom professionals and between newsroom professionals and the public.

Based on our research, we suggest that future collaboration should consist of two successive commitments. First, collaboration should focus on the internal structures of the newsroom. Before an organisation can deepen its engagement with the public, today's fast-changing media landscape demands that the organisation reshape its goals and vision. Argyris (1982) contends that double-loop learning is important when organisations have to make decisions in rapidly changing and uncertain contexts. These institutions must not merely readjust established working patterns; they must endeavour to holistically reconsider their goals, strategies, and learning systems. This shift requires not only a unified managerial vision (which is not currently the case in most newsrooms), but it also mandates a change in the mindset of journalists – a change aimed at greater acknowledgement and understanding.

Traditional journalists currently define ethical standards. And, as in many organisations, the dominant group often has a more significant role in the decision-making process (Bloor and Dawson, 1994). New, upcoming subcultures in organisations, such as online journalists, can seek several strategies. Either they conform to the established ethics or they seek legitimacy by creating their own standards (Bloor and Dawson, 1994; van Maanen and Barley, 1984). We propose a new strategy that contains a degree of cross-pollination, but does not require the fusion of a converged newsroom that can lead to new dilemmas (Tameling and Broersma, 2012). We suggest that, while working in their own expertise, online and established journalists should create more dialogue in which journalists can learn from each other and acknowledge that different working processes and ethical standards exist for different platforms. Such mutual understanding and acknowledgement can be a first step to a fruitful collaboration that is not forced. Similarly, research has shown that the increasing number of visual and graphic designers within newsrooms also demands more understanding, collaboration, and an integration of different norms in order to communicate with the public (Lowrey, 2002). However, increasing acknowledgement of different subcultures only works if the hierarchical differences are diminished, with a greater focus on each other's expertise. This reconsideration of journalistic practice can be the first step in moving away from news desks as separate islands.

Once the internal vision of the online strategy is set, and a majority is on the same page, external collaboration should then be stimulated. Because citizen contributors can openly collaborate with professional reporters working within newsrooms, the entry of user-generated content will likely further flatten the long-standing internal hierarchy of journalistic production (Bruns, 2005; Deuze, 2009). This emergent, less autonomous kind of journalism will reshape the mindsets of traditional journalists. Deeper engagement within narrow segments of an audience can be stimulated as journalists of all platforms labour together.

Collaborating with the public should, ideally, be a way to improve the newsgathering process. In this regard, knowledge-centred newswork differs from other conceptions of collaborative newsmaking in that the current model seeks to reach niche segments of the public who possess particular insights on the topic at hand. An example of such engagement lies in the Public Insight Network developed by American Public Media. News outlets in the United States can subscribe to the Network, which consists of a database of individuals who have self-identified (mainly via social media requests sent by the member news organisations) as bearing in-depth expertise on various subjects. In the heat of a deadline, journalists can file a query into the digital system and immediately locate expert members of the public with whom to speak, thereby building a more robust 'Rolodex of powerful sources' (Skoler, 2005: 20). This incorporation of a wider spectrum of voices into the reporting process could have significant impacts upon ethical debate in that newsmaking is no longer as insular a process. In the Netherlands, a similar case can be found at the public broadcaster NOS with its NOS Net. This database consists of a nationwide network of 'experts', such as teachers, police, nurses, and tenants, who can inform the news organisation on issues within the working and living environment (NOS, 2013). According to the editor-in-chief, the newsroom can use NOS Net to assess 'what people know and not so much what people think' (de Haan, 2011: 145).

Elements of knowledge-centred newswork also seem to exist within crowdsourced, data-driven journalism projects. For example, more than 20,000 users of the *Guardian's* website combed through 700,000 expense claims filed by members of parliament, identifying specific instances of financial mismanagement (Andersen, 2009; Weinberger, 2011). These collaborative experiments, however, do not mean that the authority of journalists is lost. Professional journalists should ultimately judge the selection, sourcing, and verification processes; they are still the ones ultimately making ethical judgements. But the public's more direct involvement in the newsmaking process means that journalists will likely be held to greater standards of transparency and ethical accountability.

These two tenets of support for more internal collaboration and external involvement could lead towards this structure of knowledge-centred newswork, if managerial leaders have a stake in its success. Here, the final objective is coping with the changing media landscape while improving journalistic quality and professional skills.

Conclusion

For news organisations, the emergence of internal convergence and external collaboration is creating uncertainties about the future of news and journalistic practices. At the same time, our research has revealed that journalism practitioners have not abdicated the central mission of newswork. Journalism today remains vitally integral to societal knowledge production, and the practice of accurate newsmaking can still largely be circumscribed around this function (Downie and Schudson, 2011; Gans, 2007; Kovach and Rosenstiel, 2010). In short, as media theorist James W. Carey (1997: 333) presciently advised, 'What unifies the practice [of journalism] across time, media, and organisations is its democratic context.' While the sovereignty of individual media institutions has greatly diminished, newsrooms – as the long-standing nexus of journalistic activity – still possess ample abilities to produce complex news products that would be arduous for non-institutional players to complete independently (Downie and Schudson, 2011; Kreiss et al., 2011).

Yet today's journalists no longer occupy their privileged position in the knowledge-production process; professional practitioners no longer autonomously transmit knowledge downwards from their place atop the knowledge hierarchy. Instead, without losing their professional authority, newsworkers must horizontally engage with informed citizens and their professional colleagues towards the ethical discovery of news within a networked world. In this regard, collectively navigating the emergent ethics of convergence and collaboration can ultimately strengthen journalism for the digital age. However, to move towards knowledge-centred newswork, two main challenges need to be overcome. First, the traditional professional autonomy and defensive attitude of professional journalists, which hinders a fruitful understanding of others' work – whether that of peers or citizens – must be confronted and tempered. Second, while speed and reliability might seem to be two journalistic values that contradict one another – what Witschge and Nygren (2009) identify as a disconnect between old and new media logic – our research shows that attempts must be made to balance and to reconcile these seemingly contradictory aspects of journalistic work. Therefore, although several informational, organisational, and cultural bottlenecks must still be surmounted, our research shows that journalism has reached a point where deeper engagement both internally and externally can positively reshape and improve newsworkers' work while simultaneously allowing them to hold onto their professional roles and commitments in the digital era.

Note

All web addresses in this chapter were last accessed in June 2013.

References

Achtenhagen, Leona, and Raviola, Elena (2009) 'Balancing Tensions during Convergence: Duality Management in a Newspaper Company', *International Journal on Media Management*, 11(1): 32–41.

Ahmad, Ali N. (2010) 'Is Twitter a Useful Tool for Journalists?', *Journal of Media Practice*, 11(2): 145–55.

Andersen, Michael (2009) 'Four Crowdsourcing Lessons from the *Guardian*'s (Spectacular) Expenses-Scandal Experiment', *Nieman Journalism Lab*, 23 June: www.niemanlab.org.

Argyris, Chris (1982) *Reasoning, Learning, and Action: Individual and Organizational* (San Francisco: Jossey-Bass).

Bakker, Tom, and Paterson, Chris (2011) 'The New Frontiers of Journalism: Citizen Participation in the United Kingdom and the Netherlands', in Kees Brants and Katrin Voltmer (eds), *Political Communication in Postmodern Democracy: Challenging the Primacy of Ethics* (Basingstoke: Palgrave Macmillan), 183–99.

Bloor, Geoffrey, and Dawson, Patrick (1994) 'Understanding Professional Culture in Organizational Context', *Organization Studies*, 15: 275–95.

Boczkowski, Pablo (2004) *Digitizing the News* (Cambridge, MA: MIT Press).

Brants, Kees, and de Haan, Yael de (2010) 'Taking the Public Seriously: Three Models of Responsiveness in Media and Journalism', *Media, Culture and Society*, 32(3): 411–28.

Bruno, Nicola (2011) *Tweet First, Verify Later? How Real-Time Information is Changing the Coverage of Worldwide Crisis Events* (Oxford: Reuters Institute for the Study of Journalism, University of Oxford): http://reutersinstitute. politics.ox.ac.uk.

Bruns, Axel (2005) *Gatewatching: Collaborative Online News Production* (New York: Peter Lang Press).

Bruns, Axel (2008) *Blogs, Wikipedia, Second Life, and Beyond: From Production to Produsage* (New York: Peter Lang Press).

Bruns, Axel (2010) 'News Produsage in a Pro-Am Mediasphere: Why Citizen Journalism Matters', in G. Meikle and G. Redden (eds), *News Online: Transformations and Continuities* (London: Palgrave Macmillan), 132–47.

Carey, James W. (1993) 'The Mass Media and Democracy: Between the Modern and the Postmodern', *Journal of International Affairs*, 47(1): 1–21.

Carey, James W. (1997) 'Afterword: The Culture in Question', in E. Munson and C. Warren (eds) *James Carey: A Critical Reader* (Minneapolis, MN: University of Minnesota Press), 308–40.

Cassidy, William P. (2005) 'Variations on a Theme: The Professional Role Conceptions of Print and Online Newspaper Journalists', *Journalism and Mass Communication Quarterly*, 82(2): 264–80.

Cassidy, William P. (2007) 'Online News Credibility: An Examination of the Perceptions of Newspaper Journalists', *Journal of Computer-Mediated Communication*, 12(2): 478–98.

Castillo, Carlos, Mendoza, Marcelo, and Poblete, Barbara (2011) 'Information Credibility on Twitter', paper at International World Wide Web Conference (WWW 2011).

Christensen, Clayton, Skok, David, and Allworth, James (2012) 'Breaking News: Mastering the Art of Disruptive Innovation in Journalism', *Nieman Reports*, 66(3): 6–20.

Chung, Deborah, S., Eunseong, Kim, Trammell, Kaye, D., and Porter, Lance, V. (2007) 'Uses and Perceptions of Blogs: A Report on Professional Journalists and Journalism Educators', *Journalism and Mass Communication Educator*, 62(3): 305–22.

Davis, Michael (2010) 'Why Journalism is a Profession', in Christopher Meyers (ed.), *Journalism Ethics: A Philosophical Approach* (Oxford: Oxford University Press), 91–102.

de Haan, Yael (2011) 'Between Professional Autonomy and Public Responsibility: Accountability and Responsiveness in Dutch Media and Journalism', PhD thesis, University of Amsterdam.

Deuze, Mark (2004) 'What is Multimedia Journalism?', *Journalism Studies*, 5(2): 139–52.

Deuze, Mark (2008) 'The Professional Identity of Journalists in the Context of Convergence Culture', *Observatorio (OBS*) Journal*, 7: 103–17.

Deuze, Mark (2009) 'The People Formerly Known as the Employers', *Journalism*, 10(3): 315–18.

Deuze, Mark, and Dimoudi, Christina (2002) 'Online Journalists in the Netherlands: Towards a Profile of a New Profession', *Journalism*, 3(1): 85–100.

Deuze, Mark, and Paulussen, Steve (2002) 'Research Note – Online Journalism in the Low Countries: Basic, Occupational and Professional Characteristics of Online Journalists in Flanders and the Netherlands', *European Journal of Communication*, 17(2): 237–45.

Domingo, David (2008) 'Interactivity in the Daily Routines of Online Newsrooms: Dealing with an Uncomfortable Myth', *Journal of Computer-Mediated Communication*, 13(3): 680–704.

Downie, Leonard, and Schudson, Michael (2011) 'The Reconstruction of American Journalism', in Robert McChesney and Victor Pickard (eds), *Will the Last Reporter Please Turn out the Lights: The Collapse of Journalism and What can be Done to Fix it* (New York: New Press), 55–90.

Dupagne, Michel, and Garrison, Bruce (2006) 'The Meaning and Influence of Convergence: A Qualitative Case Study of Newsroom Work at the Tampa News Center', *Journalism Studies*, 7(2): 237–55.

Gans, Herbert J. (2003) *Democracy and the News* (Oxford: Oxford University Press).

Gans, Herbert J. (2007) 'Everyday News, Newsworkers, and Professional Journalism', *Political Communication*, 24(2): 161–6.

Gerring, John (2007) *Case Study Research: Principles and Practices* (Cambridge: Cambridge University Press).

Gillmor, Dan (2004) *We the Media: Grassroots Journalism for the People, by the People* (Sebastopol, CA: O'Reilly Media).

Gowing, Nic (2009) *Skyful of Lies and Black Swans: The New Tyranny of Shifting Information Power in Crisis* (Oxford: Reuters Institute for the Study of Journalism, University of Oxford): http://reutersinstitute.politics.ox.ac.uk.

Gubrium, J. F., and Holstein, J. A. (eds) (2002) *Handbook of Interview Research: Context and Method* (Thousand Oaks, CA: Sage).

Hermida, Alfred (2010) 'From TV to Twitter: How Ambient News Became Ambient Journalism', *Media/Culture Journal*, 13(2).

Hermida, Alfred (2011) 'Tweets and Truth: Journalism as a Discipline of Collaborative Verification', paper at 'The Future of Journalism' conference, Sept., Cardiff University: www.caerdydd.ac.uk/jomec/resources/foj2011/foj 2011-Hermida.pdf.

Hermida, Alfred (2012) 'Social Journalism: Exploring How Social Media is Shaping Journalism', in Eugenia Siapera and Andreas Veglis (eds), *The Handbook of Global Online Journalism* (Chichester: John Wiley & Sons, Inc.), 309–28.

Johnstone, John W. C., Slawski, Edward, J., and Bowman, William, W. (1976) 'The Professional Values of American Newsmen', *Public Opinion Quarterly*, 36(4): 522–40.

Joyce, Mary (2007) 'The Citizen Journalism Web Site "OhmyNews" and the 2002 South Korean Presidential Election', *Berkman Center Research Publication*, 15: 2–21.

Kovach, Bill, and Rosenstiel, Tom (2010) *Blur: How to Know What's True in the Age of Information Overload* (New York: Bloomsbury).

Krause, Monika (2011) 'Reporting and the Transformations of the Journalistic Field: U.S. News Media, 1890–2000', *New Media and Society*, 33(1): 89–104.

Kreiss, Daniel, Finn, Megan, and Turner, Fred (2011) 'The Limits of Peer Production: Some Reminders from Max Weber for the Network Society', *New Media and Society*, 13(2): 243–59.

Lasica, J. D. (2003) 'Blogs and Journalism Need Each Other', *Nieman Reports*, 57(3): 70–4.

Lasorsa, Dominic (2012) 'Transparency and Other Journalistic Norms on Twitter', *Journalism Studies*, 13(2): 402–17.

Lewis, Seth, Kaufhold, Kelly, and Lasorsa, Dominic (2010) 'Thinking about Citizen Journalism: The Philosophical and Practical Challenges of User-Generated Content for Community Newspapers', *Journalism Practice*, 4(2): 163–79.

Lowrey, Wilson (2002) 'Word People vs. Picture People: Normative Differences and Strategies for Control over Work among Newsroom Subgroups', *Mass Communication & Society*, 5(4): 411–32.

Lowrey, Wilson (2011) 'Institutionalism, News Organizations and Innovation', *Journalism Studies*, 12(1): 64–79.

McQuail, Denis (2005) *McQuail's Mass Communication Theory* (London: Sage).

Merrill, John (1974) *The Imperative of Freedom: A Philosophy of Journalistic Autonomy* (New York: Communication Arts Books).

Mitchelstein, Eugenia, and Boczkowski, Pablo J. (2009) 'Between Tradition and Change: A Review of Recent Research on Online News Production', *Journalism*, 10(5): 562–86.

Muthukumaraswamy, Karthika (2010) 'When the Media Meet Crowds of Wisdom', *Journalism Practice*, 4(1): 48–65.

Newman, Nic (2009) *The Rise of Social Media and its Impact on Mainstream Journalism* (Oxford: Reuters Institute for the Study of Journalism, University of Oxford): http://reutersinstitute.politics.ox.ac.uk.

NOS (2013) *Dossier NOS Net*: http://nos.nl/dossier/128677-nos-net.

Park, Robert Ezra (1940) 'News as a Form of Knowledge: A Chapter in the Sociology of Knowledge', *American Journal of Sociology*, 45(5): 669–86.

Paulussen, Steve, and Ugille, Pieter (2008) 'User Generated Content in the Newsroom: Professional and Organisational Constraints on Participatory Journalism', *Westminster Papers in Communication and Culture*, 5(2): 24–41.

Paulussen, Steve, Heinonen, Ari, Domingo, David, and Quandt, Thorston (2007) 'Doing it Together: Citizen Participation in the Professional News Making Process', *Observatorio (OBS*) Journal*, 1(3): 131–54.

Quinn, Stephen (2005) 'Convergence's Fundamental Question', *Journalism Studies*, 6(1): 29–38.

Rainie, Lee, and Wellman, Barry (2012) *Networked: The New Social Operating System* (Cambridge, MA: MIT Press).

Robinson, Sue (2011) 'Journalism as Process: The Organizational Implications of Participatory Online News', *Journalism and Communication Monographs*, 13(3): 137–210.

Sakaki, Takeshi, Okazaki, Makoto, and Matsuo, Yutaka (2010) 'Earthquake Shakes Twitter Users: Real-Time Event Detection by Social Sensors', *Conference Proceedings: 19th International World Wide Web Conference (WWW 2010)* (New York: ACM Press), 851–60.

Shirky, Clay (2008) *Here Comes Everybody: The Power of Organizing without Organizations* (New York: Penguin Press).

Singer, Jane B. (2004a) 'More than Ink-Stained Wretches: The Resocialization of Print Journalists in Converged Newsroom', *Journalism and Mass Communication Quarterly*, 81(4): 838–56.

Singer, Jane B. (2004b) 'Strange Bedfellows: The Diffusion of Convergence in Four News Organizations', *Journalism Studies*, 5(1): 3–18.

Skoler, Michael (2005) 'Fear, Loathing and the Promise of Public Insight Journalism', *Nieman Reports*, 59(4): 20–2.

St John, Burton, and Johnson, Kirsten A. (2012) *News with a View: Essays on the Eclipse of Objectivity in Modern Journalism* (Jefferson, NC: McFarland & Co.).

Tameling, Klaske, and Broersma, Marcel (2012) 'Crossmediale dilemma's: De zoektocht naar convergentie bij Nederlandse nieuwsmedia', *Tijdschrift voor Communicatiewetenschap*, 40(3): 231–50.

Tameling, Klaske, and Broersma, Marcel (2013) 'De-converging the Newsroom: Strategies for Newsroom Change and their Influence on Journalism Practice', *International Communication Gazette*, 75(1): 19–34.

Thurman, Neil (2008) 'Forums for Citizen Journalists? Adoption of User Generated Content Initiatives by Online News Media', *New Media and Society*, 10(1): 139–57.

van Maanen, John, and Barley, Stephen. R. (1984) 'Occupational Communities: Culture and Control in Organizations', *Research in Organizational Behavior*, 6: 287–365.

Ward, Stephen (2004) *The Invention of Journalism Ethics: The Path to Objectivity and Beyond* (Montreal: McGill-Queen's University Press).

Weaver, David H., and Wilhoit, G. Cleveland (1986) *The American Journalist: A Portrait of U.S. News People and their Work* (Bloomington, IN: Indiana University Press).

Weaver, David, H., Beam, Randal, A., Brownlee, Bonnie, J., Voakes, Paul, S., and Wilhoit, G. Cleveland (2006) *The American Journalist in the 21st Century: U.S. News People at the Dawn of a New Millennium* (Mahwah, NJ: Lawrence Erlbaum).

Weinberger, David (2011) *Too Big to Know: Rethinking Knowledge Now that Facts aren't the Facts, Experts are Everywhere, and the Smartest Person in the Room is the Room* (New York: Basic Books).

Witschge, Tamara, and Nygren, Gunnar (2009) 'Journalism: A Profession under Pressure?', *Journal of Media Business Studies*, 6(1): 37–59.

Yin, Robert K. (1989) *Case Study Research: Design and Methods* (London: Sage), vol. 5.

14

Can the Ethics of the Fourth Estate Persevere in a Global Age?

Ejvind Hansen

Due to the development of transnational communicative and economic structures, nation states are increasingly unable to be the starting point for journalistic regulation. In this chapter, therefore, I raise the question of whether it is possible – and desirable – to have transnational rules for ethically good journalism. In order to answer that question, I take the classical distinction between deontological and consequentialist approaches as my starting point, arguing that the persistence of the distinction demonstrates that ethical considerations should be thought of in *both* deontological and consequentialist terms. In other words, ethical evaluations should focus upon the meeting between normative ideals and factual realities. This meeting is always up for debate because ideals can challenge reality, just as reality can challenge ideals. Ethical questions thus always raise a fundamental 'maybe'.

Traditionally, the ideals of journalists have been articulated in close affiliation with ideas of the Fourth Estate. However, due to our globalised communicative structure, this articulation is in need of revision. I argue that ethical demands change because the structure of internet-based publics changes: on one hand, the community structure of the internet fragments the publics; on the other hand, the socially and discursively weak agents become increasingly invisible. I suggest that journalistic products are ethically urgent insofar as they both bring communities together and give voice to the inarticulate or voiceless. I argue that in order to substantiate this approach, it is important to articulate rules because rules further the possibility of deliberating disagreements.

The notion of deliberating disagreement is at the core of ethical discussions. I suggest that Habermas's discourse ethics account may serve as a starting point for articulating a robust body of journalistic ethics. However, two moderations are important. First, the rules and codes should be articulated against a 'globalised we', rather than against the nation state. Second, it is important to realise that the rules do not robustly prescribe *what to do*. They should serve as a starting point for articulating and discussing *disagreements*. No interests, communities, or voices should per se be excluded, but that is not the same as arguing that we should accept every practice. The openness of the 'maybe' does not call for global agreement but rather for the possibility of discussing disagreements.

What does it mean to be ethical?

To be ethical means to act according to ethical norms. Norms for good journalism are, however, not necessarily ethical. For instance, in order to be a good journalist, it is important to be truthful, impartial, representative, critical, accurate, empathetic, skilful, and respectful of deadlines. But none of these norms are, by themselves, ethical. Consider this example. Certainly in most cases, it is ethically preferable to be truthful; however, we can think of instances in which the ethical value of truthfulness is – at least disputably – an open question. Most journalists agree, for example, that some notions of privacy trump the quest for truthfulness. Another example relates to the claim that journalists should be able to present complex issues in an accessible manner. It is an open question, however, whether this is a good (in the ethical sense) thing to do. Is it really a good thing that complex issues are simplified in the presentation? Is it even a good thing that the issues are made publicly accessible at all? In some respects, accessibility is a good thing; it helps less informed or less educated agents understand complex aspects of the world. We could also argue, however, that the accessibility may be ethically costly. In some cases, the accessibility of the presentation may delude readers, listeners, or viewers into thinking they understand the matter at hand and, in the light of this delusion, they start to have strong opinions about that issue. In some cases, it may be more desirable that we know about our *ignorance*, rather than being slightly informed, thinking we know the fundamentals.

In order to reflect upon the ethical value of journalism, then, it is certainly important to settle what it means to be ethical. The history of philosophy demonstrates that this is a complex issue. I will not go into details in this context, but since the eighteenth century it has been common to distinguish between deontological and consequentialist approaches (a third, virtue-based, approach will be discussed later in this chapter). As is widely recognised, classic representatives of the deontological position include Immanuel Kant (1785, 1788), Jürgen Habermas (1983), and John Rawls (1999). The consequentialist approach is represented by John Stuart Mill (1863) and Peter Singer (1993).

Deontological theorists claim that for acts or decisions to be ethically valuable, they need to be based on ethically valuable motives – whether or not we act according to our duties. Alternatively, consequentialist theorists claim that ethical value stems from the consequences of the acts. So, to take an example, if we are to assess the ethical value of work done by *News of the World* journalists from a deontological perspective, we must evaluate the motives of the employed journalists. From a consequentialist perspective, it is the outcomes of their practices that are most important. In this particular case, deontologists and consequentialists will probably not differ much in their final verdict; both the motives and the outcomes resulting from the phone hacking scandal were problematic. However, in other cases, we can see bad consequences stemming from good intentions, and good consequences in spite of less-than-flattering motives.

In itself, this distinction does not help us much in giving clear standards because the obvious next question is: what does it take for motives or consequences to be 'good'? The history of philosophy is crowded with varying accounts of how to answer this question. In certain respects, we can say that the main insight we have gained through philosophical discussions is that, to a large extent, a substantiation of the good will be dependent on culture-relative ideas and norms.

However, another insight can be gained from the persistence of the distinction between deontology and consequentialism. Neither can be refuted because they are, in a certain sense, both right. In order to articulate why certain motives are inherently good, we have to be able to show that they, at least *ceteris paribus*, lead to consequences that we find desirable. If it could be argued that a certain motive would inevitably lead to bad consequences, it would probably be difficult to defend it as morally good. Likewise, it is difficult to refute the deontological intuition that luck-based good consequences are of less moral value than good consequences that were intentionally reached.

Robert Nozick (1981: sect. 5) has sought to articulate this insight in a push–pull dialectics of ethical actions. On one hand, good actions need to be *pushed* by agents' awareness that good actions do lead to something desirable for me (good consequences); on the other hand, good actions also need to be *pulled* by an awareness of, and respect for, the value of the other as a unique individual (p. 454). Nozick's idea that the push has to be conceived in egoistically good consequences (what's in it for me) is probably too narrow; however, his articulation of the self-interested ego turns out to be less crude than it appears at first sight. According to Nozick, the self-interest that should motivate us to be ethically good is the interest in being of value for others (pp. 409ff.).

For the purpose of this chapter, the latter point is crucial: to be human – to act in the world – is never merely factual. The facticity of human lives is always embedded in values. We can (at least to some extent) choose to live worthless lives but, as ethical creatures, that is not value-neutral. Every human being and activity is thus situated at the crossroads between values and worldly affairs. Deontology's focus on motives highlights the values and ideals of the acting agents, while consequentialism's focus on outcomes highlights worldly affairs. Deontologists focus upon what is *sought* (having intentions means wanting to change something in the world), while consequentialists focus upon what is *actually* done. This is not to say that deontologists ignore reality and consequentialists ignore values and ideals. The point is merely that the dispute about what is primary in determining ethical value is futile.

Therefore, in order to assess the ethical value of practices, we need to evaluate the meeting between motives and consequences. In other words, the ethically good is defined by ideals and values (motives of the agents) in their meeting with reality (consequences). In order to have ethical values, it is necessary that we, on one hand, have ideas about how the world *ought* to be (values, motives for action). On the other hand, these motives cannot exist independently of how the world actually *is* (how the world 'reacts' to our actions – the consequences). Ethical evaluations have to happen at the meeting point of established ideals and experiences of goodness/justice (see Derrida, 1992, 1993).

Traditional journalistic values

What, then, are the established ideals of journalism? Good journalism is defined by reaching the goals of journalism. To decide the *ethical* value of journalism, one thus needs to take the reflection one step further: is it an ethically good thing to realise the goals of journalism? Often this reflection leads to affirmative answers by referring to the role of journalism as the Fourth Estate: journalism is ethically good because it enlightens citizens through critically investigated information. Hereby the citizens are empowered to act as competent political agents, and the political establishment is (to some extent) prevented from abusing its powers.

However, traditionally, the notion of the Fourth Estate has been closely linked with clearly defined democratic political nation states. The Fourth Estate is thought of as an informative and critical link between citizens and political decision-makers, both of which are defined in terms of a juridical set of rules that give citizens and political decision-makers certain rights, privileges, limitations, and obligations. The set of rules is conceived of as enforcing certain interests of the nation state and the individuals within it.

Therefore, the notion of the Fourth Estate is conceived in a context for which the reach of political jurisdictions is clearly defined; the nation state is the pervasive maximum horizon of political decisions. (Foreign policy is also defined as the management of national interests outside of the nation.) The role of the journalist is to keep an eye on the established powers of the nation state, and his or her ethical obligation is to empower the citizens of the nation state to act in competent ways. In order to make certain that the media live up to these ideals, media are given certain privileges (e.g. privileged access to events), but they are also regulated – or self-regulated – in various ways (e.g. the Canadian Broadcast Standards Council, the United Kingdom's Ofcom and Press Complaints Commission, Denmark's Press Council, and the United States' Federal Communications Commission and Federal Trade Commission).

Journalism was thus born as a regulated mediator between state-defined institutions and agents. This is, however, gradually changing. Informational, communicational, economic, and political powers increasingly travel across national borders – a development that is facilitated by the emergence of the internet and embodied in multinational companies and institutions like the World Trade Organization, the International

Monetary Fund, the World Bank, etc. (More elaborate accounts of the challenges of the nation state in relation to the public sphere can be found in Hansen, 2012.)

In relation to journalism, national mass media are challenged by competition from other, less nationally restricted communicative media. Due to their transnational capabilities, these media are not easily regulated through traditional legal means, and we cannot expect them to feel obliged towards Fourth Estate-oriented ideals in every country. Insofar as the transnational media are successful, the traditional media will thus be tempted to imitate the successful competitors – even though this may lead in directions that do not necessarily support citizen empowerment. And the identification of citizens with the nation state is, therefore, less self-evident.

New structures calling for revised values

We now arrive at the question of whether the idea of the Fourth Estate can be transferred to this new informational, economic, and political setting, given that the public of the media is less attached to specific political units. Is it possible, beyond the borders of nation states, to articulate *ethical* rules for regulation of media? If not, how then are we going to regulate media? Which norms will define what ethically good journalism in a transnational setting is?

To return to the above discussion about ethical value, one could say that the question of ethically good journalism is challenged insofar as journalism is now produced by media that are transnationally defined. Traditionally, however, ethical questions have been defined within national bodies, and ideals have reached towards the common good of the nation state. Good journalism was defined by facilitating a diverse and competent democratic public sphere in which urgent problems were dealt with, and citizens felt represented by the political establishment (Habermas, 1962, 1992). Even within the horizon of the nation state, this was not easily accomplished due to the diversity of citizen interests, but the *idea* of a common interest between the nation state and its citizens served as a normative standard that could be brought up in critiques of the prevailing journalistic practices. Discussants could disagree about what actually should be thought of as the common interest – political ideologies are mainly defined through such disagreements – but having pointed out certain public issues as those of common interest, it was not possible to claim that they should be ignored in public media.

In the new setting, however, it is less obvious what 'common' means. Who is the 'we' in a globalised communicative structure? Globalised communication does not mean that everybody communicates with everybody; in that case, the 'globalised we' would simply be everybody. Globalised communication is rather defined by a lack of *firm* boundaries. The globalised public sphere is characterised by multiple communities with clearly defined internal ideals, rules, and norms. But unlike the ideals, rules, and norms of the nation states, those of internet-based communities are not obliged towards inclusion of the weak, the poor, and the inarticulate. Internet-based publishers certainly have clearly defined ideals (based on target group analyses). Otherwise they would not be able to maintain an audience. Sometimes these ideals may be ethical in character, but structurally they are not necessarily so. Internet-based communities are not ethically responsible for the weak and the inarticulate. If you do not fit into the norms and ideals of a community, you will have to find another place to be. This is different in the communities of the nation states. If you do not fit into the norms and ideals of the nation state, you cannot merely go somewhere else; the political and administrative body of the nation state is forced to include you – in one way or another. What then do the social challenges of the shift from nation-state-based publics to informationally structured, global publics mean for the role of journalism?

In a situation where nation-based regulation of the public sphere seems to be challenged, a search for alternatives becomes urgent. Is it possible to frame communicative structures in ways that can facilitate fruitful and inclusive considerations?

Handling the ethical impasse

The situation today is that the old norms for good journalism are being gradually undermined and no clear alternatives are in sight. This is certainly a problem because ethical considerations thus become uncertain. However, in returning to the initial framing of this chapter, I will argue that there are also certain ethical gains in this uncertainty.

In answering the question of whether good journalism is a good thing, we have seen that this question only makes sense if it makes sense to have doubts about the answer. Ethical questions need to contemplate the dialectic relationship between our ethical ideals and the reality in which they are embodied. The ideals challenge reality, just as reality may sometimes challenge our ideals. Ethical questions are what make us uncertain about what we do. As soon as we are too certain about the ethical value of our work, we are wrong. In the case of journalism, the traditional nation-state-based narrative of the ethical value of journalism had become, in a certain sense, too strong; the Fourth Estate narrative had become established as a tradition with only narrow space for uncertainty.

Today, if we are to answer the question of whether good journalism is a good thing, we have to realise that the proper answer is: maybe. The maybe represents the typical frustration between philosophers and scientists on one hand and journalists on the other. The maybe is a weak qualifier in the journalistic argument analysis. However, this maybe is a very strong one. It urges journalists not to silence the voices of doubt through normative 'autopilots' that immunise journalists' practices against critique.

The uncertainty is, however, only fruitful if it is not situated in a complete vacuum. Just as ethical ideals that are too firm hinder a dialectical relationship, this relationship can also be hindered by a situation in which the globalisation of communication infrastructures leads to a situation with *no* journalistic norms (due to the external pressures).

In the previous sections, we saw that there are two main challenges to an internet-based public sphere. First is that there is no clearly defined common 'we'; internet-based communities can be quite self-contained, and it is not necessary to relate to other communities except when the participants find it pertinent. Second, care for weak and inarticulate voices is not certain; internet-based communities are not automatically ethically responsible for the weak and inarticulate. Not fitting into the norms and ideals of a community means you have to find another place to be. This is a marginalisation of weakness. The physically poor and weak are still visible; we see them in the streets, in the hospitals, in the nursing homes. Those who are virtually weak, however, tend to become invisible because, on the internet, you have no other existence than communicative existence.

I suggest that new approaches to journalism ethics should take this situation as its starting point. Journalistic products are ethically urgent insofar as they (a) bring communities together and (b) raise the voices of the inarticulate. After all, the ethical implications of social invisibility have been well articulated (see Couldry, 2010; Honneth, 2003). The task of ethical journalism should be to articulate and establish accounts of the 'globalised we'.

The main challenge with this account is substantiating it. What legitimises the journalistic account of the 'globalised we'? And what are the standards that ensure the journalistic account is relevant and adequate? The first step towards these answers is realising that the journalistic account can never be globally completed. Just as the ideals of the Fourth Estate were regulative ideals that could never be adequately met, an aim towards the 'globalised we' is essentially an ideal that cannot be actually completed. (I have elaborated the claim of essential journalistic inadequacies in Hansen, 2013.) The 'globalised we' should serve as an ideal that actual practices are measured against. Are journalists trying to connect, and succeeding in connecting, communities and raising the voices of the inarticulate? If yes, that is ethically praiseworthy.

However, this first step does not refute the objection that there are some communities and some voices that, according to common under-standing, should not be facilitated or raised in the public sphere. Examples could be communities or voices that infringe on privacy, distribute security-violating information, etc. This then calls for a second step in articulating the new ethics of journalism: according to which values should the selection happen? Is it possible to articulate culturally independent norms that could serve as guidelines for journalists in their concrete selection of relevant voices?

The need for 'rules'

In order to respond to these questions, I suggest that we return to the philosophical history of ethics. The distinction between consequentialist and deontological approaches focuses on action: consequentialism reflects upon the consequences of actions, while deontology investigates the 'why' of actions. Alternatively, virtue ethicists suggest that ethics should focus on the agent: an action is ethically right if it is what virtuous agents would do in the circumstances. A virtue is a character trait, and virtues are necessary in order for human beings to flourish or live well. (The classical formulation of virtue ethics was given by Aristotle, tr. and ed. 1976; in recent years, the most influential revitalisation of virtue ethics has been carried out by MacIntyre, 1981.)

In light of the complexities arising from the globalisation of communication, it would seem obvious to redirect ethical reflections from rules of action to virtues of character. The cultural, regional, structural, and religious variations in the world seem to make it impossible to articulate rules for action that take its complexities into account. In other words, the demands for ethical journalistic action in China are, in many respects, not comparable to the demands in South Africa, Denmark, or Colombia. Returning to the virtue ethics approach, one might expect that a focus upon the virtues of each individual journalist may reveal less cultural variation. Even though the journalist in China is situated differently than the journalist in South Africa, Denmark, or Colombia, it may be argued that they are all still ethically demanded to act justly, courageously, and honestly (see Thomas Bivins' chapter in this volume). I am, however, not convinced that the virtue ethics approach will entirely solve the challenges of global relativity. There are, in my mind, two problems with this approach.

First, virtues are not necessarily ethical. Take the example of courage. Intuitively, most of us would agree that it is a good thing to be a courageous journalist. But what does it mean to be a courageous journalist? Journalists like to refer to Bob Woodward and Carl Bernstein as paradigmatically courageous journalists who, together with courageous sources, uncovered information that led to the Watergate scandal. Following this narrative, we may say that the courage of Woodward and Bernstein led to the fall of something unethical, and courage is thus ethically praiseworthy. However, at other times, the ethical value of courage is less obvious. In editorial offices with strong Fourth Estate ideals, it would probably take quite a lot of social courage for individual journalists to accept bribery and produce journalistic products that are clearly 'purchased' by strong interest groups. In this case, most of us would probably agree that courage is not ethically praiseworthy because we sympathise more with the prevailing normativity rather than the courage to break with it. The point here is that virtues are only ethically praiseworthy if they serve interests that we praise ethically.

Second, the virtue ethics approach turns an ethical question into a personal question of investigating my own conscience. Certainly, as outsiders, we may praise Woodward and Bernstein for courage in the Watergate case, but maybe they were not actually driven by courage. What if they were driven by the desire for recognition and prestige? MacIntyre's revitalisation of virtue ethics is very conscious of the internal character of virtue ethics (MacIntyre, 1981: 258). Ethical questions cannot be reduced to internal evaluations of the relationship between my actions and the person I would like to be. The reflection upon what kind of person I would like to be – what are my virtues – may be part of my ethical self-reflections. But if these reflections are independent of my social existence – how my existence influences other human beings – they are no longer ethical. The social or worldly consequences of my virtuous character should be part of ethical reflections.

Ethical reflections or discussions must have a genuine critical impetus. In other words, ethical deliberations implicate reflections upon whether or not concrete actions or states of affairs are ethically valuable. However, with the virtue-based approach, such reflections tend to be individualised, and mutual critical exchanges become very difficult. I am not convinced that this is a satisfactory starting point for ethical reflections on journalism because practices can be immunised against critique if they focus solely on the virtues.

I suggest that a rules-based focus is necessary when we engage in mutual ethical evaluations of our actions – rules understood as prescriptive articulations of what it means to act ethically, but also rules understood as prescriptions that are challenged by the consequences that follow from the ethical efforts. This does not have to preclude the virtue focus, but virtues cannot stand as ethical landmarks without rules. Unlike virtues, rules are not necessarily internalist in focus. In addition, rules have two further advantages. First, the level of detail is higher in rules. Second, rules are *intrinsically* articulable. It is possible to act according to rules that are not actually articulated (e.g. when we follow rules unconsciously), but it does not make sense to claim the existence of rules if they cannot be articulated – at least subsequently.

The main challenge against rules-based ethics does, however, persist: the regional, cultural, and religious plurality of the world makes it difficult to reach consensus about the legitimacy of concrete ethical rules. As we have seen, however, virtue ethics are also challenged by this problem. Having accentuated the radical 'maybe' in ethical discussions, I will certainly not argue that journalists can have ethical rules that unequivocally prescribe what to do in concrete situations. That would entail the death of the 'maybe'. The gain of ethical rules is not their prescription of what to do, but rather that they are something we can argue about. Rules are fruitful for such discussions because of their intrinsic articulability and proficiency of detailing. This makes it possible to locate disagreements in the prevailing normativity, which is a fruitful starting point for deliberative exchanges and discussions. The problem with virtue ethics is that it is difficult to disagree that we should act justly, courageously, and honestly. The main disagreement often resides in defining what it means to do this.

In cases of disagreement about ethical evaluations of concrete actions, it is easier to locate the disagreements if the subject is well-defined. Do we disagree about the interpretation of the action (how the action is articulated and which ethical reflections follow from this articulation)? Are we discussing the relevance or proficiency of prevailing rules in relation to the action? Does the meeting between ethical ideals and worldly affairs call for new kinds of action or for new ethical rules?

Similar discussion can certainly take place in a virtue ethics approach, but the problem is that it is difficult to discuss the virtues as such. Is it actually possible (truly) to discuss whether we should be just, courageous, or honest? I think not. The discussion, therefore, ends in vaguely defined norms, and it becomes difficult to locate actual disagreements because, even though we seem to agree that we should be just, the disagreement may reside in the fact that our concepts of justice differ. Ethical discussions often have to take one step further to reveal *what kinds* of justice, courage, and honesty we endorse. And in this clarification we will, as argued above, have to refer to reflections on what kinds of actions and consequences would follow. And this will take us back to the rules-based starting point.

Rules for the 'globalised we'

In 'Force of Law' Derrida (1992: 17) argued that the founding question or aporia of ethical questions stem from the following problem:

> How are we to reconcile the act of justice that must always concern singularity, individuals, irreplaceable groups and lives, the other or myself as other, in a unique situation, with rule, norm, value or the imperative of justice?

Derrida's point is that singular, concrete acts are always in tension with articulated norms and rules because norms and rules need to be general, and thus abstract, whereas singular acts are concrete, manifold, diverse, etc. General norms and rules focus upon certain aspects – to the detriment of others – and the aporia of justice stems from the persistent question: are the normative rules just? Are they based on 'good' abstractions? Is it the 'important' aspects of reality that are highlighted in the rules? New concrete actions always challenge the rules because it may be that they embody or enlighten new important aspects of reality that were not thought of when articulating the prevailing rules.

The important point in our context is that rules are necessary because then we can have the dialectical reflection upon their possible failure. Without rules, there is no ethical 'maybe'. The rules constitute a *tension* between reality and ideals.

The question of how we substantiate the ethical task of articulating and establishing accounts of the 'globalised we' now becomes: what rules will help journalists act ethically in deciding what interests deserve to be brought to public attention and what interests do not? The archetypal ethical rule is the categorical imperative, which was initially formulated by Immanuel Kant (1785). It states that we should act only according to those maxims that can be willed as a universal law. The categorical imperative has since been challenged in many ways. As noted above, Habermas presented his own discourse ethics translation of the imperative: 'Only those norms can claim to be valid that meet (or could meet) with the approval of all affected in their capacity *as participants in a practical discourse*' (1990: 66; italics in the original).

In order to handle the challenges of the 'globalised we', it is important to realise that articulation of the rules can no longer be accomplished against the framework of the nation state. In a previous paper (Hansen, 2012), I have argued that rules for freedom of expression should be articulated independently of the nation state (because expressions travel across nation states), and a similar argument could be put forward in relation to journalism ethics: increasingly, journalists operate across borders; nationally framed ethical rules will not sufficiently cover all journalists.

National codes for good journalism thus no longer suffice. Initiatives that seek to unite ethical codes across national borders are, therefore, important. The International Federation of Journalists and its Ethical Journalism Initiative (http://ethicaljournalisminitiative.org) is one step in this direction, but it is largely thought of within the frame of the nation state; membership, for example, is primarily possible for national trade unions. An upcoming initiative that is more globally defined is the Center for International Media Ethics (www.cimethics.org), which gradually seems to be heading towards a global set of ethical guidelines for journalists.

Certainly, the level of detail in these approaches does not constitute a fully fledged ethics of journalism. As mentioned earlier, we need to articulate ways in which this radical notion of openness can be narrowed. And as noted in previous sections, some interests *should* be excluded; journalists should not, for example, further communicative infringements of privacy or distribute security-violating information. The point is that the challenge of narrowing should be articulated in rules, rules that are intrinsically disputable. I suggested previously that journalistic products are ethically urgent insofar as they both bring communities together and raise the voices of the inarticulate. Should these two endeavours also include those who distribute security-violating information or invade other agents' privacy or intimacy? It may be argued that they are excluded from the common we, and they are discursively weak and inarticulate (at least as public voices). Should journalists be willing to raise the voices of groups such as, for example, hacker communities or terrorist groups?

In the end, I would like to conclude by affirming the answer: yes, we *should* seek to bring such communities closer to mainstream publics by raising their voices. This doesn't mean we should support or legitimise the communities' practices; journalists should not, for example, help groups distribute harmful information. Rather we should make it possible for the communities to articulate their interests and desires. Being willing to raise the voices of discursively weak and inarticulate communities doesn't mean we should accept the views represented by such groups. Rather we should be ready to listen to their views and arguments – to challenge ourselves by the 'maybe' that they could articulate, but also to challenge back, arguing against their views. The point is that such discussions will be based on the openness of the ethical 'maybe', but the openness is not absolute; it happens in the dialectical meeting between normative ideals and factual realities. All sides of the discussions will have to demonstrate that their views lead to fruitful meetings.

It should be clear by now that the exact shape of the rules is not something that can be articulated in this context. In fact, for the argument posed, the exact shape is not even decisive. In order for the rules to reach something close to global consensus, it is certainly important that they have broad ethical appeal for journalists. But the main benefit of ethical rules is not that they are true or right. The main benefit is that we achieve a starting point for *disagreeing* – or to be more precise, a starting point for *discussing* disagreement. The rules will not give us ethical certainty; they will show us the impossibility of certainty. And that *uncertainty* is the necessary starting point for action.

Good journalists have to navigate within this paradox in their everyday practices. The traditional narrative has broken down, and we need to articulate new ones (Hansen, 2011, 2013). Journalists who actually understand the implications of this paradox – and the resulting 'maybe' – will never again be the same. But they will become better journalists. That is for certain.

Note

All web addresses in this chapter were last accessed in June 2013.

References

Aristotle (1976) *The Nicomachean Ethics*, tr. J. A. K. Thomson (Harmondsworth and New York: Penguin).

Couldry, Nick (2010) *Why Voice Matters: Culture and Politics After Neoliberalism* (Los Angeles and London: Sage).

Derrida, Jacques (1992) 'Force of Law: The "Mystical Foundation of Authority"', in D. Cornell, M. Rosenfeld, and D. Carlson (eds), *Deconstruction and the Possibility of Justice* (New York: Routledge), 3–67.

Derrida, Jacques (1993) *Spectres de Marx: L'état de la dette, le travail du deuil et la nouvelle internationale* (Paris: Galilée).

Habermas, Jürgen (1962) *Strukturwandel der Öffentlichkeit: Untersuchungen zu Einer Kategorie der Bürgerlichen Gesellschaft* (Frankfurt am Main: Suhrkamp).

Habermas, Jürgen (1983) 'Diskursethik: Notizen zu Einem Begründungs-programm', in *Moralbewusstsein und Kommunikatives Handeln* (Frankfurt am Main: Suhrkamp), 53–125.

Habermas, Jürgen (1990) 'Discourse Ethics: Notes on a Program of Philosophical Justification', in T. McCarthy (ed.), *Moral Consciousness and Communicative Action*, tr. C. Lenhardt and S. W. Nicholsen (Cambridge: Polity Press), 43–115.

Habermas, Jürgen (1992) *Faktizität und Geltung: Beiträge zur Diskurstheorie des Rechts und des Demokratischen Rechtsstaats* (Frankfurt am Main: Suhrkamp).

Hansen, Ejvind (2011) 'Den Dialog-udfordrende Journalist', in R. Buch (ed.), *Forandringens journalistic: 40 års tilbageblik* (Aarhus: Forlaget Ajour), 97–117.

Hansen, Ejvind (2012) 'Freedom of Expression in Distributed Networks', *tripleC – Cognition, Communication, Co-operation*, 10(2): 741–51.

Hansen, Ejvind (2013) 'Aporias of Digital Journalism', *Journalism: Theory, Practice and Criticism*, 14(5): 678–694.

Honneth, Axel (2003) 'Unsichtbarkeit: Über Die Moralische Epistemologie von "Anerkennung"', in *Unsichtbarkeit. Stationen einer Theorie der Intersubjektivität* (Frankfurt am Main: Suhrkamp), 10–27.

Kant, Immanuel (1785) *Grundlegung zur Metaphysik der Sitten* (Hamburg: Felix Meiner).

Kant, Immanuel (1788) *Kritik der Praktischen Vernunft* (Hamburg: Felix Meiner).

MacIntyre, Alasdair C. (1981) *After Virtue: A Study in Moral Theory* (Notre Dame, IN: University of Notre Dame Press).

Mill, John Stuart (1863) 'Utilitarianism', in G. Williams (ed.), *Utilitarianism, On Liberty, Considerations on Representative Government* (London: Everyman's Library), 1–67.

Nozick, Robert (1981) *Philosophical Explanations* (Cambridge, MA: Belknap Press of Harvard University Press).

Rawls, John (1999) *A Theory of Justice* (rev. edn, Cambridge, MA: Belknap Press of Harvard University Press).

Singer, Peter (1993) *Practical Ethics* (2nd edn, Cambridge: Cambridge University Press).

15

Ethics in the Age of the Solitary Journalist

Wendy N. Wyatt and Tom Clasen

As the central hub and the beating heart of news organisations everywhere, the newsroom has served as a defining feature of modern journalism. Open spaces buzzing with activity. Phones ringing. Keyboards clattering. Clocks ticking. Editors leaning over reporters' shoulders reading copy. Fluorescent lights shining down on empty coffee cups that have been pushed aside. Notes. Lots of notes. Organised chaos. The image has become almost cliché. Even people who have never stepped foot in a newsroom could describe one, thanks to depictions in film, television, and theatre.

But the newsroom is more than simply a physical site for newsmaking. It is the quintessential symbol of journalism and, therefore, also important in the ethical sense. A newsroom's behaviours constitute the ethical profile of the entire organisation or – if the case is high-profile enough – of the entire profession. Individual journalists may see the distinction between the ethically best and worst of their peers, but the public often does not. When it comes to issues of press responsibility and behaviour, it is the newsroom that the public almost always calls to account.

Despite its power as a site for newsmaking and as a symbol for ethical (or not) journalism, the newsroom is not inevitable. In the United States at least, the newsroom as we know it didn't emerge until the second half of the nineteenth century (Nerone and Barnhurst, 2003), and many indicators suggest that it may be on its way out. In an age when journalism is undergoing fundamental change, so, too, is the newsroom. Most observers of news media predict that the journalism of tomorrow will look much different than it does today. No one can perfectly predict what will endure and what will change, but many indications point to a diminishing role for what has been the embodiment – in the physical and ethical sense – of modern journalism.

So what happens when something so central to journalists', scholars', educators', and the public's conception of journalism goes away? More specifically, what happens to journalism ethics in an age when more and more journalists work in isolation? What is lost, and what may be gained? Those questions are the focus of this chapter. To address them, we consider how the newsroom – as both the locus for journalists' work and a powerful symbol of journalism itself – has affected journalism ethics. What we find is a complex newsroom culture that has brought with it both goods and harms. With the diminishment of the newsroom and the organisational culture it helped create, we argue that the challenge becomes one of holding onto the best parts of that culture while leaving behind those that inhibit ethical practice. In the end – and if we can get it right – journalism in a solitary age may allow not only for the maintenance of journalism ethics but for its enhancement.

Before addressing what may be to come if newsrooms are shuttered and journalists go it alone, we turn to the abundance of evidence that supports the emergence of a solitary age.

The dawn of a solitary age

The newsroom's decline has been much lamented. What Daniel Hallin (1994) referred to as the 'high modern' period of news culture in the United States, one in which the newsroom reached the pinnacle of its development, is being threatened by economics and by technology (Nerone and Barnhurst, 2003). The same is true in other Western countries. Newsrooms are getting smaller by the year, and while the figures are constantly evolving, the statistics provide some sense of what's happening to the size of newsrooms in the United States and United Kingdom.

By 2011, American newspaper newsrooms had lost 28% of their news professionals since the turn of the century (American Society of News Editors, 2012). One indication that the trend would continue came in 2013 when the *Chicago Sun-Times* laid off its entire photojournalism staff, announcing that it would rely on freelancers and reporters. Television news has experienced a similar trend; in 2012, staff sizes at the three US network newsrooms were less than half the size they were in the 1980s

(Project for Excellence in Journalism, 2012). US news magazines have also shed large numbers of newsroom jobs. For example, as of 2011, *Time* magazine had cut staff positions every year since 2005 (Israely, 2011). In radio, even as the number of all-news stations has increased, the trend towards more syndicated programming has meant less local staff. The only bright spot in legacy US newsrooms seems to be in local TV news where median staff size has remained constant during the last five years (Project for Excellence in Journalism, 2012).

In the United Kingdom, in late 2011, the National Union for Journalists was fighting to defend up to 300 journalists' jobs, including 100 at *The Times* and *Sunday Times*, between 60 and 80 at the *Guardian*, up to 20 at the *Independent* and the *Evening Standard*, and more than 20 at Thomson Reuters (*The Journalist*, 2011–12). The beginning of 2012 brought further news of downsizing. The *Daily Telegraph* and *Sunday Telegraph* cut 30 jobs (Greenslade, 2012a), and Trinity Mirror made 75 cuts that amounted to 19% of its editorial workforce (Greenslade, 2012b).

How, then, are legacy news organisations filling their pages, broadcasts, and websites? One way is through outsourcing. This, in fact, was offered as the top trend to watch at the 2012 International Newsroom Summit sponsored by the World Association of Newspapers and News Publishers. According to Erik Bjerager, World Editors Forum president, 'Well-paid journalists in old media are frequently exchanged for freelancers or external content companies with lower costs' (World Association of Newspaper Publishers, 2012). Journatic is an example of one such company. Before a scandal erupted over fabricated bylines, it provided content to the *Houston Chronicle*, *San Francisco Chronicle*, *Chicago Sun-Times*, *Chicago Tribune*, and *Newsday* (Wasserman, 2012).

Speakers at the newsroom summit weren't the first to predict a future dominated by outsourcing. A 2009 issue of *American Journalism Review* warned journalists that if they weren't already working in a free-agency economy, they soon could be (Macy, 2099). Each year, through buyouts and layoffs, large numbers of journalists are finding themselves with a new description on their business cards: work for hire.

When journalists do manage to hold onto their jobs, they often find themselves working in far different environments than what the traditional newsroom provided. In the UK, journalists at the *Independent*, *i*, the *Independent on Sunday,* and the *Evening Standard*, all owned by Alexander Lebedev, received an email in June 2012 announcing that some would begin working from home. This resulted from a plan to consolidate the four titles onto a single floor in rented office space (Greenslade, 2012c).

Other journalists who still come to the office find themselves operating as 'one-person newsrooms'. What used to be an endeavour undertaken by teams of reporters, photographers, and editors has become a solitary enterprise. TV organisations, for example, are using more 'backpack' journalists who report, write, shoot, and edit their own stories. Small TV stations have been doing this for years, but the practice has now expanded to larger organisations as well. In 2011, more than 15% of large-market newsrooms in the US reported that they mostly rely on sojos – solo journalists (Project for Excellence in Journalism, 2012). Even American news networks have adopted the practice for foreign bureaux. In late 2007, ABC dispatched seven correspondents to form solo bureaux in different countries, a practice used by newspapers with their foreign bureaux even prior to the digital age. As of January 2011, this allowed the network to have an editorial presence – even if that presence means one person – in 19 cities around the world (Kumar, 2010–11).

Beyond TV, journalists working in other formats are being asked to go it alone, juggling most duties that used to require a team, as well as new duties such as blogging, posting to social networking sites, and filing stories on the web. When John Schwada, a former Los Angeles political reporter, visited students from the University of Southern California (USC) specialised graduate programme in convergent journalism, he commented on the 'alone-ness' of the new journalists. Most of them don't see themselves working in a traditional newsroom or having a regular editor (Schwada, 2011). Schwada is himself a victim of cutbacks; after 15 years at his station, he was let go in 2011 when the station wanted to find someone more versatile.

Many students from USC will likely find themselves joining colleagues who have left legacy organisations to work for web-based news sites that have never known a traditional newsroom. A number of successful sites such as MinnPost.com have small staffs of reporters, most of whom built their reputations at legacy organisations. But at MinnPost, the newsroom is all but non-existent and much of the website's material comes from freelancers (Singer, 2010a). Dozens of other entrepreneurial enterprises share these characteristics – whether they are small sites with one or two full-time employees and a hyper-local focus (AOL's Patch sites) or large and influential sites with an international reach (Huffington

Post or Worldcrunch). In all of these models, journalists' work is done in a largely solitary way.

All of this evidence suggests that journalists are already beginning to experience a fundamental shift in the way their work life is structured. To consider the ethical implications of this shift, we turn next to newsroom influences that will likely diminish or disappear altogether and consider whether those changes should be mourned or welcomed.

The newsroom as moral compass

The newsroom is a complex and contradictory environment. It's a place where professionals who value independence and autonomy as core principles are subject to significant socialisation effects. It's a place that allows for attachment in a professional life dominated by detachment. And it's a place that has been simultaneously praised for fostering behaviour that makes journalists and the public proud but also condemned for creating a culture that encourages unethical behaviour or looks the other way when it happens. The significant body of literature on newsroom sociology has examined in detail the influences that have accumulated over time 'as layers of practices and ideals from different formations have sedimented on top of each other' (Nerone and Barnhurst, 2003: 436). Yet, taken as a whole, that literature stops short of making a conclusive judgement about whether the newsroom is beneficial or harmful to journalism ethics.

What we do know is that, in the American context at least, the newsroom has played a central role in creating journalists' professional identities – enabling them to claim an 'exclusive social status and role' (Deuze cited in Singer, 2010a: 128) – and it has been crucial in informing their ethical values, their commitments, and their behaviours. The newsroom has affected not only the ways in which journalists make hard decisions about difficult ethical dilemmas but also the ways in which they go about their everyday work.

In all three of David Weaver and Cleveland Wilhoit's seminal studies of American journalists – conducted in 1982, 1992, and 2002 – the authors found that newsroom learning was an important influence on journalists' ethics. In fact, it consistently topped the list with between 82 and 88% of journalists in each study claiming that newsroom learning was an influence (Weaver et al., 2007). Other influences were family upbringing, co-workers, and senior editors, reporters, and directors. When the authors examined four groups of influences – newsroom context, family and religion, continuing education, and college experiences – the newsroom context cluster emerged as the most powerful set of factors influencing journalists' ethics.

And the learning that happens in the newsroom frequently seems to be the 'right' kind of learning in terms of ethics. As much as some critics relish claiming that journalism ethics is an oxymoron, Lee Wilkins and Renita Coleman have discovered otherwise. In their study of journalists' moral development, Wilkins and Coleman found that, while ethical lapses do occur, they are 'more than counterweighted by good decisions made daily by reporters and editors' (2005a: 52). Of course, the journalists who have fabricated and plagiarised stories or those who have hacked people's phones gain the notoriety, but we tend to forget about all the journalists making good decisions and doing ethically justifiable work everyday.

Wilkins and Coleman (2005b) used the defining issues test (DIT) to measure journalists' moral development and found that only philosophers, seminarians, and medical students and doctors scored higher. Below journalists were, among others, lawyers, graduate and undergraduate students, business professionals, and adults in general. Journalists did well not only on the paper and pencil test but were also able to balance competing values, anticipate harms and goods, and consider their duties to multiple stakeholders. One caveat is important here: moral development measures ethical reasoning, not ethical behaviour. It's possible that someone could think one way and act another, but strong moral reasoning skills certainly enable strongly ethical behaviour. Journalists' reasoning skills, which are developed in important ways by what happens in the newsroom, should enable journalists to act in ethically praiseworthy ways. Certainly, then, if the newsroom goes away, an important influence on ethics would also go away, and this has the potential to jeopardise journalists' moral development.

We think that a lost newsroom, leading to a potentially solitary work life, would also mean other losses for journalism ethics. Although autonomy and independence are hallmarks of the Western journalism tradition, we are not convinced by the existentialist claim that journalists should be driven by authentic selfhood (see Merrill, 1994). Just as no man or woman stands alone, no journalist stands alone. The African concept *ubuntu* can be loosely translated into 'I am because of others', and journalists certainly *are* because of other journalists. In fact, as Cliff

Christians et al. (2012) have argued, our relationships with others define the good and shape our ethical problem-solving. Moral agency comes from these relationships, and newsrooms have served as important spaces that allow journalists to develop their relationships with each other and, subsequently, their socially constructed identities as journalists.

What do these newsroom-enabled relationships yield? First is a sense of solidarity and shared purpose. Newsroom colleagues are comrades – brothers- and sisters-in-arms. They are people who share the same moral commitments and who, through those commitments, have taken up the identity 'journalist'. As Sandy Borden and Chad Tew have argued, lots of people are capable of 'snapping good pictures, checking facts and telling good stories', but journalists have intention; they have committed to the role of journalist – committed to 'living' and 'being' a journalist – not only to doing the job of journalism (2007: 301). The *Washington Post*'s Judy Mann went so far as to say that 'the business and what it stands for is, to many of us, about as close as we come to having a religion' (1981: B1).

Being a journalist means acting in ways that align with the profession's moral narrative. This narrative comes in part from the profession itself – the institutional culture of journalism (Weaver et al., 2007) – but far more important is the organisational culture of the newsroom. This moral narrative is shared through mentors and role models in the newsroom. From an Aristotelian perspective, these moral heroes are the bearers of tradition who, through their actions, help others develop virtuous characters. When a newsroom has a strong role model – or a number of them – it can serve as an incubator for journalists who exhibit traits of honesty, courage, compassion, fairness, and trustworthiness.

The newsroom, then, creates an all-important discursive community within itself. From a Habermasian perspective, engagement with others is essential to the moral life (see e.g. Habermas, 1990). One person's – in our case, one journalist's – perspective is necessarily limited. Therefore, ethics must not be done in isolation. The best way forward is to seek out the ideas, insights, and opinions of others, and the newsroom provides an intentional space, 'a centre of moral attention' (Christians et al., 2012: ix) for discourse that can inform decision-making and action.

Much in the literature supports the claim that newsrooms provide an important discursive community. Although journalists have at their disposal codes of ethics and other documents to help guide their ethical behaviour, Weaver and his co-authors, together with other scholars, contend that journalists 'receive far more effective guidance through personal conversations than through documents' (2007: 162; see also Battistoli, 2008; Hill-Wagner, 2007). These personal conversations can involve everything from sharing cautionary tales to collectively grappling with a dilemma for which no precedent exists.

The newsroom community has also served a self-policing function. Multiple levels of oversight in the newsroom – both formal and informal – help keep journalists honest. John Long, ethics chairman for the National Association of Press Photographers, suggested that peer pressure is a valuable asset:

> If you are a staff of one (or a freelancer), you have no one looking over your shoulder ... If you look at some of the great falls from grace over the past years, you can see how many of the major ethical blow-ups came from photographers who were working in isolation, or freelancing, or both. (2012: 20)

While the newsroom polices the members of its community, it simultaneously provides them with protection. Journalists who do the right thing in the face of pressure to act otherwise can find supporters, defenders, and advocates in their newsroom colleagues. Sometimes the defence is a public one, which may extend to formal legal protections, but more often it happens within the walls of a newsroom where journalists get private support and encouragement.

Finally, the newsroom community has provided a place for journalists to let off steam and to relieve pressure. This was first noted by Herbert Gans in his seminal study of *CBS Evening News*, *NBC Nightly News*, *Newsweek*, and *Time*, when he observed journalists voicing their strong opinions about issues 'they can neither express in their stories nor keep bottled up inside' (1979: 187). For a profession whose work is done largely in the glare of the public, newsrooms – many of which are protected by a security guard in the lobby – provide a backstage space where journalists can let down their guard and be themselves among a community of peers.

The dark side of newsroom culture

Much of the discussion above is based on a discursive newsroom community that creates and develops journalists with strong moral compasses. That argument, however, hinges on a key assumption: that the community itself is an ethically robust one. The literature shows that there is more than one side to the story of newsroom culture. For all of the benefits newsrooms can bring to journalism ethics, there is an equal – perhaps even greater – number of harms. Before we mourn the decline of the newsroom and paint a bleak picture of journalism ethics in the solitary age, the darker side of newsroom culture must be considered. The departure of the newsroom may, in fact, mark the departure of much that was detrimental to ethical journalism.

We have argued that newsrooms are a key site for constructing journalists' identities and cultivating their values, commitments, and behaviours. The potential is certainly there for newsrooms to serve as strongly positive socialising influences. However, a good deal of the literature portrays newsrooms as ethically bankrupt spaces.

Multiple studies have found that newsroom culture is among the most defensive of any industry (Briggs, 2012). Newsrooms tend to be autocratic, hierarchical, aggressive, power- and status-driven, competitive, and slow to change (Everbach, 2006). 'People working in newsrooms have long enjoyed the luxury of thinking their business was different from other businesses' (Briggs, 2012: 21), and this attitude has served to effectively shut off journalists from the public they purport to serve. Nearly all of journalists' working relationships have tended to be with sources and colleagues, and 'actual readers or viewers [have] rarely touched the working lives of most journalists' (Singer, 2010b: 95). In fact, some scholars claim that newsrooms don't only isolate journalists from the public, they actually foster a disdain for that public. As John Pauly noted, 'the profession's contempt for the public it rhetorically reveres can be stunning' (2009: 21).

This attitude is clearly troubling, and it doesn't bode well for journalism ethics. As James Carey described, a bond between the press and the public has been central to journalism's guiding philosophy:

> *The god term of journalism – the be-all and end-all, the term without which the entire enterprise fails to make sense – is the public. Insofar as journalism is grounded, it is grounded in the public. Insofar as journalism has a client, the client is the public. The press justifies itself in the name of the public: It exists – or so it is regularly said – to inform the public, to serve as the extended eyes and ears of the public, to protect the public's right to know, to serve the public. The canons of journalism*

> *originate in and flow from the relationship of the press to the public. The*
> *public is totem and talisman, and an object of ritual homage. (1987: 5)*

What we see, then, is a disconnect between theory and practice. Instead of journalists adopting a view that they exist to serve the public, they learn to see the world outside the newsroom 'as existing only to feed their needs inside the newsroom' (Patterson and Urbanski, 2006: 843).

The theory/practice divide isn't only illustrated through attitudes about the public. We can see another example of the divide when we consider the scarcity of newsrooms marked by conversation. Although a newsroom provides space for sorting through ethical dilemmas, this space doesn't guarantee an active, discursive community. In some newsrooms, conversations may never get started. A defensive newsroom culture doesn't foster in journalists the ability to deliberate and solve problems in group settings (Campbell, 2002). In other words, just because journalists are working *next to* each other doesn't mean they're working *with* each other. Busy journalists find little time for what they may see as idle chatter, particularly as the digital age demands more from everyone. Competitive journalists don't see an advantage in seeking or offering input. And journalists working in a toxic environment, which Maggie Patterson and Steve Urbanski (2006) claim many newsrooms can be, are unlikely to view the newsroom as a helpful or healthy place for conversations about ethics. Therefore, despite the opportunities, evidence shows that 'ethics discussions occur only rarely in most newsrooms' (Branham, cited in Weaver et al., 2007: 159). The spaces that are so central to journalists' identities are often spaces defined by moral muteness (Bird and Waters, 1989), where 'ethical issues do not enter into discourse at either an individual or organisational level' (Drumwright and Murphy, 2004: 11). Journalists are morally mute when they fail to recognisably communicate their moral concerns (Bird, 1996); instead they either say nothing or 'communicate in ways that obscure their moral beliefs and commitments' (p. 16). Ethics discussions may also be stalled by a newsroom inflicted with moral myopia, 'a distortion of moral vision, ranging from short-sightedness to near blindness, which affects an individual's perception of an ethical dilemma' (Drumwright and Murphy, 2004: 11). In this instance, moral issues fail to come into focus; journalists in a newsroom simply don't recognise issues as *moral* issues.

Silence doesn't always prevail. In some newsrooms, discussions are happening, yet they're not always the right kinds of discussions.

Conversations about ethics can fail in multiple ways. Although peer pressure can be an ethically positive force, it can also lead journalists down problematic paths. We know that journalists receive more guidance from peers than from documents, but peers may also tell tales of cutting ethical corners or bending ethical rules; documents, however, do not. Narratives that set low ethical bars lead to newsrooms that practise what Howard Good called 'no-fault ethics' (2001: 40).

Newsroom conversations about ethics may also be too narrow. As John Pauly argued, they are often focused on one decision at one moment as it relates to one story. Journalists rarely grapple with ethical questions at a broader level – those, for example, that deal with the social implications of their work (Pauly, 2009).

And newsroom conversations about ethics rarely represent authentic discourse in the Habermasian sense. For Habermas, authentic discourse – what he calls communicative action – requires participation by all stakeholders, or at the very least by people who can serve as proxies for stakeholders who aren't at the table. Newsrooms tend to be homogeneous places; they are exclusive sites for people who come at the news from the perspective of newsmaker. Even when news organisations take steps to recruit diverse talent, 'too often those voices are squelched by an insistence on conformity' (Mohl, 2002: 3). And historically, conformity has developed from a newsroom culture largely defined in white, male terms.

This emphasis on conformity is yet another example of a theory/ practice disconnect that occurs in the newsroom. Although autonomy and independence are principles that journalists routinely trumpet, strong socialisation influences coupled with demanding production pressures have led journalists – knowingly or not – to become conformists who vociferously protect the status quo. Journalists are, therefore, 'inclined to define journalism in terms of limited newsroom conceptions' (Adam, 2002: 9), which too often leads the profession to mock 'even modest attempts to change its practices' (Pauly, 2009: 21).

But change is what some media ethics scholars insist is needed. Stephen Ward (2012), for example, calls for a shift to a more global focus in journalism ethics. This reconceptualisation would mean that journalists act as agents in a global public sphere who serve a global public; in their work, they would aim at promoting non-parochial understandings of issues. Cliff Christians is also an advocate for change. The next generation of journalism ethics, he contends, should leave behind its emphasis on professional codes and practitioner conventions; instead it 'ought to arise from and be accountable to the general morality' (Christians, 2010: 208). The reliance on specific journalistic principles such as truth seeking, accountability, independence, and minimising harm should shift to a reliance on universal values inscribed in the common good.

Unfortunately, being open to change – much less being committed to making that change happen – is beyond the capacity of defensive newsroom cultures. In 1997, Jay Rosen (cited in Stepp, 1997: 35) described newsroom culture this way:

> *The practical demands, the production demands have come to rule the intellectual life of the newsroom. We're talking about a system where nobody is reading, nobody is experimenting, nobody is lifted out of the routine. The newsroom isn't constituted as a learning environment.*

Newsrooms may experience 'moments of alternative thoughts' (Kunelius and Ruusunoksa, 2008), but those moments are fleeting. Visionary thinking is quickly replaced by the struggle to keep up and to compete both with other new organisations and with colleagues who, too, want the prize-winning scoop that attracts the editor's attention and fuels the much-yearned-for career surge (Patterson and Urbanski, 2006).

Hopes for ethics in the solitary age

We began work on this chapter with a fear that journalism ethics could be entering a dark age. Without the defining symbol of the newsroom, how could journalism forge ahead in an uncertain time, one marked by a struggling business model, paradigmatic changes in the way information is shared, declining public trust, and, of course, monumental ethical lapses? Even if the newsroom has never been perfect, it seemed to us the place that offered the best hope for building on what journalism has done ethically right over the years and then working to make it better. We worried that losing a newsroom community could mean losing a space for journalists to engage with ethical dilemmas they now face, but it could also mean losing a space for them to imagine journalism ethics as the profession finds its new way.

We're now less worried and even a bit optimistic (some may call it idealistic). We've discovered that the best things newsrooms brought to journalism ethics don't, in fact, depend on a newsroom. And newsrooms cannot – or are not – providing some of the most important things that journalists need to grow in ethically sophisticated ways.

Journalists need diverse discursive communities. They need bonds with other journalists but also a reconnection to their audiences. They need 'moments of calm reflection' (Pauly, 2009: 21) and an intellectual life 'lifted out of the bureaucratic settings in which [they] are likely to operate' (Adam, 2002: 9). And as they learn to become journalists – through formal or informal means – they need an education that spurs their moral imaginations and prepares them to work in a profession that will look very different from the one their teachers knew.

Working as a solitary journalist means that the preordained newsroom community won't be there, but journalists can and should work to form and/or join new – and dare we say better – communities. Some of these will be physical; others will be virtual. Some will be local; others will be global. Regardless of the particular form a community takes, its chances of authentically representing multiple perspectives are far better than those provided by a community comprised entirely of journalists who have been socialised into an established newsroom orthodoxy. The goal is to find communities that, taken together, can come close to approximating Habermas's ideal of communicative action.

Engaging in this kind of community involvement may strike some as counter to the journalistic norm of detachment and independence. After all, one reason that journalists' working relationships have tended to be exclusively with colleagues and sources is to ensure, if nothing else, the appearance of professional distance. We, however, argue in favour of a journalism of *attachment*. Others support that argument. Jim Carey spoke of journalists as 'partner[s] with the rest of us – no more or no less' (1987: 14). And Rob Anderson et al. (1994: 74) described their vision of journalism, which necessitates attachment, like this:

> *To fulfil its responsibilities, journalism must consider its role as a listener and facilitator, hearing and heeding society's many voices; generating dialogue; contributing to understanding; and helping people and communities live, work, and govern together.*

All of this relates to journalists' need to reconnect with their audiences – with members of the public – and solitary journalism provides new opportunities for pursuing this connection. Jane Singer contends that journalists and audiences have much to learn from each other, and journalists' engagement with members of the public 'can go a long way toward enhancing understanding, strengthening relationships and fostering opportunities for greater trust in the news media' (Singer, 2010b: 97–8). Even more importantly, democracy, as 'an inherently collaborative public undertaking' can be enhanced by journalism that shares the same features (p. 98). Of course, all of this depends on journalists being motivated to engage. Admittedly, the question of motivation is a difficult one for ethics; no ethical framework can satisfactorily address it. What we can hope is that when journalists who have been resistant to engagement step out of what has been the dominant newsroom culture, they will see its value. Sometimes the motivation isn't sufficient until we know fully what's at stake if we don't engage.

The opportunity that the solitary age provides for journalists to form connections with their audiences does not – and should not – preclude them from retaining bonds with each other. In a post-newsroom era, journalists will still need a sense of professional identity, and that identity is fostered through interaction with others who do the same work. Journalists will still need peers with whom they can bounce off ideas, let off steam, and simply share the triumphs and travails of their work. Like other communities to which journalists belong, peer communities can be real and virtual, local and global. Our hope is that journalists will be able to experience the kind of professional camaraderie that makes working life better while simultaneously reaching beyond the exclusive communities of their peers to form new connections with outsiders.

With the trend towards solitary journalism already under way, what kind of evidence, if any, is emerging that the ideal for engagement envisioned here can be achieved? Are journalists starting to reach out to each other and to members of the public to build the relationships that will make journalism better? Yes and no. As they have always done, traditional associations provide regular opportunities for journalists to connect with each other in both real and virtual environments. If journalism associations can find ways to remain relevant, there's no reason they should go the way of newsrooms. The digital age is also providing new virtual venues for journalists to connect with each other and with the public. The European Journalism Centre sponsors an online journalism community (http://community.ejc.net) designed to help journalists link to other media professionals from around the world. Its 3,500 members can participate in online forums, join groups on special topics, post blogs, and chat with other members. The Poynter Institute in the United States hosts a website (poynter.org) with some similar features. Of course, social media such as Facebook and Twitter are the preferred method for many – journalists and otherwise – to build community and engage in conversation, even if it is only 140 characters at a time.

Are journalism associations, websites, Facebook, or Twitter providing the ideal model? Are they going to create the community needed to better develop the ethical compass of the solitary journalist? At this point, probably not. These opportunities for engagement are often useful, but many of the conversations are no more ethically rich than the newsroom conversations they may replace. But they do provide a start – a glimpse of what may be further developed. Journalists and others who care about making journalism better will need to bring their collective creative talents to bear on imagining how ethically promising communities can be developed. And, of course, they will need the motivation to do it, which, for some, will require a shift in attitude that welcomes engagement. Truth be told, journalism culture is still today dominated by newsroom culture. Until a critical mass of journalists find themselves working alone, perhaps for now we can only hope that the seeds of what we advocate in terms of engagement can be planted.

Being part of diverse discursive communities is essential for journalists and for journalism ethics, but solitary journalists can also benefit from solitude. There is a value to being alone that can enhance journalism ethics. Robert Kaplan has argued that journalism should cultivate loneliness – the 'first-hand, solitary discovery of local knowledge best associated with old-fashioned travel writing' (2006: 49). He contends:

> The best writing, literary or journalistic, occurs under the loneliest of circumstances, when a writer encounters the evidence first hand without any one of his social, economic, or professional group nearby to help him filter it, or otherwise condition his opinions. (p. 50)

Working outside of a newsroom allows journalists to break free of the professional caste in which they have been enveloped. They can approach stories with a fresher perspective, unchained from norms that so often tend to limit or even inhibit good journalism. And this freedom can surely benefit journalism ethics as well, for a journalist who can experience 'independence of thought and experience' (Kaplan, 2006: 49) is in a better position to engage in sophisticated moral reasoning than someone who simply follows the crowd.

How, then, do we prepare future journalists for the solitary age? How do we shift journalism education, and specifically journalism ethics education, away from its focus on newsroom-driven work? First, we must ensure that those who teach ethics have an understanding of the discipline that reaches beyond professional codes and norms. The newsroom 'war stories' that an ethics teacher brings to the classroom – or the workshop – will become less germane and less helpful. Even many of the more sophisticated case studies that appear in textbooks and professional journals will lack relevance for someone who will work in a much-altered profession.

We envision journalism ethics education structured around three key ideas, the first of which relates to its goals. Even in a landscape undergoing remarkable change, we endorse a set of goals introduced nearly 30 years ago by Daniel Callahan (1980) of the Hastings Center. The goals, which apply to all ethics teaching, include:

1. stimulating the moral imagination;
2. recognising ethical issues;
3. eliciting a sense of moral obligation;
4. tolerating ambiguity and disagreement; and
5. developing analytical skills.

On the surface, Callahan's goals appear rather humble; they say nothing about teaching people what the right thing to do is. But we argue that anyone who achieves these five things is necessarily better equipped to figure out *how* to do the right thing.

Our second key idea for the structure of journalism ethics education heeds Cliff Christians's call for a return to a focus on the general morality. Here, the emphasis is placed on our ethical life as human beings rather than specifically as journalists. We are asked how we can contribute to the common good through honouring the universal principles of truth seeking, respect for the sacredness and dignity of all others, and a commitment to non-violence, which is best expressed through the golden rule (Christians and Cooper, 2009). The solitary age itself is a catalyst for this renewed focus, and ethics education must take advantage of the environment provided by it to foster an ethics that, as Christians argues, arises from and is accountable to the general morality.

Finally, and perhaps most importantly, education should emphasise discursive ethics; it should teach future journalists the absolute centrality of engagement with others from diverse communities, and it should give journalists skills in interacting with those communities. In this sense, ethics education that focuses on building cultural competence, on honing skills in speaking and listening, and on reconciling competing views that will likely be expressed in any discursive environment becomes more important than studying codes or reading case studies. One place to begin this work is through the cosmopolitan ethics of Martha Nussbaum (1997), Kwame Anthony Appiah (2006), and others. Education that does these things necessarily helps foster moral development – helps develop future journalists who can approach ethics with the sophistication it deserves.

As we conclude, we don't want to leave the reader with an impression that our vision for journalism ethics in the solitary age is a utopian one. Many of the pressures that have led journalists to act in unethical ways in the past will most certainly live on in the solitary age. We don't envision an end to production and deadline pressures, economic worries, the competitive instinct, or a desire to please. Journalists will have to continue negotiating these challenges. Yet the potential opportunities that a post-newsroom age provides give us optimism that journalism ethics can find its way in a new era and serve both journalism and the public better.

Note

All web addresses in this chapter were last accessed in June 2013.

References

Adam, G. Stuart (2002) 'Notes toward a Definition of Journalism', in Roy Peter Clark and Cole C. Campbell (eds), *The Values and Craft of American Journalism: Essays from the Poynter Institute* (Gainesville, FL: University Press of Florida), 7–40.

American Society of News Editors (2012) *Total and Minority Newsroom Employment Declines In 2011 But Loss Continues to Stabilize*, 4 Apr.: www.asne.org.

Anderson, Rob, Dardenne, Robert, and Killenberg, George (1994) *The Conversation of Journalism: Communication, Community and News* (Westport, CT: Praeger).

Appiah, Kwame Anthony (2006) *Cosmopolitanism: Ethics in a World of Strangers* (New York: W. W. Norton).

Battistoli, Bruno (2008) 'Transmission, Translation and Transformation: Communication of Ethical Codes in the Newsroom', paper at conference of International Communication Association.

Bird, Frederick B. (1996) *The Muted Conscience: Moral Silence and the Practice of Business Ethics* (Westport, CT: Quorum Books).

Bird, Frederick, and Waters, James (1989) 'The Moral Muteness of Managers', *California Management Review*, 32(Fall): 73–88.

Borden, Sandra L., and Tew, Chad (2007) 'The Role of Journalists and the Performance of Journalism: Ethical Lessons from "Fake" News (Seriously)', *Journal of Mass Media Ethics*, 22(4): 300–14.

Briggs, Mark (2012) *Entrepreneurial Journalism: How to Build What's Next for Journalism* (Los Angeles: Sage).

Callahan, Daniel (1980) 'Goals in the Teaching of Ethics', in Daniel Callahan and Sissela Bok (eds), *Ethics Teaching in Higher Education* (New York: Plenum Press), 61–80.

Campbell, Cole C. (2002) 'Journalism Enlarged: Stuff that Matters', in Roy Peter Clark and Cole C. Campbell (eds), *The Values and Craft of American Journalism: Essays from the Poynter Institute* (Gainesville, FL: University Press of Florida), 58–70.

Carey, James W. (1987) 'The Press and Public Discourse', *Center Magazine*, 20(2): 4–32.

Christians, Clifford G. (2010) 'The Ethics of Privacy', in Christopher Meyers (ed.), *Journalism Ethics: A Philosophical Approach* (New York: Oxford University Press), 203–14.

Christians, Clifford G., and Cooper, Thomas W. (2009) 'The Search for Universals', in Lee Wilkins and Clifford G. Christians (eds), *The Handbook of Mass Media Ethics* (New York: Routledge), 55–68.

Christians, Clifford G., Fackler, Mark, and Ferré, John P. (2012) *Ethics for Public Communication: Defining Moments in Media History* (New York: Oxford University Press).

Drumwright, Minette E., and Murphy, Patrick E. (2004) 'How Advertising Practitioners View Ethics: Moral Muteness, Moral Myopia, and Moral Imagination', *Journal of Advertising*, 33(2): 7–24.

Everbach, Tracy (2006) 'The Culture of a Women-Led Newspaper: An Ethnographic Study of the Sarasota Herald-Tribune', *Journalism and Mass Communication Quarterly*, 83(3): 477–93.

Gans, Herbert (1979) *Deciding What's News* (New York: Random House).

Good, Howard (2001) 'We Need Ethics Examples', *Quill*, 89(3): 40.

Greenslade, Roy (2012a) 'Up to 30 Jobs Go at Telegraph Titles', Greenslade Blog, 30 Jan.: www.theguardian.com/media/greenslade/2012/jan/30/telegraphmedia group-downturn.

Greenslade, Roy (2012b) 'Trinity Mirror's Job Cuts are Sad – But that's 2012 Newspaper Reality', Greenslade Blog, 1 Feb.: www.theguardian.com/media/greenslade/2012/feb/01/trinity-mirror-downturn.

Greenslade, Roy (2012c) 'Independent Titles and Standard Face Radical Cost-Cutting Proposals', Greenslade Blog, 22 June: www.theguardian.com/media/greenslade/2012/jun/22/independent-titles-standard-radical-costcutting.

Habermas, Jürgen (1990) *Moral Consciousness and Communicative Action*, tr. Christian Lenhardt and Shierry Weber Nicholsen (Cambridge, MA: MIT Press).

Hallin, Daniel (1994) *We Keep America on Top of the World: Television Journalism and the Public Sphere* (New York: Routledge).

Hill-Wagner, Mary (2007) 'Tell Me a Story: How Narratives Shape Reporters' Ethics', paper at conference of National Communication Association.

Israely, Jeff (2011) 'Building a News Org in Order to Support Good Journalists', *Nieman Journalism Lab*, 22 Feb.: www.niemanlab.org.

Journalist, The (2011–12) 'Up to 300 Fleet Street Jobs under Threat', Dec. 2011– Jan. 2012: 5.

Kaplan, Robert D. (2006) 'Cultivating Loneliness', *Columbia Journalism Review* (Jan./Feb.): 48–51.

Kumar, Priya (2010–11) 'Backpack Journalism Overseas', *American Journalism Review* (Dec. 2010/Jan. 2011): www.ajr.org.

Kunelius, Risto, and Ruusunoksa, Laura (2008) 'Professional Imagination in Newspaper Newsrooms', paper at conference of International Communication Association.

Long, John (2012) 'What Keeps you Honest?', *News Photographer Magazine* (Jan./Feb.): 20.

Macy, Beth (2009) 'Hunkering down', *American Journalism Review*, 31(3): 38–43.

Mann, Judy (1981) 'The Respect for Truth Deeper than we Thought', *Washington Post*, 17 Apr.: B1.

Merrill, John C. (1994) *Existential Journalism* (rev. edn, Ames, IA: Iowa State University Press).

Mohl, Jeffrey (2002) 'Think Outside the Newsroom', *Quill*, 90(9): 3.

Nerone, John, and Barnhurst, Kevin G. (2003) 'U.S. Newspaper Types, the Newsroom, and the Division of Labor, 1750–2000', *Journalism Studies*, 4(4): 435–49.

Nussbaum, Martha (1997) 'Citizens of the World', in *Cultivating Humanity: A Classical Defense of Reform in Liberal Education* (Cambridge, MA: Harvard University Press), 50–67.

Patterson, Maggie Jones, and Urbanski, Steve (2006) 'What Jayson Blair and Janet Cooke Say about the Press and the Erosion of Public Trust', *Journalism Studies*, 7(6): 828–50.

Pauly, John (2009) 'Is Journalism Interested in Resolution, or Only in Conflict?', *Marquette Law Review*, 93(1): 7–23.

Project for Excellence in Journalism (2012) *The State of the News Media 2012*, 19 Mar.: www.journalism.org.

Schwada, John (2011) 'At USC: Journalism 1.0 Meets Journalism 7.0', *LA Observed*, 13 Sept.: www.laobserved.com.

Singer, Jane B. (2010b) 'Journalism Ethics amid Structural Change', *Daedalus*, 139(2): 89–99.

Singer, Jane B. (2010a) 'Quality Control: Perceived Effects of User-Generated Content on Newsroom Norms, Values and Routines', *Journalism Practice*, 4(2): 127–42.

Stepp, Carl Session (1997) 'Can this Relationship be Saved?', *American Journalism Review*, 19(3): 32–6.

Ward, Stephen J. A. (2012) *Global Media Ethics* (Madison, WI: Center for Journalism Ethics, School of Journalism and Mass Communication, University of Wisconsin-Madison): http://ethics.journalism.wisc.edu/resources/global-media-ethics.

Wasserman, Edward (2012) 'Factory Age News for the Digital Era', *Unsocial Media*, 16 July: www.ewasserman.com.

Weaver, David H., Beam, Randal A., Brownlee, Bonnie J., Voakes, Paul S., and Wilhoit, G. Cleveland (2007) *The American Journalist in the 21st Century: U.S. News People at the Dawn of a New Millennium* (Mahwah, NJ: Lawrence Erlbaum Associates).

Wilkins, Lee, and Coleman, Renita (2005a) 'Ethical Journalism is Not an Oxymoron: In Ethical Decision-Making, Journalists Compare "Very Favorably with Those Who Work in Other Professions"', *Nieman Reports* (Summer): 52.

Wilkins, Lee, and Coleman, Renita (2005b) *The Moral Media: How Journalists Reason about Ethics* (Mahwah, NJ: Lawrence Erlbaum Associates).

World Association of Newspapers and News Publishers (2012) *11th International Newsroom Summit Executive Summary* (May): www.editorsweblog.org.

Index

RISJ/I.B.TAURIS PUBLICATIONS

CHALLENGES

Transformations in Egyptian Journalism
Naomi Sakr
ISBN: 978 1 78076 589 1

Climate Change in the Media: Reporting Risk and Uncertainty
James Painter
ISBN: 978 1 78076 588 4

Women and Journalism
Suzanne Franks
ISBN: 978 1 78076 585 3

EDITED VOLUMES

Media and Public Shaming: The Boundaries of Disclosure
Julian Petley (ed.)
ISBN: 978 1 78076 586 0 (HB); 978 1 78076 587 7 (PB)

Political Journalism in Transition: Western Europe in a Comparative Perspective
Raymond Kuhn and Rasmus Kleis Nielsen (eds)
ISBN: 978 1 78076 677 5 (HB); 978 1 78076 678 2 (PB)

Transparency in Politics and the Media: Accountability and Open Government
Nigel Bowles, James T. Hamilton and David A. L. Levy (eds)
ISBN: 978 1 78076 675 1 (HB); 978 1 78076 676 8 (PB)

The Ethics of Journalism: Individual, Institutional and Cultural Influences
Wendy N. Wyatt (ed.)
ISBN: 978 1 78076 673 7 (HB); 978 1 78076 674 4 (PB)